W9-DDO-346

Instagram® For Business For Dummies® 2nd Edition

Published by: **John Wiley & Sons, Inc.**, 111 River Street, Hoboken, NJ 07030-5774, www.wiley.com

Copyright © 2021 by John Wiley & Sons, Inc., Hoboken, New Jersey

Published simultaneously in Canada

For general information on our other products and services, please contact our Customer Care Department within the U.S. at 877-762-2974, outside the U.S. at 317-572-3993, or fax 317-572-4002. For technical support, please visit https://hub.wiley.com/community/support/dummies.

Wiley publishes in a variety of print and electronic formats and by print-on-demand. Some material included with standard print versions of this book may not be included in e-books or in print-on-demand. If this book refers to media such as a CD or DVD that is not included in the version you purchased, you may download this material at http://booksupport.wiley.com. For more information about Wiley products, visit www.wiley.com.

Library of Congress Control Number: 2020950826

ISBN 978-1-119-69659-9 (pbk); ISBN 978-1-119-69660-5 (ebk); ISBN 978-1-119-69662-9 (ebk)

Manufactured in the United States of America

SKY10025559_031021

Contents at a Glance

Table of Contents

Introduction

Are you ready to have some fun? We hope you are! Because Instagram is all about entertainment and creating exciting content. Because you've chosen this book, we know you're ready to get down to business creating an Instagram account that will not only help you grow your business but also be something you enjoy!

With more and more people joining Instagram every day, the social media app continues to grow at unprecedented rates. But with that growth comes a lot of noise and saturation from people who don't quite understand how to use the platform effectively. However, after reading this book, you'll have the tools and tactics necessary to build a successful Instagram profile.

About This Book

The purpose of *Instagram For Business For Dummies,* 2nd Edition is to help you use Instagram effectively. But as you can see by the number of pages in this book, that purpose is easier said than done!

Instagram really is as simple as uploading a photo. But for strategic business use, you should employ a number of marketing and traffic-generating tactics, which we explore in this book. And as Instagram adds more features to the platform, such as IGTV and Reels, understanding how to create this additional content is just as important.

Instagram is an interactive and community-focused platform, so we hope you are looking forward to building a community around your brand.

We take you through every step of creating and uploading content to Instagram, writing effective captions that get your audience to take action, finding hashtags that help you get more exposure, building your audience, and using all the fun features built into Instagram.

Foolish Assumptions

When writing this book, we assumed that you

>> Have a business or are getting ready to start a business

>> Have a website for your business

>> Know your target customer audience and know that they're using Instagram

>> Want to use Instagram effectively to drive real business results

>> Don't want to look like an amateur, even if you're new to using Instagram

>> Are committed to devoting time and energy to build a presence on Instagram that will reflect your brand

If these assumptions are correct, this is the right book for you! We're confident that the tactics and information here will help you achieve your goals.

Icons Used in This Book

To make things easier and ensure that you don't miss important details, various icons appear throughout this book. Here's what the different icons look like and mean.

TIP

The Tip icon is a small piece of expert advice that will save you time and make your experience on Instagram easier to master.

REMEMBER

Because we cover a lot of details and information, every now and then we throw in a Remember icon to remind you of important details we've already covered. We know you're reading every juicy detail of the book; the Remember icon just helps resurface some of those tidbits.

TECHNICAL STUFF

Who doesn't love a little geek-fest on technical jargon? Okay, a lot of people! We've pulled out these paragraphs so you can understand the technical aspects of using Instagram without getting overwhelmed.

WARNING

Yes, this book has a few warnings. When you see a Warning icon, please take a few extra moments to understand the effect of what we're saying. You're not going to blow up your Instagram account or do anything irreparable, but we want to save you from any headaches we can.

Beyond the Book

In addition to what you're reading right now, this book also comes with a free, access-anywhere cheat sheet that provides a handy list of Instagram lingo, steps for sharing posts directly, and more. To view the cheat sheet, simply go to `www.dummies.com` and type **Instagram for Business For Dummies Cheat Sheet** in the Search box.

Where to Go from Here

The first few chapters dive into how to set up a new Instagram account. If you already have an Instagram account, you can skip the first chapter, but we encourage you to check out Chapter 2 because it contains information on how to set up an effective profile. Don't worry, you can easily update or edit anything you've already started!

After that, we have a ton of information on creating better content and getting strategic with your Instagram content. If you want to focus on specific areas, look at the Table of Contents for guidance.

If you run into trouble, check out Chapters 21 and 22, which are dedicated to troubleshooting Instagram issues. And if you're looking for inspiration, read Chapters 23 and 24.

It's time to jump into all the fun of Instagram that we've been talking about! Enjoy the book.

1

Creating Your Profile

Install Instagram on your smartphone, tablet, or Windows computer.

Set up your Instagram business profile to draw followers like moths to a flame (or whatever trite saying applies).

Prepare your business goals for your Instagram profile so you can reach the most customers.

IN THIS CHAPTER

» Finding Instagram apps for your device or computer

» Deploying Instagram apps on Windows and Mac computers

» Installing Instagram apps on mobile devices

» Using Instagram on the web

» Launching Instagram on your computer or mobile device

Chapter **1**

Installing Instagram

The good people at the Instagram division of Facebook realized long ago that many people use Instagram with all their computing devices, not just smartphones. What's more, they knew that if business owners were going to adopt Instagram as the de facto photo-sharing app, Instagram had to be available everywhere: on smartphones, tablets, computers, and even the Instagram website.

If you haven't installed Instagram yet, this is the chapter you need to read. We start by showing you where to find Instagram on the web, and then you find out how to install the Instagram app on computers, smartphones, and tablets.

Next, you see how to use Instagram on the web in case you're using a computer or device that either doesn't or can't have Instagram installed, such as a company smartphone that allows only company-approved apps. Finally, you launch the Instagram app on your computer or device so you can scratch that itch and start Instagramming.

Moving Instagram to the Launch Pad

If you don't have Instagram installed on your smartphone (or your computer), search in one of the following locations to find and download the app:

- >> **iPhone or iPad:** App Store

- >> **Android smartphone or tablet:** Google Play Store

- >> **Windows:** Microsoft Store

- >> **Mac:** App Store

In the iPhone example shown in Figure 1-1, the brightly colored bar at the top of the page indicates where you can download the app.

REMEMBER

If your workplace has a BYOD (Bring Your Own Device) policy, pass this book around to the people in your company so they can refer to the appropriate section in this chapter for installing Instagram on their computer or device.

FIGURE 1-1:
Get the iPhone Instagram app by clicking Get at the top right.

Installing on a Computer

Instagram was designed for a smartphone, but in a business setting you'll be more likely to view it at your desk while you're working. Otherwise, you'll have to keep looking from your computer screen to your smartphone.

Fortunately, the Instagram app is available for Windows and the Mac, so you can view, like, and comment on photos and videos from other Instagram users. However, you can't use your computer's webcam to take pictures or shoot video.

TIP

Feel free to skip ahead to the "No App? No Problem: Instagram Is on the Web" section to learn how to use the Instagram website. (This information should go in your brain's "be prepared" file.) Then continue reading to the end of the chapter to learn how to log in to Instagram.

Installing on a Windows PC (sort of)

The Windows version of Instagram is a Windows 10 app. As any Windows 10 user knows, Microsoft is trying to make Windows the best of both worlds by offering apps that can run on both Windows on computers and the Windows Mobile 10 operating system. (Good luck trying to find anyone using Windows Mobile 10 on a smartphone.)

Windows PC users can install the Instagram app from the Windows Store or the Instagram website. Here's how to install the app from the Windows Store:

1. **Click the Start icon in the taskbar.**

2. **Click Store in the list of programs or click the Start tile in the Start menu.**

3. **In the Search box, type Instagram.**

4. **In the list that appears below the Search box, click Instagram.**

5. **Click the Get button, as shown in Figure 1-2.**

   After the Windows Store installs the Instagram app on your computer, the Get button in the Store window changes to Launch.

6. **Click Launch to start the app.**

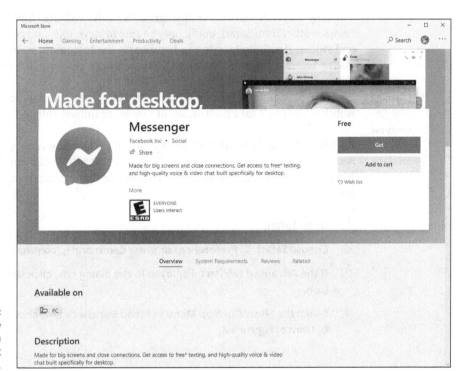

FIGURE 1-2: Click Get in the upper-right area of the Microsoft Store window.

If you prefer to install the Windows app from the Instagram website, follow these steps:

1. **Navigate to the Instagram website at** `www.instagram.com`.

2. **Click the Sign Up link in the Instagram web page.**

    The Store window appears in front of your browser window.

3. **Click the Install button (refer to Figure 1-2).**

4. **After installation, start the app by clicking the Launch button.**

Now you can skip ahead of the rest of the class and start Instagramming by going to the "Starting to Gram Instantly" section.

Installing on a Mac (sort of)

Instagram doesn't have a Mac version of its app available to download, as you'll discover if you search for Instagram in the App Store. If you try to download the app from iTunes by clicking Get on the Instagram app page, you'll see the Get button change to Downloading for a few seconds, and then the button will change back to Get.

The only way you can access Instagram is on its website. And if you use a web browser other than Safari, you'll only be able to view, like, and comment on photos and videos. Fortunately, you can bamboozle the Instagram website into thinking you're accessing the website on the iPhone so you can upload photos.

REMEMBER

You can only upload photos from your Mac from the bamboozled Instagram website. You can't take photos, shoot videos, or upload videos.

An article by Lewis Painter on the Macworld UK website (`www.macworld.co.uk/how-to/mac-software/instagram-for-mac-3641569/`) tells you how to do this. But rather than make you go to the website for this information, we tell you how here:

1. **Open Safari.**

2. **Choose Safari ⇨ Preferences or press Command+, (comma).**

3. **If the Advanced tab isn't displayed in the dialog box, click the Advanced icon.**

4. **Select the Show Develop Menu in Menu Bar check box, shown at the bottom of Figure 1-3.**

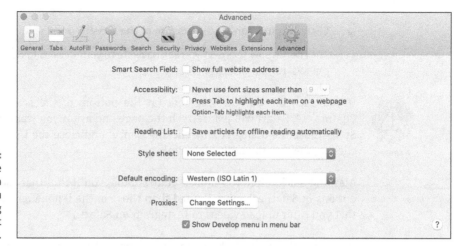

FIGURE 1-3:
Display the
Develop menu in
the Safari menu
bar by selecting
the check box at
the bottom.

5. **Close the window.**

The Develop option now appears in the menu bar.

6. **Click Develop, move the mouse pointer over User Agent, and then click Safari—iOS 13.1.3—iPhone in the side menu.**

REMEMBER

Apple is always improving its iOS, so the version in the side menu will be newer than 13.1.3 by the time you read this.

7. **Open the Instagram website and log in.**

The Instagram home screen appears, as shown in Figure 1-4.

FIGURE 1-4:
To upload a
photo, click the
plus icon.

8. **Click the plus icon, at the bottom of the screen.**

The File window opens so you can navigate to your desired folder and add photo(s) to your Instagram profile.

WARNING

If you click the Use the App link (at the bottom of the screen, as shown in Figure 1-4), Safari will just refresh the page and ask if you want to open the App Store. Close the dialog box by clicking Cancel and close the Use the App link by clicking the X to the right of the link.

Alas and alack, after you upload your photos, you'll find that the photo-editing options in Safari are more limited than those in the iPhone app. (And remember that you can't upload videos to Instagram on Safari.)

If you'd rather upload photos to Instagram by using an app, check out the two apps that the Instagram website lists: Flume and Uplet. A discussion of third-party apps is beyond the scope of this book, so please visit the Instagram website for that information.

Now that you have Instagram doing your bidding on your Mac, start using Instagram by moving ahead to the "Starting to Gram Instantly" section.

Installing on Instagram's Native Platform

The first version of Instagram, which was available for download on October 6, 2010, was for iPhone users. It was a wise decision: The popularity of the iPhone combined with Instagram's ease of use when it came to sharing photos resulted in more than one million registered Instagram users by the end of 2010. (Ten years later, there are about one billion users on iPhone and Android platforms.) You can install the iPhone app not only on your iPhone but also on your iPad if you prefer to use your tablet. (If you have an Android smartphone or tablet, don't worry. We have you covered in the next section.)

Installing on an iPhone

It's easy to download Instagram from the App Store to your iPhone:

1. **Tap the App Store icon.**

2. **Tap the Search icon in the lower-right corner of the screen.**

3. **Tap the Search box, at the top of the screen, and start typing the word** Instagram.

   After you type the first few letters, Instagram appears at the top of the results list.

4. **Tap Instagram in the results list.**

   The app information appears on the screen, as shown in Figure 1-5.

5. **Tap Get.**

   If you need to sign into the App Store, type your password in the Sign In to iTunes Store window and then tap Buy. If you have a newer iPhone that doesn't have a Home button, follow the prompts to complete your transaction. If your iPhone has a touch button and you use Touch ID instead of typing your password, place the appropriate finger or thumb on the Home button.

6. **Tap Open.**

FIGURE 1-5:
The Instagram app in the iPhone App Store.

The next time you want to open Instagram, swipe to the Home screen that has room for icons — because that's where you'll find the Instagram icon.

Now Instagram is ready for you to start using it, so move ahead to the "Starting to Gram Instantly" section.

Installing on an iPad

Instagram has yet to create a native app for the iPad, which is another one of life's great mysteries (but not at the level of where missing socks go). However, you can use the iPhone app on the iPad.

Here's how to install Instagram on an iPad:

1. **Tap the App Store icon.**

2. **Tap the Search icon in the lower-right corner of the screen.**

3. **Tap the Search box, at the top of the screen, and start typing the word Instagram.**

   After you type the first two or three letters, Instagram appears at the top of the results list.

4. **Tap Instagram in the results list.**

5. **In the upper-left corner of the screen, tap Filters ⇨ Supports.**

6. **Tap iPhone Only, as shown in Figure 1-6.**

7. **Tap the Instagram app's Get button (see Figure 1-7).**

   If you need to sign into the App Store, type your password in the Sign In to iTunes Store window. Then tap Buy. Or if you use Touch ID, place the appropriate finger or thumb on the Home button instead.

8. **Tap Open.**

Now that you've installed Instagram on your iPad, go straight to the "Starting to Gram Instantly" section to learn how to start using Instagram.

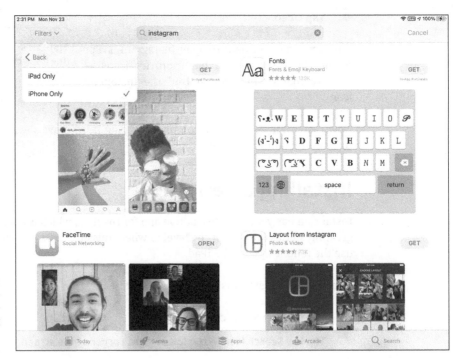

FIGURE 1-6:
Yes, tap iPhone Only when you're installing Instagram on your iPad.

FIGURE 1-7:
The Instagram
app is in the
upper-left corner.

Instagram Has Android Covered, Too

After Instagram was satisfied with the development of its app on the iPhone, staffers turned their attention to developing Instagram for the Android platform. On the first day the app was released, in April 2012, more than a million users downloaded it.

Here's how to install Instagram from the Google Play Store:

1. **Tap the Play Store icon on the Home screen.**

   If the Play Store icon isn't on a Home screen, tap Apps on the Home screen and then tap Play Store in the Apps screen.

2. **Tap the Search box at the top of the screen, and start typing the word** Instagram.

   After you type, Instagram appears in the results list.

3. **Tap Instagram in the results list.**

   The app information screen shown in Figure 1-8 appears.

4. **Tap Install.**

5. **Tap Open.**

It's time to start Instagramming, so skip ahead to the "Starting to Gram Instantly" section.

No App? No Problem: Instagram Is on the Web

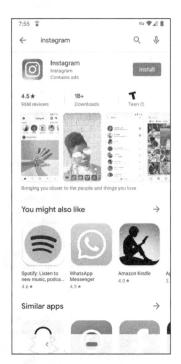

If your company doesn't allow you to install unauthorized apps on company smartphones, you can still access the Instagram website on your smartphone or computer, but there is less functionality.

FIGURE 1-8:
Tap the Instagram icon to read more about the app.

Open the Instagram website by typing `www.instagram.com` in your browser's address bar. You can log in to Instagram on the web in one of two ways:

>> **Instagram username and password:** Type your Instagram username in the Username box and then type your password in the Password box. Then click or tap Log In.

>> **Facebook account:** If you prefer to use your Facebook account, click or tap Log In with Facebook. (If your browser doesn't have your Facebook account information stored in a cookie, the Facebook window appears on your screen so you can type your username and password.) Then click or tap the Log In As button.

REMEMBER

If you haven't created an Instagram account yet, bookmark this page and read Chapter 2 to learn how to create an effective profile.

After you log in, you see the home page with the latest photos and videos from users you follow. The top of the screen features the Instagram logo at the left, the Search box in the center, and five icons to the right of the Search box, as shown in Figure 1-9.

FIGURE 1-9:
The Search box is at the top of the page.

>> **Home icon:** Opens the home page. When you're on the home page, this icon is black.

>> **Paper airplane icon:** Opens the Direct Message page so you can read private messages from, and send private messages to, other Instagram users.

>> **Compass icon:** Opens the Explore page so you can view a list of posts from other users whom Instagram thinks you may want to follow. To follow a user, click the Follow button.

>> **Heart icon:** Displays a list of notifications, such as when someone comments on one of your photos or videos.

>> **Profile icon:** Displays your Profile page.

If you're on the Explore or Profile page, you can return to the home page by clicking the Home icon or the Instagram logo.

Scroll down the screen to see photos and videos from other Instagram users you follow. You can double-click the photo or click the heart icon to like the photo. You can also add a comment: Click the comment icon (a text bubble) to open the post page shown in Figure 1-10, click Add a Comment, type the comment, and then press Enter.

Note the three dot icon to the right of the person who posted the photo. (If you're following this person, the icon appears to the right of the word *Following*, as in Figure 1-10). Click this icon to open a pop-up menu that enables you to report the photo or video as inappropriate, unfollow the user, open the post, share the post, copy a link to the post, embed the photo on a website, or cancel the action and close the menu.

Starting to Gram Instantly

If you've installed the Instagram app on your Windows PC or smartphone, you should use those versions instead of the tablet versions or the website because they have more functionality. And if you have a choice between using a PC or a smartphone, remember that iPhone and Android smartphone versions of Instagram have the most functionality of all.

REMEMBER

You can also use the smartphone version of the Instagram app on your iPad or Android tablet.

Starting Instagram on a computer

To open Instagram on your Windows PC, click the Start icon in the taskbar and then click Instagram in the apps list on the left, as shown in Figure 1-11. Alternatively, you can click the Instagram icon in the Start menu.

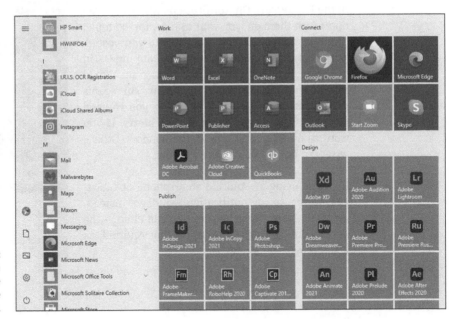

FIGURE 1-11:
The Instagram app is in the I section of the apps list.

After you launch the app for the first time, it will ask you to sign in using your Instagram username and password or to log in with your Facebook account.

If you don't have an Instagram account, click the Sign Up link at the bottom of the window. The signup screen asks you to log in with Facebook or create an Instagram account by clicking the Sign Up with Phone or Email link. From there, you'll be able to use the Signup Wizard to create an account.

TIP

Want to launch Instagram from your taskbar? Simply right-click the Instagram icon in the taskbar and click Pin to Taskbar.

Starting Instagram on a mobile device

If you're using Instagram on an iPhone, iPad, or Android device, you can start the app by tapping its icon, as shown in Figure 1-12.

If you're using Instagram on an iPhone or iPad, you'll be asked to turn on Instagram notifications in the Please Turn On Notifications window. If you don't turn them on, you won't know, for example, if one of your followers likes a photo you posted. Turn on Instagram notifications by tapping OK in the window. Next, you see the Instagram Would Like to Send You Notifications window. This seems redundant, but Instagram is asking you to send your notifications with sounds and alerts. If you want to do this, tap Allow in the window. Otherwise, tap Don't Allow in the window.

If you're using an Android smartphone or tablet, you won't see a notification window. Instead, you'll see your home screen. You can change the notification settings in Instagram for Android, as you discover in Chapter 21.

FIGURE 1-12:
The Instagram icon appears in the second row of icons on this iPhone.

Chapter 2

Setting Up Your Profile

After you install the Instagram app on your mobile device, the first major task you face is setting up your profile. Your profile should accurately represent your business brand — and appeal to your target audience.

In this chapter, we show you how to set up the different components of your profile. Although a profile has several parts, establishing the right username immediately is the most important. Proper selection at the beginning ensures that you don't have to make unwanted changes in the future or compensate for an irrelevant username as your business grows. If you set up your Instagram profile foundations to align with your brand, you'll be able to edit additional components as you grow and better drive business results from your Instagram account.

Professional Profile Practices

Your *Instagram profile* is both your first impression to potential customers and new visitors as well as your consistent branded message to your existing audience. Your profile should be recognizable to your audience and showcase the value you provide as a business. See Figure 2-1.

Instagram profiles are comprised of the following six components: username, profile photo, name, bio, website URL, and business address (optional). In addition, profiles that have upgraded to a business account, such as the account in Figure 2-1, have connection buttons. We talk more about all these elements in the coming sections.

Profile photo   Username

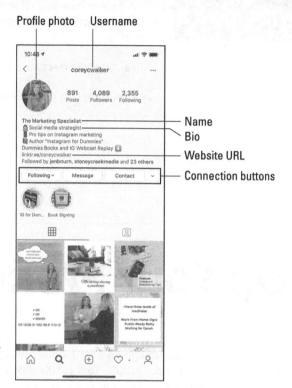

Name
Bio
Website URL
Connection buttons

FIGURE 2-1:
An Instagram profile consists of these standard components.

Your profile should be consistent with the branding and messaging you use on other online marketing platforms but also align with the styling and formatting that appeals to Instagram users. Note too that you need to design your profile according to Instagram's formatting and character restrictions. These limits and restrictions are discussed in more detail later in this chapter.

Choosing a name and username for your business

Your name and username are two of the most important components of your Instagram profile because they are the only two parts of your profile that are searchable. When users type a keyword or name in the Search field on Instagram, the app looks at only the username and name fields of accounts to determine if an account is relevant to that search query.

REMEMBER

The *username* is the string of characters at the top of a profile. The *name* is the bold text below the profile photo. If you want your business to be found by a keyword or phrase, be sure to include it in either the name or username for your account.

Choosing the best username

You must select a username when you set up a new Instagram account. Your *Instagram username* is how you are recognized on Instagram. All activity, from the content you post to how you engage with others, is associated with your username. The username is at the top of the profile, as shown in Figure 2-2.

Your username is the component of your Instagram URL that defines your account. It's delineated with the @ symbol when referring to you as a user. The URL for your Instagram account is

```
http://instagram.com/yourusername
```

When you interact on Instagram, the username appears as

yourusername

An Instagram username is limited to 30 characters and must contain only letters, numbers, periods, and underscores. You can't include symbols or other punctuation marks as a part of your username.

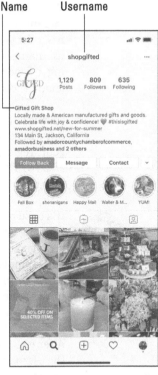

Name   Username

© Gifted

FIGURE 2-2:
The username of your account is listed at the top of your profile.

Choose a username that represents your brand, is recognizable, and, if possible, distinguishes what you do. Your username might be simply your business name or an adapted version of your business name, such as @louboutinworld, instead of Christian Louboutin. Or you might also include a word or two that describes your business industry or niche to further define who you are, such as @yorkelee_prints.

TIP

Choosing a username that is different than your business name may confuse Instagram users as to whether or not your account is the official account for your business. It's best to keep variations as minimal as possible to avoid confusion.

During the registration portion of your Instagram account, you're prompted to select your username. If the username you selected is available, a check mark will appear. If someone is using that username, an X will appear in the username field. Keep selecting alternatives until you find an available username.

Usernames are provided on a first-come basis. If you're signing up for a new Instagram account using the web version, Instagram will populate an available username for you. Delete this username and type one that represents your brand. If the username you want to use is unavailable, you can use alternative options by adding periods or underscores to the username, using abbreviations, or adding another word.

There is little you can do to have an existing username transferred to your account if it's in use or was previously used by another account. If another account is using your registered trademark as its username, visit `https://help.instagram.com/101826856646059` for information on how to file a claim of trademark violation.

TIP

It's good practice to read your username objectively before finalizing it. When you combine more than one word, without spacing, into a single username, the arrangement of the letters may read differently or inappropriately to others. For example, @yourusername might be read as "You Ruse R Name" instead of "Your Username." When this is the case, consider adding periods or underscores to separate the words within the username as follows: @your.username or @your_username.

After you select a username, all content linking to your profile is associated with the username's URL. If you want to change the username at some point, your URL would change and you would need to update all backlinks and links to that profile accordingly. This is why it's best to choose the right username when setting up your profile.

If you do want to change your username, follow these easy steps:

1. **Go to your profile on Instagram on either your mobile device or your computer.**

2. **Tap or click Edit Profile.**

3. **In the Username field, type the new username.**

4. **Save your changes.**

   To do so, tap the check mark, Done, Save, or Submit button (depending on the device you're using).

Choosing the best name

Your *Instagram name* is visible only when someone visits your profile directly. The name appears in bold below the profile photo (refer to Figure 2-2).

Your profile will perform better in searches and look more professional if the name and username are different. Having a name that's different from your username provides double the opportunity for keywords and searchable criteria in the Instagram app. Power users on Instagram take the time to craft good username and name components.

Unlike your username, which is one word, your name should be in proper sentence structure with capital letters and spacing. Your name (like your username) is limited to 30 characters, including spaces.

You can use your actual name or business name as your name on Instagram. Or you may choose to use an abbreviation or a commonly recognized description of your business. For example, if your business is a pizza restaurant called Farm Fresh Pizza, your username might be farm.fresh.pizza and your name might be Best Pizzeria in Boston.

TIP

You can be found in more searches on Instagram if you include a keyword or phrase in your name or username or both. If you didn't put a defining keyword in your username, you should include one in your name field, in addition to your actual name. For example, in Figure 2-2, the keywords *Gift Shop* were added to the name field.

The name on your profile is not tied to your URL or other defining aspects of Instagram, so you can change it at any time. Consider adding or changing keywords, as necessary, to appeal to your target audience on Instagram.

If you want to change your name, do the following:

1. **Go to your Instagram profile, and tap or click Edit Profile.**

2. **In the Name field, type the new name.**

3. **Save your changes.**

   To do so, tap the check mark, Done, Save, or Submit button (depending on the device you're using).

Choosing a profile photo that attracts customers

The *profile photo* on your account, as well as your username, is associated with all your activity. When you post anything to Instagram or engage with other users in any way, your profile photo is visible.

Your profile photo should represent your brand and be recognizable to others. If your company is actively using other social media platforms, its Instagram profile photo should be the same as the one used on other platforms. In this way, you create cohesion across your online media and assure your customers that they found the correct account when searching for you.

TIP

Profile photos on Instagram are cropped to a circle, so your photo should fit properly within that crop. Don't use a logo or an image that loses valuable content when cropped to a circle.

The profile photo on your profile page appears larger than anywhere else on Instagram. When interacting with others, the profile photo is a thumbnail (small) version. Choose an image that isn't too busy, overwhelming, or cluttered with text, because the image will become difficult to decipher as a thumbnail.

The best profile photos are high resolution so that they have a clear object of focus, contain a simple background, and don't pixelate. (In a *pixelated* photo, a low-resolution image is enlarged too much and the individual square pixels become obvious, making the image blurry.)

Writing a Bio That Draws in Followers

Your *Instagram bio* is a short description on your profile that tells people about your business. This description is similar to a 30-second elevator speech and is how you convince new visitors to follow your account.

Most people will read your bio only the first time they visit your profile. Your bio is the first impression you give to new viewers and should accurately convey the message you want to share.

Deciding what information to include

Before you start writing your bio, choose at least two or three key aspects of your business to highlight. These should be traits that will connect emotionally, in some way, with your ideal target audience, such as the examples shown in Figure 2-3.

You also need to determine the voice and style of your bio. If your brand is known for being humorous and witty, your Instagram bio should reflect that same style through words and relevant emojis. In contrast, if your brand is professional and classy, your bio should not be silly and humorous.

© Stephanie Carls/@stephanie.carls (right)

FIGURE 2-3: Effective Instagram bios immediately convey value to the visitor.

To market effectively on Instagram, you must know your target audience and how they're using Instagram. Your bio should be written in a way that connects with the people in that specific demographic. Determine the characteristics that you most want to connect with in that audience and write your bio accordingly. For example, in Figure 2-4, the target audience is people who want to learn about video marketing and how to create their own videos. The bio is written to appeal to that audience.

The Instagram bio is limited to 150 characters, including spaces. The bio is designed to be one single paragraph of information, but you can use formatting techniques to add spaces and line breaks.

REMEMBER

If a bio is too long to fit on the profile page, a More link appears. Tap this link to view the full bio on the screen.

TIP

Because Instagram was designed to be used on a mobile device, it's best to format your bio on a mobile device so that you retain the correct formatting and alignment. If you write your bio as a paragraph, it will have different line breaks on a computer because its screen width is wider than a screen on a mobile device.

Include the emojis and symbols on your device's keyboard in your bio to create visual appeal and to better connect with your audience. To add emojis, you must open the emoji keyboard on your mobile device. An iOS user should tap the smiley face at the bottom of the keyboard. An Android user can tap the smiley face to the left of the spacebar. (If you don't see a smiley face, tap and hold down on the globe icon to display a pop-up menu, where you can select the smiley face icon.)

Instagram is a visual platform, and having icons in the bio helps yours stand out from others. You have many emojis to choose from. If the traditional funny face and cartoonish emojis don't translate to your brand's style, use simple emoji symbols such as squares, diamonds, triangles, and arrows to add color and visual content without detracting from your professional style.

Generally, hashtags are not a good idea in Instagram bios. If people click the hashtag in your bio, your profile page closes and the hashtag gallery results appear instead. The exception is if you have a unique branded hashtag. For example, @shopgifted encourages followers to use the #thisisgifted hashtag to have their photos showcased on their account (see Figure 2-5). We talk about using hashtags on Instagram in Chapter 8.

Formatting your bio

You can edit or create your bio by tapping the Edit Profile button in your Instagram profile. In the Edit Profile screen, shown in Figure 2-6, go to the Bio field and insert the text for your bio. Save any changes when you're finished. Please note that Figure 2-6 shows the setup for a business profile.

Android users can format a bio completely in Instagram. If you want to include line breaks and spacing, tap the Return or Enter key (on the keyboard of your mobile device) at the end of the line.

© @owenvideo

FIGURE 2-4:
The Instagram bio for @owenvideo is designed to appeal to people interested in video marketing.

© Gifted

FIGURE 2-5:
A hashtag in your Instagram bio can be helpful for branding.

TIP

Your bio can be edited and rewritten as often as you want. It's a best practice to review your bio every six months and verify that the information is still accurate and relevant. If something should be revised, go through the editing steps used to set up your initial bio to change the text.

If you run marketing campaigns or have seasonal content or promotions, you can update your bio to align with these events.

Using a call to action to drive website traffic

The last line of your bio should be a call to action (CTA) that directs visitors to click the URL listed below it. (We cover this URL setup in the next section.) The call to action should be clear, actionable, and specific to the action you're asking visitors to do.

Do not simply write *Visit our website* or *Click below.* Instead, use something like *Get your free ebook here* or *Shop our new styles now.* Include a down-arrow emoji at the end of the CTA that points to where the URL will appear in the bio (refer to the example in Figure 2-4).

FIGURE 2-6:
Add your bio in the Edit Profile screen.

As with the rest of your bio, the CTA can be edited as often as you like. Experiment with different wording to determine which drives the best number of clicks to your website.

Choosing a website link that encourages clicks

The most effective way to generate website traffic from Instagram is the link in your bio. To maximize your website traffic, make sure that the URL in your bio takes visitors to the exact page you're promoting. For example, if you're promoting an opportunity to sign up for your newsletter but the link goes to your website home page where there's no place to sign up, you'll lose potential registrants. In this case, you want the link to go directly to the website page where the signup form is located, making it easy for your Instagram audience to sign up quickly.

Your URL can be updated or changed as frequently as you like. You might have a default web page for your profile but change it to coincide with a promotion or campaign you're running on Instagram. After that campaign is complete, you can change the link back to your default.

TECHNICAL STUFF

To accurately track your Instagram traffic, you need to do more than upload a direct link to your website. If someone clicks the link in your bio from Instagram on the desktop, Google Analytics records it as referral traffic from Instagram. When someone taps the link in Instagram on a mobile device, a new browser is opened. Google Analytics doesn't properly track that traffic for you. Instead, it considers opening the new browser *direct* traffic, not social media referral traffic.

Although Google Analytics is tracking that traffic for you, it's categorizing it alongside all other direct traffic to your site, not as a click-through from Instagram. As a result, you may look at your website traffic and be convinced that Instagram is not driving any significant traffic, when it may be sending much more traffic than you're aware of.

To correct this, use a link shortener that provides trackable data on the number of clicks. The link shorteners Bitly, goo.gl, and Rebrandly are the most reliable and safe options. Each provides a data analysis of each link to enable you to track how many clicks you're generating.

To use a link shortener, follow these simple steps:

1. **Find your long-form URL (the direct link from your website) and copy it.**

2. **Open the link shortener website of your choice.**

3. **Paste the long-form URL in the link shortener website.**

    The link shortener generates a short link.

4. **Customize the short URL to match your branding or page.**

5. **Copy the short URL and paste it as your URL in your Instagram bio.**

TIP

Most link shorteners generate a link with random letters and numbers, such as `http://bit.ly/2X4y6`. This doesn't look professional, and visitors might find the link confusing or might question the link's validity. You can simply customize the link to reflect your brand. For example, if your long-form URL is `http://jennstrends.com/blog`, the short-form one might be `http://bit.ly/JTBlog` or `http://bit.ly/JennsTrendsBlog`.

Taking Advantage of a Business Profile Upgrade

In late 2016, Instagram introduced business profiles to Instagram. Before this feature rolled out, all profiles on Instagram looked identical. Now brands have the capability to stand out from regular accounts and can benefit from a variety of features available only to business profiles.

By upgrading to a business profile on Instagram, you get features such as the following:

>> Easy-to-access connection buttons that make it easy for your customers to email you, call you, or get directions to your location

>> An industry listing that informs visitors as to what you do as a business

>> In-app analytics to best monitor what is and isn't working in your content strategy

>> The ability to boost posts from your Instagram profile and run ads on Instagram

>> The ability to manage your Instagram comments and engagement through your Facebook page

TIP

The Contact button feature means people can call or email you, providing you with additional ways to connect directly with your customers and close more sales!

To upgrade to a business profile on Instagram, you must have a Facebook business page to which you can connect. Instagram advertising is managed through the Facebook Business Manager, and even if you don't plan to run ads, Instagram requires you to connect to a Facebook business page.

WARNING

You can connect only one Facebook page to one Instagram profile. If you manage multiple Instagram accounts and want to upgrade them all, they must each connect to a separate Facebook page.

Now that you've set up your Instagram account, as outlined in this chapter, you can easily upgrade your account to a business profile, following a few steps outlined next.

Connecting to a Facebook page

As mentioned, you need to have a Facebook business page if you want to upgrade to an Instagram business profile. Then you follow a few easy steps to connect your Instagram account to your Facebook business page and set up your contact information.

To upgrade your Instagram account to a business account, do the following:

1. **Log in to Instagram on your mobile device, and tap Edit Profile.**

    The Edit Profile screen appears, as shown in Figure 2-7.

2. **Select the Switch to Professional Account option.**

3. **Swipe your way through the screens that highlight the value of business profiles.**

4. **When you get to the last screen, tap Continue.**

5. **Swipe up and down the Select a Category screen to view suggested category names.**

6. **If you don't see the category name in the list, tap Search Categories and type the kind of business you have.**

    As you type, categories that most closely match what you typed appear below the Search Categories box. Continue typing characters to narrow the search results.

7. **Tap the category that best describes your business in the list.**

8. **If you don't want your category to appear in your profile, tap the Display on Profile slider button to Off.**

9. **Tap Done.**

10. **The Business option is selected in the Are You a Business? screen, so tap Next.**

11. **In the Review Your Contact Info screen, update or add information as necessary (see Figure 2-8).**

    Information from your Facebook page, including your email address, phone number, and location, is imported, as shown in Figure 2-8. The info shown here determines which contact information (email, phone, and directions) appears when a user taps the Contact button in your profile.

    You can edit your contact information at any time.

12. **Tap Next to connect to a Facebook page.**

    If you manage only one Facebook page, that page is selected automatically. If you manage multiple Facebook pages, they will appear in the list of options. Select the page to which you want to connect.

13. **Complete the steps to finish your business profile.**

    You can connect with your Facebook page if you want. To complete your profile, add your website and bio, post three photos or videos (which Instagram encourages you to do every week), and invite friends.

Your Instagram account is now set up as a business profile!

FIGURE 2-7:
The Edit Profile screen has an option for upgrading to a business profile.

FIGURE 2-8:
Edit the contact information for your profile.

Navigating your business profile

Now that you've upgraded to a business profile, you'll see some new features on your profile, as shown in Figure 2-9.

Business profile features allow you to make the most out of your Instagram account by tracking your account analytics, promoting your posts, and providing information to your audience about how to contact you:

>> Tap the menu icon (three lines), in the top-right corner, and then tap Insights in the menu that appears to view your profile analytics. As you post content and build your audience, new information will be recorded in your analytics.

>> The Promotions button allows you to create a paid advertising campaign based on content in your profile.

>> The category you selected appears in gray below your name. If you decided not to display the category under your name, perhaps because it didn't describe your business, you see your bio instead.

>> The contact information you set up when upgrading your account appears on your profile when your visitor taps the Contact button, making it easy for your audience to contact you. (A Contact button appears in Figure 2-9.)

After upgrading your account, your new business profile appears to people visiting your profile, as shown in Figure 2-10. They also see your other connection buttons (Following, Message, and Contact in Figure 2-10) and industry listing.

Even though you have these additional features as a business profile, your profile characteristics, such as your username, name, bio, and URL, remain the same.

FIGURE 2-9:
Business profiles provide features not available to a regular Instagram account.

FIGURE 2-10:
Instagram users view your business profile with these added features.

Chapter **3**

Hitting Your Target Audience

You can take fabulous photos and create cute graphics to promote your business on Instagram all day long, but putting a plan in place is crucial for true success. If it seems like there's no rhyme or reason to the posts from some businesses, it's because there isn't. But you're different. You want to do it right, which is why you're reading this book.

In this chapter, you start by determining your business goals and deciding whether you need a team to fulfill them. Then you find out how to gather post ideas by researching your competition, determining the different types of posts, and putting your content into an organized content schedule. Finally, the chapter gets more techie, showing you how to schedule and analyze your posts to save time and create a more successful campaign.

Organizing Your Marketing Goals and Roles

Before you dive deeply into how to take the perfect Insta-awesome photo, you should establish your business goals for the account. Instagram is a wonderful platform, but it's best to know your business reasons for joining before you start posting.

Here are some of the top reasons why businesses join Instagram:

>> **Brand awareness:** Make your brand recognized by potential customers.

>> **Engagement:** Meet and interact with your potential customers.

>> **Increase web traffic:** Drive traffic to your website or blog.

>> **Content distribution:** Disseminate useful information about your product.

>> **Lead generation:** Collect data for list building and sales prospecting.

>> **Community building:** Gather a community of people who love and engage with your brand.

>> **Customer support:** Answer questions, field complaints, and accept compliments.

Assembling your Instagram team

Of the seven business reasons for using Instagram, you might have only one or you might have them all! The number of reasons you choose dictates the roles and responsibilities in managing your account. And your budget plays a big role in determining whether you or a team shoulder those responsibilities. Regardless of the number of people, certain functions must be established for your business to be successful on Instagram.

Social media manager

Generally, the *social media manager* is responsible for the account's big picture. In regards to your business goals, the social media manager plans the strategy of the account and might assist in hiring team members for the other roles (discussed next). The social media manager also creates the account, manages passwords, and sets up the profile page. Details on how to do all these tasks are in Chapters 1 and 2. If you're a one-person team, you'll take on the role of social media manager and all the other roles described in this section.

Content creator

The *content creator* creates and organizes all content to be shared in the account. It's best if the content creator has experience with photography and graphic design because Instagram is visual and success on the platform requires professional imagery. The content creator may also be responsible for posting, scheduling, and storing posts to be shared later. Details about creating a content calendar are detailed later in this chapter.

Community manager

The *community manager* is in charge of engagement. This person should be regularly following other accounts, and liking and commenting on posts from other Instagrammers. A community manager should be actively listening to your audience and those in your online community so he or she can anticipate problems or take advantage of opportunities to promote the brand. The community manager is the PR arm of your Instagram account.

Campaign manager

Promotions, contests, and giveaways are used to attract more followers. The *campaign manager* manages them all. A promotion might include paid advertising or working with other accounts for shared exposure. The campaign manager works closely with the content creator, often providing a storyboard of ideas.

Analytics manager

The *analytics manager* tracks all data in the account. Followers, post performance, campaign results, hashtag winners, you name it — the analytics manager tracks it. After this data is collected, the analytics manager shares it with the team so they can make informed decisions about what is and isn't working.

Determining your brand voice

Does your brand have a consistent voice? For instance, if someone doesn't see your physical branding (logo, colors, imagery), could he or she recognize that the content was from you simply by the words that were written?

Establishing a consistent brand voice is important, especially if you have several content creators. Here's how to get started:

>> **Review several samples of your content and pull the pieces that you feel best represent what you (and your team, if you have one) want to convey as your brand.** Figure out what they all have in common. Also note which items don't fit so you'll know what you don't want your brand voice to sound like.

>> **Choose three words that best describe your brand from the pile of sample content.** For instance, a daycare might choose *nurturing, diverse,* and *joyful.* Then further break down how these words will be expressed by your brand. For example:

- Nurturing: Loving, safe, cuddly, warm, kind, patient

- Diverse: Multiple programs, cultural awareness, inclusive

- Joyful: Happy, fun, musical, laughter

>> **If you have a team, ensure that they're on board with the brand voice and the associated words.** Show them your favorite pieces of content that embody these words so they have a good understanding about how you want them used.

>> **Review your brand voice at least every six months to make sure it's still working.** Look over a large sample of content to see how your brand voice has been carried out, and adjust anything that isn't working. You may even discover a new word that you'd like to incorporate!

Envisioning your look

After you have an understanding of your brand's voice, it's time to work on your brand's look. Although most people consider the logo to be the main element of a brand, you need to consider a lot more. In the context of Instagram, your content, not the logo, is usually the focal point of your profile. However, your logo makes a good starting point upon which to base other elements.

A logo is a distinctive symbol that the public can easily identify as part of your brand. Think of some of the brands you see regularly, such as Target, Apple, and Starbucks. One look at their logo and you instantly know which company is represented.

Logos can be designed in a variety of ways:

>> As an object that's easily associated with the product or service, such as the smoking wine bottle from Smoking Gun Wines (see Figure 3-1, left).

>> As an abstract symbol that isn't obviously related with the product or service, such as the symbol that the Marketing Specialist uses with the company name (see Figure 3-1, center).

>> As a wordmark logo, in which the name of the business is the logo set in a consistent font and color, such as the Jenn's Trends logo (see Figure 3-1, right).

FIGURE 3-1:
These logo types illustrate an easily associated product or service (left), an abstract symbol (center), and a wordmark logo (right).

The company's color palette, brand voice, values and, of course, brand name should all be integrated with the logo. A professional graphic designer can work with you to select colors, advise on fonts that enhance your brand voice, and assist in drawing or selecting visual objects to represent your brand. A graphic designer is also familiar with the different file types necessary for print versus online and should provide the logo in several formats for different uses. We recommend that you use a professional for this instead of creating a logo on your own.

After your logo is created, you'll likely have one or two colors established with your brand. Next, develop a fuller color palette of complementary colors that you can use in your marketing content. Remember to consider your brand voice when selecting these colors. Most colors illicit a mood (for example, blue is calming and red can mean anger), so do some research or have your graphic designer help create a full color palette when he or she develops your logo.

Next, focus on creating a consistent style for your images. Choices for your images can vary by using the following:

>> Photography, illustrations, videos, or any combination thereof: In Figure 3-2, left, @kailochic uses photography exclusively as its Instagram style. In Figure 3-2, center, @ahrynscott uses video as its style.

>> Text overlays on all, some, or no images: In Figure 3-2, right, @mollymarshall-marketing uses text overlays on many of her images.

FIGURE 3-2: Instagram business accounts often showcase one image style, such as photography (left), videos (middle), or text overlays on images (right).

© Kara Whitten (left), Ahryn Scott (middle), and Molly Marshall Marketing (right)

>> **Only certain colors:** @laurabriedis.design uses purple and green as the dominant colors in all the images chosen for her Instagram style, as you can see in Figure 3-3, left.

>> **Only certain subject matter:** In Figure 3-3, right, @bruce_the_office_cat features one cat hanging around the office as the main subject in all its images.

FIGURE 3-3: Instagram business accounts often stick to a color scheme (left), or one subject matter (right).

© Laura Briedis (left), ©Graphics and More (right)

By setting your business goals, assembling your team (even if that team is just you), determining your brand voice, and envisioning your look, you've provided a good foundation. Now you're ready to start thinking about your posts. Read on to find out how to find post ideas.

Gathering Post Ideas

If you've completed the steps outlined earlier in this chapter, you can now get down to the fun part: finding post ideas! Researching your competition, deciding on a post type, and creating a content calendar are covered next to keep you on the path to an awesome Instagram page!

Researching your competition

Chances are you already have a good idea about who your competition is offline, especially if your business serves customers locally. If you have several business names to research, finding them on Instagram is fairly easy if they each have an account.

Here are two easy ways to find the Instagram accounts of your competitors:

>> Go to their websites and see whether they have a link to their Instagram accounts. If so, click the link or Instagram icon.

>> Go to Instagram directly and click the magnifying glass at the bottom of the page to display the Search field. Then tap in the Search field and type the business name (see Figure 3-4) and see whether the business appears. Tap the name to go to the account.

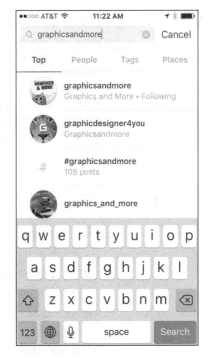

FIGURE 3-4:
Type a business name in the Search field, and look for its Instagram account in the list that appears.

TIP

If you're using the second research method, several accounts might have similar names. If you can't distinguish which one is the correct account, use the first method to verify that you've found the correct one.

After you locate a competitor's Instagram account, look at its profile page. Some businesses take more care with their profile page than others. Ask yourself the following:

>> Does the profile page have an easily identifiable username?

>> Is the account set up as a business account? (Email or Contact buttons are displayed on business accounts, as shown in Figure 3-5.)

>> Does the page explain what the business does in a simple way?

>> Does the business include a link to its website or another resource?

>> Are photos, images, and videos used in a cohesive way?

>> Does the page have an Instagram story running?

Look at what your competitor has done. Can you learn any lessons, good or bad, for your own profile? For more information about creating a winning profile, see Chapter 2.

Next, tap the most recent post that the competitor's account posted. Take note of the image and caption. Does the post

>> Have an intriguing image, video, or photo?

>> Use text overlays that might include a quote, phrase, or statistic?

>> Use filters? If so, is one filter used consistently?

>> Have a caption? If so, does it make you want to know more?

>> Use hashtags? If so, how many?

Go through this set of questions with several of your competitor's posts. Note which of them received the highest engagement (most likes and comments). Also note the posts that received low engagement.

FIGURE 3-5:
A business profile can display buttons for Contact or Email, and other action items.

If you'd like to get more technical, set up an Excel spreadsheet using the preceding questions as column headings and note similarities between winning and losing posts. Repeat the process with other competitors. Then use the information to craft posts that are more attractive to your target audience.

TIP

This process doesn't need to be restricted to competitor research. Feel free to see what other brands are doing successfully on Instagram and determine whether their techniques can be translated to your business.

Determining post content

If you did the research described in the last section, you'll have a good idea of what content is working (and what's not) for your competitors and other brands. Now that you have the data you need, plus the work you've done on your brand, you're ready to go!

You should now know the following:

>> Your brand voice

>> Your color palette

>> Whether you'll be using photography, illustrations, video, or all three

>> Whether text overlays will be used sometimes, always, or never

>> Whether you'll be using a filter and, if so, which one

>> Your caption style

>> How many hashtags you'll use (for information on hashtag research, head to Chapter 9)

If you're still struggling for content ideas, think about the following quick, effective content ideas for your posts:

>> How-to articles related to your industry (by using a link in the bio)

>> Product or service success stories and testimonials (by using a link in the bio)

>> Case studies (by using a link in the bio)

>> Weekly hashtag themes, such as #TBT (Throwback Thursday) or #WCW (Woman Crush Wednesday)

>> Holidays

>> Behind-the-scenes photos of your staff

TIP

For more post ideas, see Chapter 24.

After you have the type of content for your posts figured out, the next step is creating a content calendar.

Creating a content calendar

A *content calendar* is an excellent way to get your content organized. It forces you to think strategically, which is far better than putting last-minute random content on your profile. It also provides an easy way to share plans with your team and offers a complete snapshot at the end of the year for planning the next year. An Instagram content calendar should

>> Include one to six months of planning.

>> Tie in with your other marketing functions and campaigns.

>> Account for holidays (including wacky ones such as #NationalDonutDay) if you choose to celebrate them.

>> Account for major industry events.

>> Include dates of product or service launches.

>> Include space for regularly scheduled tips, articles, and how-to's.

>> Save space for curated content from others.

>> Set aside dates for tying in Instagram stories and video with your regular Instagram posts.

>> Note whether a post will be a paid ad and how much you'll spend.

If you want to start simply, set up a content calendar in Excel or Google Sheets. Create a worksheet for each month of the year, and then type each day of the week across the top. On the left, separate the rows by weeks, for instance, September 1 — September 6, 2020, as shown in Figure 3-6. Add a row below each date if you also plan to do Instagram stories on a regular basis.

Days/Weeks	Monday	Tuesday	Wednesday	Thursday	Friday	Saturday	Sunday
September 1-6 Post							
Stories							
September 7-13 Post							
Stories							
September 14-20 Post							
Stories							
September 21-27 Post							

FIGURE 3-6: A simple content calendar set up in Excel.

After you set up the framework, start filling in known items, such as holidays, events, promotions, and contests you've planned. You'll be surprised how quickly your content calendar fills up, but there will still be several empty spaces. These empty spaces are the perfect spot for setting dates for tips, articles, how-to's, infographics, and curated content from others. See Figure 3-7 for an example of a content calendar for an outdoor equipment retailer.

If you've been on other social media platforms for a while, you may have tons of this content waiting to be reformatted for Instagram. But if you're new to social media, a brainstorming session is helpful for thinking of creative new posts.

FIGURE 3-7:
This content
calendar shows a
one-month plan
for an outdoor
equipment
retailer.

Days/Weeks	Monday	Tuesday	Wednesday	Thursday	Friday	Saturday	Sunday
September 1-6 Post	Labor Day	Campfire s'mores	Best hiking article	Tent sale promo	Mt. Lassen photo	25% off tents this weekend	
Stories	Parade video	Boomerang of campfire	Jax on hike	Walk-thru of best tents in store		C'mon down to the sale!	
September 7-13 Post	Lake Tahoe photo	Mountain biking event photos			20% off hiking equip		
Stories	Boating on Tahoe video	Behind the scenes of biking events			Pics of hiking shoes on sale		
September 14-20 Post	#GoCamping promo with user generated photos all week						
Stories	Send us your camping photos! Camper takeover!						
September 21-27 Post	Backpack sale		Fall camping article		#FreeCarabinerDay		Backpack sale
Stories	Sara modeling backpacks		Leaves falling video - get ready for Fall		Carabiners falling from bin video		

Now that you have a plan, you can move on to creating the content. Chapters 4 and 5 have in-depth information about taking photos and creating videos. If you plan on creating posts with text overlays or other designed images, dozens of apps make it quick and easy for anyone. Here are some to try out:

>> **Adobe Spark** (https://spark.adobe.com): Social media graphic templates to repurpose, including one for Instagram stories

>> **Canva** (www.canva.com): Social media graphic templates, photography, fonts, and images available for free or $1

>> **PicLab** (http://museworks.co/piclab): Features for creating photo collages and specialty sticker overlays

>> **PicMonkey** (www.picmonkey.com): Templates, design elements, and collages

>> **Typic** (www.typicapp.com): Filters, creative text overlays, and stickers

>> **WordSwag** (http://wordswag.co): Backgrounds and free photography plus several fonts and suggested famous quotes available for text overlays

In the next section, you find out about the best places to store and schedule all this glorious content.

Evaluating third-party scheduling and analytics platforms

Excel and Google Sheets are excellent tools for planning the timing, topics, and titles of posts, but they're not meant to be used to store images for posting later. Luckily, several platforms allow you to store, schedule, and analyze your

Instagram posts. But unlike Facebook or Twitter, Instagram has a tricky little clause in its terms and conditions that doesn't allow you to schedule a post; Instagram prefers that people post in the moment.

Several platforms offer a work-around for this snag — allowing you to upload and store your image and caption in advance. After you load the material, you can schedule a time for it to automatically post to Instagram. This update is handy; previously, most apps sent a push notification to your phone, and then you still had to publish the post yourself.

Third-party platforms are excellent for planning ahead visually. Scheduling allows you to see what the images you plan to post look like together, so you can ensure that your page will be as visually appealing as possible.

Another function that many third-party platforms offer (and many businesses overlook) is analytics. You can learn quite a bit about your customers' preferences by paying attention to data.

For instance, simply looking at which posts received the highest likes or comments in the last month unveils big clues about what you should post next. You'll probably notice that certain images or background colors work better. Data can also reveal which time of day is best to post, or whether certain hashtags attract more people. For specifics on Instagram analytics, head to Chapter 13.

As of this writing, the most common third-party platforms that enable Instagram post scheduling and analytics are as follows:

- AgoraPulse
- Iconosquare
- Buffer
- Hootsuite
- Later
- Planoly
- Tailwind
- Sprout Social

Following are other services included on most of the platforms listed:

- Connections to other networks, such as Facebook, Twitter, LinkedIn, and Pinterest

>> Engagement (commenting, liking, following) with other accounts

>> The capability to share scheduled posts with other members of your team and track approvals

>> The capability to manage multiple accounts at once on a dashboard, such as the one in Figure 3-8

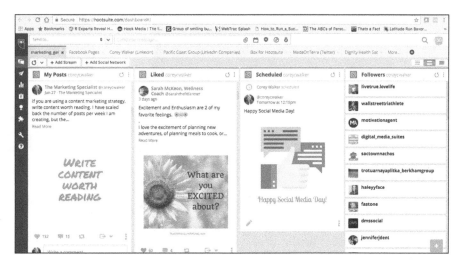

FIGURE 3-8: Many platforms, such as Hootsuite, offer a dashboard so you can see multiple streams of content in one place.

Do your homework by looking at the services available and comparing the pricing on each platform. (Pricing structures vary wildly.) Some platforms are robust but may have more than you'll realistically use. Imagine how you would use the platform on a daily basis, look at your budget, and then make your choice.

TIP

If you use multiple social media networks for your business, choose a platform that uses a dashboard so you can view all your accounts easily.

Chapter **4**

Taking and Posting Great Photos

Now that you have all your Instagram ducks in a row, it's time for those ducks to start walking around . . . and take some photos.

In this chapter, you find out how to take photos with Instagram, use editing tools to make your photos look their best, and then share photos stored on your iPhone, iPad, or Android smartphone or tablet with your followers and on other social networks.

REMEMBER

You can't upload photos when you use the Instagram website on your desktop, tablet, or smartphone browser.

All figures in this chapter were taken using the iPhone app, because that's Instagram's native platform. Don't worry, Android users — we note any differences between the iPhone and Android apps.

Taking Your Best Shot

Before you can post a photo on Instagram, you need to tell the app where to get the photo. In this section, we cover taking a photo. For details on selecting from your existing photos, see the "Uploading Photos from Your Camera Roll" section, later in the chapter.

When you first log in to Instagram, you'll see your feed on the screen. Tap the + icon at the bottom of the screen. When prompted, allow Instagram access to your phone's camera. Next, you'll see the Photo screen shown in Figure 4-1.

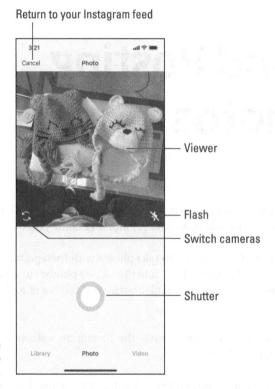

Return to your Instagram feed

Viewer

Flash

Switch cameras

Shutter

FIGURE 4-1:
Now you can take
your photo.

The good news is that you have to go through this process only once. The next time you open Instagram and tap the + icon, you won't have to enable camera access.

Note the following elements in the Photo screen:

>> The *viewer* appears in the top part of the screen.

>> The *switch cameras icon* (two circular arrows) is in the bottom-left corner of the viewer. Tap the icon to switch between your smartphone's front and back cameras.

>> The *flash icon* (lightning bolt) appears in the bottom-right corner of the viewer. Tap the flash icon to toggle the following flash modes:

- Off: This mode is the default. The flash icon has a diagonal line through it (iOS) or a hollow lightning bolt (Android).

- On: The flash icon appears without a diagonal line (iOS) or with a solid lightning bolt (Android).

- Auto-detect (iOS only): The flash icon has an *A* in the upper-right corner.

>> The *shutter button* is the large gray circle in the bottom half of the screen.

>> The *Cancel button* (iOS) or *X icon* (Android), in the upper-left corner, returns to your Instagram feed.

When you're ready to take a photo, tap the shutter button. Your phone makes a camera shutter sound, as it does when you use the phone's Camera app.

Improving Your Best Shot

The photo you've just taken appears in the viewer of the Filter screen, as shown in Figure 4-2.

REMEMBER

Instagram automatically crops the photo to a square for editing and posting. If you want the photo to have taller or wider dimensions, you must add it from your camera roll.

The screen contains the following four sections, from top to bottom:

>> The *top menu bar*, with a < (back) icon on the left, the Lux icon in the center (which you learn about later in this chapter), and the Next link on the right

>> The *viewer*, which displays your photo

>> A row of *filter thumbnail images* so you can see what your photo will look like with a filter applied

>> The *bottom menu bar*, with a Filter menu option (selected by default) and the Edit option

FIGURE 4-2:
The Filter screen.

TIP

Not interested in editing your photo? Simply tap the back icon in the upper-left corner to save your photo to your camera roll automatically and then take a new one, if you want.

Applying a filter

Below your photo in the viewer is a row of filters. Each filter includes a thumbnail image so you can see the filter's effect on your photo.

Swipe from right to left in the row of thumbnail images to view all 23 filters, from Clarendon to Nashville. (Normal is the default image, without a filter.) Tap a filter thumbnail image, and the photo in the viewer changes to show you the photo with that filter applied.

REMEMBER

To return to the original photo, tap the Normal thumbnail (refer to Figure 4-2). To continue processing the photo with a filter, either tap Edit at the bottom-right corner of the screen to edit your photo further, or tap Next in the upper-right corner of the screen to add a description to your photo. (You learn how to add a description in the "Enriching Your Photo" section, later in this chapter.)

What happens when a filter is not quite to your liking and you'd like to tweak it? You can change the intensity of any filter (except Normal) by tapping the filter thumbnail image again. A slider appears; move it to the left and right to change the intensity. The photo in the viewer changes to reflect the selected intensity. The default intensity for each filter is 100. (And yes, we checked each one.) In iOS, a frame icon appears to the right of the slider bar. When you tap this icon, Instagram automatically adds a square frame to the photo. Remove the frame by tapping the icon again.

When you've set the intensity to just the right amount, tap Done. If you're still not satisfied and want to return the photo to its original intensity, tap Cancel.

REMEMBER

Keep in mind that any filter settings will revert to the default after you leave this screen.

TIP

If you want to see how the photo with a filter compares to the original photo, tap and hold down on the viewer to view the original photo. Release your finger to see the photo with the applied filter.

Changing the order of filters

Too many filters or your favorite ones are too far down in the list? No problem. Swipe to the end of the filter list, and you'll see a Manage icon. Tap the icon to open the Manage Filters screen, shown in Figure 4-3, where you can perform three tasks: Change the order of filters in the row, add filters, and disable filters.

The filters on the Manage Filters screen appear in the same order as they do in the Filter screen. You can change the order of filters as follows:

1. **Tap and hold down on a filter name in the list.**

   After you hold down on the name for about a second, the filter name gets larger (iOS) or outlined in gray (Android).

2. **Move the name in the list.**

   As you move the filter name, other filter names helpfully move out of the way so you can see where your selected filter will appear in the list.

3. **When the filter is where you want it, release your finger.**

   The filter name appears in your desired location in the list.

That's all there is to it! To return to the Filter screen, tap Done (iOS) or the check mark (Android).

Adding a filter

When you swipe up and down in the list of filters on the Manage Filters screen, you'll see several filter names that have a hollow circle to the right of the name (iOS) or appear dimmed (Android). These filters are disabled, but it's easy to add any of them to the Filter screen.

Simply tap a dimmed filter name. The circle turns blue with a check mark (iOS) or the name turns black (Android), which means the filter is active, and you see a check mark to the right of your newly activated filter name. Tap Done (iOS) or the check mark icon (Android), and you return to the Filter screen, where you see your new filter in the row of filters.

Disabling a filter

If you decide that you don't want to include one or more filters in the Filter screen, you can disable it by tapping the filter name in the list on the Manage Filters screen. The check mark to the right of the name disappears in both iOS and Android, but in Android the filter name is also gray. (To restore the filter, just tap the disabled filter name again.)

When you're finished, tap Done (iOS) or the check mark icon (Android).

Tweaking with the editing tools

When you've finished experimenting with filters, view Instagram's editing tools by tapping Edit at the bottom of the screen. A row of editing tools appears below the viewer, as shown in Figure 4-4.

Swipe from right to left in the row of editing tools to see all 13 tools. Tap a tool to open it below the viewer.

What you see below the viewer depends on the tool you tapped. For example, when you tap the Brightness tool, a slider appears so you can increase or decrease the photo's brightness. No matter what tool you use, the photo in the viewer reflects the changes you make.

Here's what you can do with each tool:

FIGURE 4-4:
The tool name appears above each tool icon.

>> **Adjust:** You can adjust your photo in several ways by using the Adjust tool. A row of three icons and an associated slider bar appear below the photo, as shown in Figure 4-5, so you can make the following changes:

- Change the vertical or horizontal perspective of the photo by tapping the left or right icon, respectively, below the photo. After you tap the icon, it's highlighted in black. The slider bar is a series of vertical lines. Swipe left and right in the slider bar to see the change reflected in the photo. As you slide, the highlighted icon above the slider bar is replaced with a box that shows you the change amount measured in degrees.

- If the object in your photo appears tilted, tap the straighten icon in the middle of the icon row. Then swipe left and right in the slider bar to tilt the photo so that the object appears straight. As you swipe in the slider bar, a box appears in place of the straighten icon and shows you the number of degrees you're tilting the photo.

- Rotate the photo 90 degrees counterclockwise by tapping the rotate icon in the upper-right corner of the screen. Keep tapping the rotate icon to continue to rotate the photo in the viewer.

- Crop the photo to a specific area by first zooming in (touch the photo and spread your thumb and index finger apart) in the viewer. Then hold down on the photo and drag it in the viewer until you see the part of the photo you want to post on your Instagram feed. If you decide you don't want to crop the photo, zoom back out to the photo's original size by pinching your thumb and index finger together in the viewer.

In iOS, a grid appears on top of the photo to help with the adjustment. Tap the grid icon in the upper-left corner to cycle through the different grid intensities or to remove the grid.

FIGURE 4-5:
Use the slider bar in the Adjust screen to change the photo's perspective.

>> **Brightness:** In the slider bar below the viewer, slide the dot to the left to darken the photo or to the right to make the photo brighter. As you move the slider bar, the photo in the viewer darkens or brightens accordingly.

>> **Contrast:** In the slider bar, lower the intensity of dark areas and make all the colors in the image more consistent by sliding the dot to the left. Make the light areas lighter and the dark areas darker so there is a greater distinction between light and dark by sliding the dot to the right.

>> **Lux tool:** At the top center of the Filter and Edit screens is an icon that looks like a magic wand (iOS) or a sun (Android). Tap it to open the Lux tool, which you can use to quickly change the exposure level and brightness instead of using the separate Brightness and Contrast editing tools. Move the slider to change the exposure level and brightness. When you're finished, tap Done to save your changes, or tap Cancel to discard them.

If you want to undo any edits you've made, tap the Lux icon and then move the slider to its default location, 50. (The default setting for the Brightness and Contrast editing tools, however, is 0.) When you're done, tap Done. If you've undone any edits in tools other than Lux, you won't see the gray dot below the tool button.

>> **Structure:** This tool enhances the details in the photo, such as adding color in an area that appears washed out in the original. In the slider bar, slide the dot to the right to see how the tool increases the details of the photo in the viewer. If you think the photo is too detailed, slide to the left to make the photo fuzzier.

>> **Warmth:** In the slider bar below the viewer, slide the dot to the right to make the colors warmer by adding orange tones or to the left to make the colors cooler by adding blue tones.

>> **Saturation:** In the slider bar, slide the dot to the right or left to increase or decrease, respectively, the intensity of all colors in your photo.

>> **Color:** You can change the color of your photo's shadows or highlights or both, as well as change the intensity of the tint. Eight colors are available: yellow, orange, red, pink, purple, blue, cyan, or green, as you see in Figure 4-6.

- *To change the color of shadows in your photo:* Tap Shadows, if necessary (it's the default), and then tap one of the color dots.

- *To change the highlight color:* Tap Highlights, and then tap one of the eight color dots, which are the same colors as those used for shadows.

- *To change the tint intensity for the shadow or highlight color:* Tap the color dot twice. In the slider bar that appears below the viewer, slide the dot to the left or right to decrease or increase the intensity, respectively. When the intensity looks good to you, release your finger from the dot and then tap Done to return to the Color page.

>> **Fade:** Do you want your photo to look like it's been sitting in a shoebox for years . . . or decades? In the slider bar, slide the dot to the right to fade the color from your photo or to the left to add color.

>> **Highlights:** In the slider bar, slide the dot to the right to increase the brightness in bright areas of the photo. Slide to the left to darken the bright areas in the photo.

>> **Shadows:** In the slider bar, slide the dot to the right to lighten the dark areas in your photo. Slide to the left to darken the dark areas.

>> **Vignette:** This tool allows you to darken the edges of the photo so people will focus on the center of the photo. In the slider bar, slide the dot to the right to darken the photo edges.

>> **Tilt Shift:** You can blur the outer edges of your photo and keep the center in clear focus so people will automatically look at the focused area. Tap Radial below the viewer to blur all four edges of the photo and keep the center focused. Tap Linear to blur just the top and bottom edges of the photo.

FIGURE 4-6:
Tap the color dot to select a color for your photo shadow.

You can change the size of the "unblurred" area of the picture by tapping the center of the photo with your thumb and forefinger. Then spread them apart to make the area larger or together to make the area smaller. Tap Off if you don't like the changes and want to keep your entire photo in focus.

>> **Sharpen:** This tool sharpens features that aren't visible in the original photo, such as the texture on a wall. In the slider bar, slide the dot to the right and left to make the photo less and more fuzzy, respectively.

After you finish making changes to your photo, apply your effect by tapping Done. Or discard the effect by tapping Cancel.

REMEMBER

After you apply an effect, a gray dot appears below the effect's icon as a reminder that your photo now sports that effect.

Saving your changes (or not)

When you've finished using the editing tools and filters, you can do one of four things:

>> **Discard your changes** and return to the Photo screen by tapping the left arrow icon in the upper-left corner and then tapping Discard in the pop-up menu.

>> **Save your changes and continue editing** by tapping the left arrow icon and then tapping Save Draft in the pop-up menu.

>> **Discard your changes and continue editing** by tapping the left arrow icon and then tapping Cancel in the pop-up menu.

>> **Add a description** to the photo by tapping Next in the upper-right corner. The New Post screen appears, where you can add a caption and location, tag friends, and decide if you want to share the photo on other social networks. (See the next section.)

To follow along with the example in this chapter, tap Next.

Enriching Your Photo

After you tap Next in the Edit screen, the New Post screen appears, as shown in Figure 4-7. In this screen, you can add a caption to your photo, tag people who appear in the photo, include the photo's location, share the photo on other social media networks, and turn commenting on and off.

Describing your photo

To add a description to your photo, tap in the top section where it says *Write a caption*. A keyboard appears at the bottom of the screen.

REMEMBER

Captions can't exceed 2,200 characters. You'll know you've reached the limit when you keep typing and no characters appear in the caption box.

TIP

To add a blank line between paragraphs, tap the Return key after the last character of text. You can read more about formatting your caption (and the pitfalls) for the iPhone and Android smartphones at `www.jennstrends.com/how-to-format-instagram-captions/`.

When you've finished writing, tap OK in the upper-right corner of the screen. The text of your caption appears in the caption box.

To edit the caption, tap in the caption box and make your changes. When you're finished, tap OK.

FIGURE 4-7:
Add details to your photo here.

It's good to have options

Below the caption box are four options to identify people in your photo, add a location to your photo, share your photo on other social networks, and turn commenting on and off (under the Advanced Settings link at the bottom).

Tagging people

When you *tag* people, you add their Instagram usernames to your photo so they know that you posted a photo with them in it. Instagram enables you to tag up to 20 people in a single photo. To tag a person in your photo, do the following:

1. **On the New Post screen, tap Tag People.**

   The Tag People screen appears.

2. **Tap the photo to tag.**

   The Search screen appears.

3. **In the Search for a Person box, type the name of the person you want to tag, and then tap the Search key in the keyboard.**

   A list of people appears below the box.

4. **Swipe up and down in the list until you find the person you want to tag, and then tap the person's name.**

   You can tag only people who appear in the list.

5. **Repeat this process to tag more people.**

6. **When you've finished tagging people, tap Done in the upper-right corner of the screen.**

WARNING

Be sure that you tag only people who are in the photo. If you tag someone who isn't in the photo, the tagged person may report you to Instagram, and then you may be subject to "deleted content, disabled accounts, or other restrictions" per Instagram's Community Guidelines. However, if the photo contains a logo or product, you can tag the brand or company associated with the product or logo.

Adding your location

You can include your current location in the photo's description. Tap Add Location. Your smartphone or tablet asks if the Instagram app can use your location if it's the first time you are adding a location. Tap Allow in the pop-up window to continue.

In the Locations screen that appears, swipe up and down in the list of nearby locations. If you don't find your location, tap the Search box at the top of the screen and start typing. As you type, results that most closely match your search term(s) appear in the list. When you find the location in the list, tap the location name.

If you want to delete the location, tap the delete icon (X) to the right of the location. After you delete the location, you see Add Location again on the screen.

REMEMBER

After you allow the Instagram app to use your location, the next time you open the New Post window, you'll see a row of potential locations below Add Location. Swipe up in the row to view more locations. Tap the location name to select it as your location. You can still add a location by tapping Add Location and either selecting a location from the list or by typing the location in the Search box and then selecting the location in the list.

Facebook

Tap the dot to toggle the Facebook switch from left to right to log into Facebook and post your photo to your Facebook newsfeed as well as to Instagram. If this is the first time you're posting to Facebook, you'll be asked to allow Facebook to access your Instagram account.

If your shared post links to your personal account, the post is shared only with your Facebook friends. When your shared post links to your business account, the post is shared with the people who follow your Facebook business profile.

Twitter

If you want to tweet the same Instagram photo you're preparing, tap the dot to toggle the Twitter switch from left to right to log into your Twitter account. After you log in, you can share your photo and caption in a tweet. Remember that Twitter will cut off any caption that exceeds 280 characters. If this is the first time you are posting to Twitter from Instagram, you will have to allow Twitter access to your account.

Tumblr

You can post your photo to your Tumblr account as well by tapping the Tumblr dot to toggle from left to right. Tumblr opens so you can log into your account, and then you return to Instagram. When you share your photo and related information in Instagram, you'll share it to your Tumblr feed as well.

You have to tap the toggle dot every time you want to share on Facebook, Twitter, and Tumblr.

Turning commenting on and off

Before you share your photo, you may not want to take the time to read or respond to comments. You can block your followers from leaving comments about your photo. Begin by tapping the Advanced Settings option at the bottom of the New Post screen (refer to Figure 4-7). In the Advanced Settings screen, tap the Turn Off Commenting dot to toggle from left to right. To return to the New Post screen, tap the left arrow in the upper-left corner.

Tag, you're it, business partner

In your post, you can promote a *business partner* (another Instagram user with a business profile you can tag in branded content posts). Connect with the business partner by opening the Advanced Settings screen and tapping Tag Business Partner to search for the business partner. (It's a good idea to ask your prospective business partner for permission first, don't you think?) After you've tagged your business partner, you can have that person promote your post by tapping the Allow Business Partner to Promote dot. Your post will include a *paid partnership with* label, and Instagram will share the post's metrics with your business partner.

REMEMBER

When you ask your partner for permission to work with him or her, be sure your partner has a business profile. If not, you won't see the partner's profile in your search.

Write alternative text

You can write alternative, or alt, text for your photo. *Alt text* is a web standard for providing image descriptions for people with visual impairments. Writing an alt text description of your photo is not only polite but also makes your photo rank higher in search engine queries.

Posting Your Photos: Ta Da!

Your photo or photos are now ready to share with the Instagram world, so all you have to do is tap Share in the upper-right corner of the New Post screen.

After you post a photo, the home screen appears with your photo at the top, as shown in Figure 4-8. If you've posted several photos in one post (we show you how later in the chapter), you'll be able to swipe in your post to view them all. Slicker than a box of rocks.

Instagram automatically uploads your photo in the best resolution possible. When you take a photo with a smartphone or tablet that runs iOS or Android, resolution isn't an issue. However, if you upload a photo from your camera roll (on the iPhone) or gallery (on an Android smartphone), check your image settings in a photo-editing app such as Image Size (iPhone and iPad) or Photo & Picture Resizer (Android smartphones and tablets). In the app, see that the photo has a width between 320 and 1,080 pixels with an aspect ratio between 1.91:1 and 4:5. For example, if the photo width is 1,080 pixels, the height can be between 566 pixels (1.91:1 ratio) and 1,350 pixels (4:5 ratio). If your photo height is too low or high, Instagram will automatically crop it to fit the aspect ratio. The moral of this story is to check and crop your photos before Instagram does it for you (probably to your annoyance).

FIGURE 4-8:
The photo appears in your new post.

Uploading Photos from Your Camera Roll

Do you have some photos you've already shot that you'd like to share with your followers? It's easy to select one or more photos and then share them on your Instagram feed. (We show you how to upload multiple photos in the next section.) Here's how to upload photos from your camera:

1. **Tap the + icon at the bottom of the home screen.**

   The Photo screen appears.

2. **Tap Library (iOS) or Gallery (Android).**

   The Camera Roll screen appears, as shown in Figure 4-9. (Android users see the Gallery screen.) The most recent photo you saved to your smartphone appears in the viewer. Thumbnail-sized photos appear below the viewer.

3. **Swipe in the thumbnail photos to view other photos. When you find one you like, tap it.**

   The selected photo appears in the viewer. Instagram automatically crops your photo to the size of the viewer.

4. **(Optional) View the photo in its original size by tapping the resize icon (labeled in Figure 4-9).**

5. **Tap Next.**

6. **(Optional) Apply filters and edit your photo as described earlier.**

7. **Tap Next.**

   The New Post screen appears.

8. **(Optional) Write a caption, tag people, add a location, change advanced settings and recipients, and share your photo on other social networks.**

   For details, bookmark this page and read the earlier section, "Enriching Your Photo."

9. **When you're ready to share your photos, tap Share.**

REMEMBER

If you have an Apple Mac desktop or laptop and you use the Safari web browser, there's a trick you can use to upload one or more photos from your Mac to your Instagram profile. Bookmark this page and go back to Chapter 1 to learn all about it. (Windows users, you're out of luck.)

Did you notice in Figure 4-9 the icons for the Boomerang and Layout apps? You use the Boomerang app to create and post mini-videos on your feed. Your camera takes a burst of photos, and Boomerang stitches them together, creating a quick video clip that plays backward and forward — like a Boomerang flies . . . get it? (See Chapter 15 for details on using Boomerang.)

You can use the Layout app to combine multiple photos into one photo and post the combined photo on your feed without having to swipe back and forth between photos.

Selected multiple photos

Layout app

Boomerang app

Resize photo

Selected thumbnail photo

FIGURE 4-9:
The thumbnail of the selected photo appears dimmed.

Uploading Multiple Photos to One Post

You don't need to have one post for each photo. Instead, you can add as many as ten photos in your camera roll (or gallery if you use an Android smartphone) to a single post.

Selecting multiple photos

To choose more than one photo to add to a post, do the following:

1. In the main Instagram feed screen, tap the + icon.

2. Tap Library (iOS) or Gallery (Android), in the lower-left corner of the screen.

The most recent photo in your camera roll (or gallery) appears in the viewer.

3. Swipe in the thumbnail photos, and then tap the first photo you want to add.

4. Tap the select multiple icon (labeled in Figure 4-9).

The selected thumbnail appears dimmed, with a blue number 1, as shown in Figure 4-10.

5. Tap another thumbnail.

The photo appears in the viewer, and a number 2 appears next to the thumbnail. That number shows you the order in which your followers will see the photos in your post.

REMEMBER

If you select a photo but then decide that you don't want to include it, just tap the thumbnail photo. The order of your photos will change if you selected more than two photos. To deselect all photos, tap the blue select multiple icon in the lower-right corner of the viewer.

6. Continue tapping thumbnails as needed.

In Figure 4-11, we've chosen six photos. The numbers reflect the order in which we selected each photo.

7. When you have finished selecting photos, tap Next.

The Edit screen appears.

Edit the photos by tapping Next in the upper-right corner of the screen.

FIGURE 4-10:
The select multiple icon in the viewer is blue and the other viewer icons have disappeared.

FIGURE 4-11:
The most recently selected photo appears in the viewer.

TIP

To reorder the photos, you have to deselect them and then reselect them in the correct order. (Yes, this is something Instagram needs to work on.) For example, suppose you select five photos and want to move photos 3 and 4 to positions 4 and 5, respectively. First deselect photos 3 and 4. At this point, the former photo 5 becomes photo 3. Then select the former photo 3, which becomes photo 4, and then select the former photo 4, which becomes photo 5.

Applying filters and adding photos

After you have selected your photos and tapped Next, the Edit screen appears, as shown in Figure 4-12. The top of the screen displays the photo you're editing.

A row of filter types appears below the photo. Swipe from right to left in the row to view all the filters. To apply a filter to all photos in the group, tap the thumbnail image under the filter name.

At the right side of the screen, you see part of the next photo in your photo group. To see the other photos, swipe left. To add another photo to your post, swipe to the end of the row, tap the + icon, and then select the photo from the Camera Roll screen, as described in the "Uploading Photos from Your Camera Roll" section earlier in this chapter.

Editing photos individually

To edit a photo, tap it in the row of photos. The selected photo appears in the center of your screen. Now you can do the following:

>> **Add a filter.** Swipe right to left in the filter row, and then tap the filter thumbnail image. Get all the details in the "Adding a filter" section.

>> **Change the exposure and brightness levels at once.** Tap the Lux icon (magic wand on iOS or sun icon on Android) at the top of the screen. Learn more about using the Lux tool in the "Tweaking with the editing tools" section.

FIGURE 4-12:
The filter name appears above the filter thumbnail image.

>> **Perform other editing tasks.** Tap Edit, and then follow the instructions in the "Tweaking with the editing tools" section.

Tap Done in the upper-right corner when you're finished.

Adding information and sharing your photos

When your photos are the way you want them, tap Next in the upper-right corner of the Edit screen.

In the New Post screen, you can write a caption, tag people, add a location, share your photo on other social networks, and turn commenting on and off as described earlier in the "Enriching Your Photo" section.

TIP

You can't write a caption for each photo when you have multiple photos in your post. So when you write your description, the caption should describe all your photos, not just one.

When you've finished editing your photos, it's time to share them. Tap Share in the upper-right corner of the New Post screen.

Chapter **5**

Recording and Posting Great Videos

I f you've checked your competitors on Instagram and other social-networking websites (you have, haven't you?), you've noticed that they're creating and producing short videos to promote their business. And if they haven't, producing videos of your own is an opportunity to have an advantage over your competition.

Instagram added video to its smartphone apps in 2013. Sorry, Windows and Mac users; you can't upload video to Instagram from your computers without the help of a third-party app. One popular app, Gramblr, shut down in 2019, but you can check out a list of alternatives at www.saashub.com/gramblr-alternatives.

In this chapter, you learn how to record video in the Instagram app by using a smartphone or a tablet. Then you discover how to edit your video with Instagram's built-in editing tools and add a description. Finally, you find out how to share your video on Instagram and start bringing in viewers and, maybe, customers.

Recording Your Day

Instagram gives you the flexibility to record videos that are as short as 3 seconds or as long as 60 seconds. If you find that 60 seconds is too limiting, use the video as a teaser (think of it as your own movie preview) to get people to click through to your website, another video website such as YouTube, or IGTV. (We tell you all about how IGTV works in Chapter 19.)

Before you record a video, you should know your audience: People younger than 35 prefer 10-second videos, and people 35 and older prefer 30-second spots (www.adweek.com/digital/new-study-shows-millennials-prefer-short-mobile-videos-while-older-crowds-long-form-170739/). Learn more about reaching your audience in Chapter 3.

Filming with a smartphone or tablet

When you're ready to start recording a video on your iPhone, iPad, Android smartphone, or Android tablet, open the Instagram app and then tap the + icon at the bottom of the home screen. In the Library or Photo screen that appears, tap Video.

REMEMBER

The Instagram apps on the iPhone, iPad, Android smartphones, and Android tablets all work the same.

The first time you open the Video screen, a pop-up window appears, as shown in Figure 5-1. Instagram wants to access the microphone on your smartphone so it can record videos with sound. Access the microphone by tapping OK.

> "Instagram" Would Like to
> Access the Camera
> This lets you take photos and
> record video.
>
> Don't Allow   OK

REMEMBER

The next time you open the Video screen, you won't see this pop-up window. If you want to turn your microphone off and on in Instagram, access your smartphone's settings, open the Instagram settings entry, and then turn the microphone on or off.

FIGURE 5-1:
If you want to record silent videos, tap Don't Allow.

The Video screen has the following elements, all labeled in Figure 5-2:

>> The *viewer* is in the upper part of the screen. The viewer displays what your smartphone sees through its camera lens.

>> The *switch cameras icon* is in the lower-left corner of the viewer. Tap this icon to switch between the front and back cameras.

Return to your Instagram feed

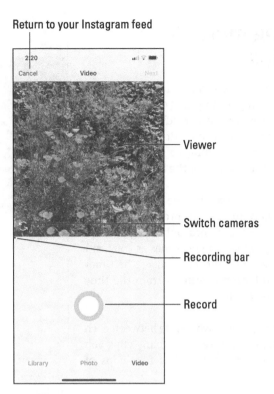

2:20
Cancel   Video   Next

— Viewer

— Switch cameras

— Recording bar

— Record

Library   Photo   **Video**

FIGURE 5-2:
Tap Cancel if you decide you don't want to record a video.

>> The *recording bar* is one of two bars just below the viewer and on the left. The recording bar represents how long you've been recording. When the recording bar is blinking, you can start recording either at the beginning of a video or after a video clip. (You find out about recording multiple video clips in the next section.)

>> The *record button* is the large gray circle in the bottom half of the screen.

Start recording by tapping and holding down on the record button. The recording bar expands as you record. (If you reach the 60-second limit, the bar spans the width of the screen and Instagram stops recording.) The amount of time you've been recording appears above the record button, as shown in Figure 5-3. When you've finished recording, release your finger from the record button.

REMEMBER

If you record for only one or two seconds, the recording bar is solid for the time you recorded. Between the recording bar and the minimum bar, you'll see a blinking recording bar. That blinking bar tells you how many more seconds you have to meet the minimum recording time to save your video.

Recording multiple video clips

To save time, you can record multiple clips in one recording. For example, suppose you're recording a video of your new restaurant. After filming the inside of the restaurant, you don't want to spend precious video time recording your move to the outside to show the exterior of the building.

After you record your first clip, release your finger. When you're ready to start recording again, tap and hold down on the record button again. You may repeat this process as many times as you want within the 60-second limit for a video. The timer above the record button continues from the time you paused the recording.

The recording bar places a white line between each clip. In this way, you can see how many clips you have. Figure 5-3, for example, has four clips of varying times.

FIGURE 5-3:
The black recording bar appears directly below the viewer.

Deleting video clips

If you decide that you want to delete the last video clip you recorded, tap Delete at the bottom of the screen. The color of the Delete text and the recording bar changes to red. Then tap Delete again. The Delete option disappears and the blinking recording bar appears so you can record a new video clip.

If you want to delete more clips, just repeat this process. Easy like Sunday morning.

Checking out your video

After you record your video, you'll want to review it before posting. From the Video screen, tap Next. You see the Filter screen, which you learn about in the next section.

WARNING

If you haven't recorded for the minimum 3 seconds, clipart of the recording bar blinks between the solid bar and the 3-second threshold line. (Admittedly, this may be hard to see.) The blinking portion of the bar tells you that you still haven't reached the 3-second limit and need to continue recording.

The video starts playing in the viewer in iOS, but you have to tap the play icon in Android. To stop playing the video, tap anywhere in the viewer. To resume, tap the play button, in the middle of the viewer, as shown in Figure 5-4.

TIP

You can toggle video sound on or off by tapping the speaker icon at the top of the page. If you've stopped your video in iOS, it will start playing after you turn the video sound on or off. In Android, you need to tap the play icon to resume playing the video.

Improving Your Video

You can improve your video in several ways: Add a filter, change the cover frame, and trim the video. In this section, you start by applying a filter to your video in the Filter screen.

FIGURE 5-4:
Begin playing the video by tapping the play icon.

Applying a filter

Below the viewer is a row of filters. (The Normal, Clarendon, and Gingham filters are shown in Figure 5-4.) The thumbnail image below each filter shows you the filter's effect on your video.

Swipe in the row of thumbnails to view all 23 filters. (Normal is the default, so it isn't considered a filter.) Tap a filter's thumbnail, and the video with the applied filter plays in the viewer.

You can change the intensity of any filter by tapping the filter's thumbnail, and then moving the slider to the left and right. (The default intensity is 100.) As you move the slider, the video reflects the change. When you've finished selecting an intensity, tap Done.

REMEMBER

The video continues to play when you apply a new filter or change the intensity of a filter. If you want to return the video to its original state, tap the Normal thumbnail.

Changing the cover frame

Instagram uses the first frame of your video to produce a *cover frame*, which is the frame that appears at the start of your video. You can change the cover frame as follows:

1. **In the Filter screen, tap Cover.**

   The default cover frame appears in the viewer and also below the viewer in a white focus box. The other frames appear next to the focus box and are dimmed, as shown in Figure 5-5.

2. **Tap and hold down on the frame in the focus box, and then drag the frame within the row.**

   As you drag, the focus box moves to another frame in your video and you see this new cover frame in the viewer.

3. **When you find a cover frame you like, release your finger.**

4. **Tap Next.**

TIP

The cover frame will appear in your Instagram feed, so be sure that the frame you select isn't blurry. You want to make a good impression on your followers as well as potential customers.

FIGURE 5-5:
Frames that aren't selected appear dimmed.

Adding details

After you take a video, you need to add some details. After all, you don't want someone scratching his head wondering what the video is about (and worse, think you're lazy). In the screen that displays your video (refer to Figure 5-4), add your caption, tags, and location by tapping Next. The New Post screen appears, as shown in Figure 5-6.

In this screen, you can add a caption, include a location where the video was recorded, share the video on other social media networks, and turn commenting on and off. The process for adding all this good stuff is described in Chapter 4.

Posting your video

When you're ready to post your video, tap Share in the upper-right corner of the New Post screen. After a few seconds, your video appears on the Instagram home screen, as shown in Figure 5-7.

FIGURE 5-6:
Your video frame appears as a thumbnail in the upper-left corner.

FIGURE 5-7:
The video plays on the home screen.

The video starts playing as soon as you view it and will play continuously every time you view the post. The video plays without sound, but you can turn on the sound by tapping the video icon in the lower-left corner of the video. Cool beans.

Uploading a Stored Video

It's easy to upload a video that you've already recorded and stored on your iPhone, iPad, or Android smartphone or tablet. Simply follow these steps:

1. **Tap the + icon at the bottom of the Instagram feed screen.**

2. **If the Library screen is not displayed, tap Library (iOS) or Gallery (Android).**

3. **Select the video you want to upload by tapping its thumbnail image in the Camera Roll or Gallery screen, as shown in Figure 5-8.**

TIP

The video plays continuously in the viewer. Stop playback by tapping anywhere in the viewer.

Instagram automatically crops your video to the size of the viewer, but you can resize the video to its original size by tapping the resize icon.

4. **(Optional) Apply a filter, change the cover frame, and trim your video.**

   These tasks are described in the "Improving Your Video" section.

5. **Tap Next.**

6. **(Optional) Add a caption and a location, specify other social networks where you want to share your video, and turn commenting on or off.**

   These tasks are the same for photos and videos. For details, see the section on enriching photos in Chapter 4.

Selected thumbnail photo

Video run time

FIGURE 5-8:
The selected video thumbnail image is dimmed, indicating that it's the video playing in the viewer.

Uploading Multiple Videos

If you've already taken videos and saved them to your camera roll (iOS) or gallery (Android), you can upload them to a single Instagram video and share it with your followers.

TIP

You can upload multiple videos to a carousel post. Read Chapter 10 to learn how to create carousel posts and use them to attract more views.

Follow these steps to upload multiple clips into one Instagram video:

1. **Tap the + icon in the Instagram feed screen.**

2. **If the Library screen isn't displayed, tap Library.**

3. **Select the first video you want to upload by tapping its thumbnail image in the Camera Roll (iOS) or Gallery (Android) screen.**

4. **Tap a second video.**

5. **Tap Next.**

   The Filter screen appears, as shown in Figure 5-9, and the first video begins playing.

WARNING

   If you add a clip that puts your video over the 60-second limit, Instagram will automatically trim the last clip so that your entire video lasts for exactly 60 seconds.

6. **(Optional) Apply a filter or change the cover or both.**

   These tasks are described in the "Improving Your Video" section, earlier in the chapter.

7. **Tap Next.**

   The New Post (Followers) screen appears.

8. **(Optional) Type a caption, add a location, share your photo on other social networks, and turn commenting on or off.**

   For more information, read the section on enriching photos in Chapter 4. All the information there applies not only to photos but also to videos, with the exception of tagging people. (You can't tag people in a video.)

FIGURE 5-9:
The first video plays automatically in the Filter screen.

REMEMBER

When you upload a video with multiple clips, you can't change the orientation of the clips to landscape or portrait. Each clip appears in its original orientation, so keep that in mind when you want to create a video with multiple clips.

3

Interacting with Others

Find your tribe of Instagram friends to follow and who will follow you back.

Uncover the etiquette of interacting with others on Instagram.

Dive into Instagram Direct to connect personally with other people.

Create and add hashtags to your posts.

Chapter **6**

Finding People to Follow

Growing your Instagram following is one of the hottest topics on Instagram. If you've spent any time there, surely you've encountered sales pitches to buy followers or purchase a crazy software program to increase likes and follows. Don't do it. Yes, it looks good having a big following, especially when starting out. However, any followers you buy are likely fake accounts, or people who would never buy from you.

In this chapter, you discover how to find followers the right way. First, you follow your Facebook friends who have Instagram accounts, and then you learn how Instagram can access the contact list on your phone to find more followers. Next, you discover ways to explore and search for followers in the Instagram app. Then you look to your competitors' and industry colleagues' follower lists for more ideas. You also learn how to develop an Insta-tribe — an online family that helps and supports you along the way. Finally, after you start getting followers, find out who is worth following back and when it's best not to bother.

Where Are My Peeps?

If you're new to Instagram, you may be wondering where to start. Instagram (and its daddy, Facebook) is happy to help you make connections. You can find people in a few different ways, as you discover in this section.

Finding your Facebook friends

Facebook has a vested interest in making Instagram grow, so it tries to encourage you to round up your Facebook friends and bring them over to Instagram. It's an easy way for you to find people.

To find friends on Facebook, follow these steps:

1. **Go to your Instagram profile page by tapping your photo at the bottom right of your phone's screen.**

2. **Tap the three lines at the top left of your screen.**

3. **Tap Discover People.**

4. **Tap the Connect to Facebook link, and then log in to Facebook.**

5. **Repeat Steps 1-3.**

   The people available to follow are displayed.

6. **Tap Follow next to any of the accounts you want to follow, as shown in Figure 6-1.**

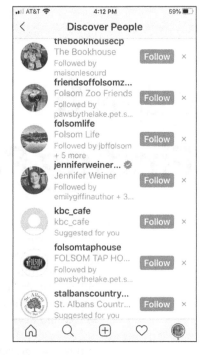

FIGURE 6-1:
Instagram displays all Facebook friends who are available to follow on Instagram.

TIP

Some of your friends may have set their accounts to private. In this case, you see Requested after you tap Follow. They need to approve you before you can view their profile and posts.

Syncing your contact list

Instagram can also connect you with the contacts stored on your phone or tablet. After you activate this feature, your contacts are periodically synced with

Instagram's servers. Instagram does not follow anyone on your behalf, and you can disconnect your contacts at any time so that Instagram cannot access them.

This feature may be best as a one-and-done in the beginning versus a constant connection for privacy purposes.

To connect your contacts, follow these steps:

1. **Go to your Instagram profile page by tapping your photo at the bottom right of your phone's screen.**

2. **Tap the three lines at the top right of the screen.**

3. **Tap Discover People.**

4. **Tap Connect, at the top of the screen, as shown in Figure 6-2.**

   Instagram syncs your contacts on your phone. The process might take a few minutes.

5. **Choose which contacts to follow by tapping Follow next to each one.**

If you change your mind at some point and want to disallow Instagram's access to your contacts, tap the three lines on your profile page, tap Settings, tap Account, and then tap Contact Syncing. Tap the Connect Contacts toggle to return it to white (off), which terminates Instagram's access.

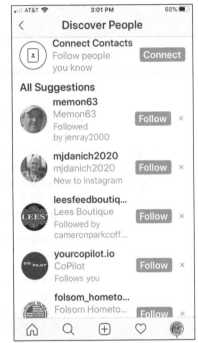

FIGURE 6-2:
Instagram can pull contacts from your phone's saved contacts for you to select to follow.

Finding New Friends

Now that you've found all your Facebook friends and contacts on Instagram, it's time to get more strategic about following the people who might have a genuine interest in your business. Instagram offers several options for exploring, searching, and suggesting new followers to you.

Exploring the Explore function

Instagram loves growth . . . and Instagram offers many ways to engage with users to keep them using the app. One way is through the Explore page, which offers photos, video posts, and stories that Instagram thinks might be interesting to you. The algorithm Instagram uses is tailored to show you content similar to the accounts you're already following and interacting with most.

Here's how to use the Explore page:

FIGURE 6-3:
The Explore page displays reels, stories, videos, and posts you might like.

1. **Tap the magnifying glass at the bottom of any screen.**

   Several reels, photos, videos, and stories are presented (see Figure 6-3).

   TIP

   If you're trying to get your posts displayed on the Explore page, note that the Instagram algorithm rarely selects graphics such as charts or infographs. It tends to favor photos or videos.

2. **Tap any photo or video that interests you.**

   Now you can scroll down to see similar additional photos and videos — like a close-up, more specific Explore feed than what's presented on the main Explore page.

3. **Tap the Instagram username at the top of any post that interests you.**

4. **Look around the page. If you like what you see:**

   a. *Like one or more photos:* Double-tap each individual photo or tap the heart icon.

   b. *Leave a comment:* Tap the photo, and then tap the comment bubble below the photo. Enter your text, and tap the blue Post link.

   c. *To follow a user:* Tap the blue Follow button at the top of the user's profile page or next to the user name when you're viewing the person's post.

   After you follow this page (if followed from the profile), Instagram offers several other accounts that it thinks you'd enjoy following. We detail this method of finding accounts to follow in the "Letting Instagram suggest users to you" section, later in this chapter.

Another avenue for exploring is to tap the buttons along the top of the Explore page. These allow you to narrow the results to certain topics, such as travel, décor, or well-being, or post types such as IGTV or Shop.

TIP

This method of finding followers is time consuming. Also, popular accounts may not be looking to follow many new people, so there's no guarantee that you'll get a reciprocal follow. However, it's always worth a shot and is a nice addition to your follower strategy.

Searching the Search feature

Another great way to find new accounts to follow is through searching Instagram. Instagram offers four ways to search: Top, Accounts, Tags, and Places.

To try out the Search feature, tap the magnifying glass on any page. The Explore page appears, as described in the preceding section. Tap the Search field at the top of the page. Top, Accounts, Tags, and Places are now available for your choosing, as shown in Figure 6-4.

FIGURE 6-4:
Search by Top, Accounts, Tags, and Places.

The *Top feature* shows you accounts that you interact with often, followed by accounts you most recently interacted with. To find new followers, search for an industry or a keyword that relates to your business or target customer. For instance, typing **real estate** presents several accounts that have *real estate* in their username or in their profile title. Scroll through those that are interesting, and follow those you like!

The *Accounts feature* can be used in a similar manner to the Top feature, but you may also choose to search by someone's name. If you have a customer list, try searching for people by name. For those that pop up, scroll through to their account and follow them if they seem to be active. Personal accounts are more likely to be private, so you will need to request access.

The *Tags feature* allows you to search by hashtag. Start simply by choosing your industry and see what appears. For example, if you're a dog trainer, start with #dogtraining. If you get too many results to be useful, add your city or state, such as #dogtrainingsacramento. Scroll through the accounts and tap the ones that call out to you. Then follow the ones that seem active and engaging. In the next chapter, hashtags are discussed in detail, and we explain more about this feature.

The *Places feature* enables you to search by location. If you're currently near your business location, the easiest way to start is to tap Near Current Location. Several nearby locations then pop up for your choosing. Tap a location near you, and then all the posts that marked that location on their post pop up. Tap some posts that catch your eye, and follow the ones you like.

REMEMBER

On all the accounts you follow, make sure to like several posts and leave a meaningful comment or two (not just an emoji). This technique greatly increases the odds that the account will follow you back.

Letting Instagram suggest users to you

As mentioned, Instagram is on a mission to grow. Therefore, its main goal is making its users happy by making their accounts grow. When you follow someone, an algorithm kicks in and displays other similar accounts that you may like following. In Figure 6-5, we decided to follow @nancysreasons. Instagram then presented many other business accounts that may be related by location or subject matter, and we can decide whether or not to follow them.

You might be wondering why you'd want to follow. They might not follow you back (but they will if they're smart). In the next section, you learn more about the benefits of keeping tabs on the competition.

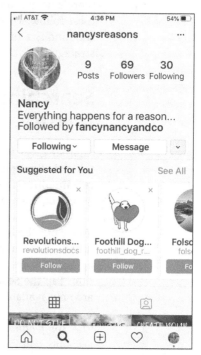

© Nancy Connolly

FIGURE 6-5:
After you follow an account, Instagram presents similar accounts you might like.

Following Your Industry

Watching your industry's Instagram accounts can help you build your following in several ways. In this section, you find out how to benefit from the earlier work of your competitors and industry icons. First, if your business serves only local customers, look at your direct, local competition. Then look more globally at bigger brands in the same industry to see the tactics they use.

Following industry hashtags is also highly productive. Does your industry hold several large conferences a year? Conferences are usually associated with a hashtag. Savvy Instagram business accounts incorporate the conference hashtag in their posts so consider searching for the hashtag to find other accounts to interact with. These accounts could be competitors or potential customers. If you're attending the event, search through the conference hashtag and follow accounts, like photos, comment, and perhaps direct message other attendees to set in-person meetings with potential customers or business partners.

Watching your competition

One of the best ways to find new followers is by researching your competitors' Instagram accounts and interacting with their followers. If they're interested in your competitor's business, they might be interested in your offerings as well. Your competitors' follower lists are like a ready-made target audience waiting just for you!

Engaging with your competitors' followers is easy. Here's how:

1. **Make a list of your top competitors.**

2. **Use the Search function to find one of them on Instagram.**

   For details on searching, see the "Searching the Search feature" section, earlier in the chapter.

3. **Go to a competitor's account, and tap the number above *followers* (at the top right of its profile page), as shown in Figure 6-6, left.**

   You see everyone following the competitor, as shown in Figure 6-6, right. You can also see accounts you both follow, who the competitor's account is following, and suggested accounts to follow.

4. **Do the following for each follower, following, or suggested account that looks interesting:**

   a. Tap the account.

   b. Like several photos and comment on at least one post.

   c. Follow the account.

5. **Repeat Steps 3 and 4 for all the competitors in your list.**

   Keep regularly engaging with these accounts, and you might just win them over to following you or becoming a customer.

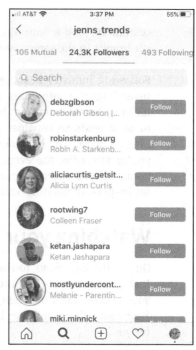

FIGURE 6-6:
You can see a competitor's followers by tapping its number of followers (left). and then deciding if you'd like to follow any of them (right).

Getting noticed by big brands

Following big brands such as Target, Maybelline, or Yoplait provides unique ideas for content or promotions done in a fresh way, but it can also yield more followers for you. How? Some big brands re-post user-generated content (content created by regular folks like you and us) from their customers, and when they do, that account can hit the jackpot on followers.

To get noticed by a big brand, follow these tips:

1. Make a list of top brands that would mesh well with your brand. For example, if you sell virtual assistant services, you might make a list of various companies that sell planners, specialty pens, and desk accessories.

2. Check whether the company re-posts images from other users by scrolling through several months of posts. Some companies are strict about their brand, and post only what has been designed by their design department. If this is the case, cross them off the list.

3. After you find a brand that does re-post user-generated content, study the posts it shares from other accounts. Do they typically like flat lays (photos where products are neatly arranged on a background and photographed from

above); photos with people, animals, or sports; a consistent filter? You might notice a pattern in what has been selected. Put your own flair on your content while making it fit the other account's style.

4. Style your photo according to the instructions in Step 3, and include the company's product with the brand label prominently displayed. Do not include other brands in the photo.

5. Add brand hashtags. Big brands often have a specific hashtag they associate with all their posts. For example, Coca-Cola recently used #KindnessStartsWith as its branded hashtag on Instagram posts for a specific campaign. If you're trying to get featured on @Cocacola, use the #KindnessStartsWith hashtag along with other hashtags that relate to the soda brand.

6. Mention the brand using its Instagram username in your written post. For instance, @coreycwalker used the hashtag #madeonterra in a post where she used the brand's bookmark in a photo. She was then featured on the @madeonterra Instagram page and was tagged back. Now @madeonterra followers might visit @coreycwalker's page to see what else she posts. See Figure 6-7 for the post featured on the @madeonterra account.

© Made on Terra

FIGURE 6-7:
Sometimes brands re-post user-generated content like this one by @madeonterra.

Deciding Whom to Follow Back

After you've employed the techniques described previously in this chapter, you'll begin to get more followers. It's a great feeling to see that number go up on your profile page, and your next decision is whether to follow those accounts back if you were not already following them. In this next section, you discover how to view your followers and decide who is best to follow back.

Viewing and following your followers

So you are starting to see more followers on your account. Now it's time to learn a simple method to follow them back. You're not required or even expected to follow someone back, but searching through your followers often yields great customer prospects. New followers appear in your notifications, but if you don't check your notifications often, it's worth checking out your follower list every few days to see whom you might want to follow back.

Checking your follower list is easy:

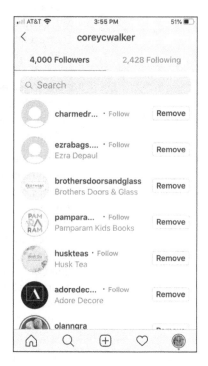

1. **Go to your profile page and click the number above *followers*.**

   All your followers appear, with the most recent followers at the top. As shown in Figure 6-8, followers you haven't followed back have a blue Follow link to the right that you can click to follow. You can also tap the Remove button to stop someone from following you without completely blocking them.

2. **Unless you recognize the username, click that name to view the user's profile page.**

3. **If you think that the user is a potential customer or partner, click the blue Follow button on his or her profile page. Otherwise, use the arrow on the top left of the page to go back to your follower list and try again.**

4. **Like a few posts and leave a meaningful comment.**

   In this way, the follower is more likely to engage with you in the future.

FIGURE 6-8:
Followers you haven't followed back have a blue Follow link to the right.

Reciprocating a follow or not

Now that you know a simple method for following back, the question is whether the account is worthy of following back. Some accounts have a habit of following accounts but then unfollowing them if they didn't follow back. You might see your numbers rise by 25, just to fall back by 22 the next day. It's a frustrating game that you should avoid.

Do follow back the following:

>> Accounts of friends, local businesses, and other people you know and like in real life (or as the kids say, "IRL")

>> Accounts in your industry, especially competitors! If they're checking up on you, it's wise to see what they're doing

>> Accounts of businesses you do business with or other related associates

>> Accounts that provide content inspiration, even if they're not in your industry

>> Accounts of people you have met on other networks, such as Facebook groups, Twitter, or LinkedIn

>> Accounts that you find personally interesting and satisfying to view and interact with, even if they're not directly tied to your business

Not every account you follow back needs to be your ultimate moneymaker. Instagram is still meant to be fun; it doesn't have to be dry and boring, even if your business is unexciting. Plus, you never know who is a friend of a friend or a cousin of someone who could be an amazing connection. Connecting with others on Instagram could be the first step in a business match made in heaven!

Don't follow back:

>> Everyone who follows you because you feel some sort of obligation.

>> Spammy accounts whose profile probably lists only a few posts and who often sell follower services.

>> Accounts that cut and paste the same generic comments. (Nothing is worse than having someone write "Love it!" when you post that your dog just died.)

>> Accounts that contain content you have no interest in personally or professionally.

>> Accounts that follow you for a few days, then unfollow you, and then follow you again a week later. They often use the #follow4follow hashtag. Stay away!

TIP

You may discover your own rules for following accounts. Keep in mind that it's okay to unfollow people too. Maybe they stopped posting, or their content no longer interests you. Clean up your feed every so often to ensure that you're viewing the best content for you and your business.

Finding Your Insta-Tribe

If you compare all the popular social networks — Facebook, Twitter, LinkedIn, Snapchat, and Instagram — the one that takes the cake on community engagement is Instagram. This section explains how to use hashtags influencers, interaction, and Instagram pods to find your ultimate Insta-tribe!

Finding or creating a community you vibe with

If you've been on Instagram for a while, you've probably seen posts talking about community and finding your tribe. But what does that mean? A *community*, or *tribe*, is a supportive group of people talking about and interacting with you and your brand on Instagram. They offer advice, give a heads up about changes on Instagram or your industry, provide support, promote your business when it makes sense, and leave comments that can help boost your posts. If executed well, your community is marketing gold.

Your first step is finding a community that fits with your brand. An easy way to do this is through hashtags. If you sell high-end baby dresses, for example, searching #baby yields several other relevant hashtags such as #babygirl, #babyboy, #babyfever, and #babyshower.

All of these hashtags are large, so by selecting one and creating a new search (as shown in Figure 6-9), you can find more specific hashtags, such as #babygirlnames, #babygirlclothes, #babygirlnursery, and #babygirlfashion. Search for people who use these niche hashtags often. Then follow them and interact with them daily by commenting and liking their posts.

While you're commenting on their posts, you'll probably start seeing other people showing up frequently on the same accounts. Follow, like, and comment on those accounts too, and before you know it, your tribe is developing!

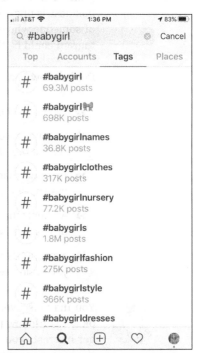

FIGURE 6-9:
Search hashtags to see Instagram's suggestions of other more specific hashtags.

To further solidify your relationship, send them a quick direct message to introduce yourself and your business. (Direct messages are covered in Chapter 8.) Because you're just meeting, it's not the time to make a sales pitch. Let the relationship flow naturally and tell them how much you enjoy the conversations you've had.

After you're in a community, certain influencers and brands may bubble to the surface. These accounts are excellent to interact with because the audience you're trying to reach sees them often. Leaving meaningful or humorous comments regularly on an influencer or a big brand account can help your following and can lead to a relationship with that influencer or brand.

You may also find your tribe completely away from Instagram. For example, Facebook groups catering to niche markets often have Instagram tribes that coincide with the group. They might have their own unique hashtags to easily identify them on Instagram. You may also discover them by following the admin of the group, and seeing the same people interacting on Instagram.

Not finding the tribe you're seeking? Start your own! Run a contest (see Chapter 12 for details) or campaign asking people to submit a photo that goes with your hashtag. For example, if you're a graphic designer, you could start a challenge using #graphicdesignotd, where designers post what they worked on that day. People love challenges like this because it provides post inspiration and an excuse to show off their work! Keep checking the hashtag for submissions, and thank everyone for participating. Then follow them, and keep coming back regularly, commenting and liking their posts. All of a sudden, a tribe is forming!

REMEMBER

With any of these methods for finding or creating your tribe, the most important element is engagement. By liking and commenting often, you get the same in return. Tribe members get to know each other on a deeper level by watching for those special posts every day. The friendships can lead to business connections, conference buddies, and more. Like the old saying goes: The more you give, the more you get back!

Deciding whether Instagram pods are beneficial

When Instagram changed from displaying posts chronologically to using an algorithm based on users' likes to show posts, many marketers panicked. It seemed like Facebook all over again — pushing people toward advertising to get their posts shown. To combat this, many savvy marketers turned to Instagram pods. A *pod* is a group of 10 to 20 accounts that usually have something in common. Maybe they're all photographers, or DIY crafters, or mommy bloggers. They all have the main goal of getting more engagement, but they don't improve your reach overall — they just rank your posts higher in the feed for the people in your pod.

This is how a pod works:

>> Instagrammers recruit several other accounts via Instagram DM (direct message) or a Facebook group. (See Chapter 8 for details on direct messaging.)

>> The people in the pod post their content on Instagram, and then share that post via a group DM set up for the pod members.

>> Pod members then click through to the person's Instagram account, liking and commenting on the post as soon as possible to help boost the post in Instagram's algorithm. Likes and comments within the first hour of a post do the most work to get a post shown more often in Instagram feeds.

>> Pod members have a responsibility to engage as often and as quickly as possible on other pod members' posts to boost engagement. Some people find the responsibility overwhelming, particularly if members of the pod post several times a day.

Does it work? Is it worth the time? The data is not clear. If you have an active group, the comments should help your engagement and likes somewhat. However, participating in a pod can be a huge time commitment and can leave you feeling tethered to your phone waiting for the next post. It's hard to run a business that way.

Often people join a pod, use it for a while, form a few good friendships, and then break up at some point due to the time commitment. You may find your Insta-tribe during this process and still interact with the same accounts from your pod after the breakup but without the pressure of commenting on-demand.

TIP

If you'd like to try a pod, start small, with no more than 15 accounts. If you like the results and can keep up, try a larger one. However, your pod should never detract from your larger audience. If you find that you have time to comment on only the same few accounts in your pod, it's best to let the pod go and get back to interacting with your audience as a whole.

IN THIS CHAPTER

» **Thinking about what you should share on Instagram**

» **Using links to share posts**

» **Sending direct messages**

» **Getting, reviewing, and responding to comments**

» **Reporting inappropriate comments**

Chapter **7**

Sharing and Commenting on Posts

This chapter tells you all about sharing your Instagram photos and videos. What's more, you'll find out how to encourage people to comment on your posts and how to send a direct message to a commenter.

You start by thinking about what you should and shouldn't share. Next, you discover how to use a link to invite other Instagram users to comment on your posts as well as how to send a direct message to other users. And if you conclude that a comment is inappropriate, you can use Instagram's built-in reporting tool to send feedback and information to the Instagram staff so they can investigate.

Before You Share, Stop and Think

Instagram provides guidelines that protect and nurture not only the larger Instagram community but also you and your business. Every social network, Instagram included, presumes that when you use its service you agree to its terms of use and any other guidelines that social network may set.

As with any social network, you need to be careful about what you post on Instagram because — as you've probably heard many times before — what's posted on the Internet stays on the Internet . . . forever.

When you share photos and videos on Instagram, you strive to promote your business in the best possible light. However, you must also abide by Instagram's Community Guidelines.

If you run afoul of the Community Guidelines, you may be reported to Instagram. The company works hard to make sure that its users are posting photos and videos that meet its standards. If yours don't, Instagram might delete your post, disable your account, or put in place what it ominously calls "other restrictions."

REMEMBER

To read the latest version of the guidelines, visit the Community Guidelines page at https://help.instagram.com/477434105621119/.

Following are the most important points in the Community Guidelines:

>> **Share only photos and videos that you've taken.** If you're using someone else's photo or video, be sure to get permission in writing, either online (such as in an email message) or on paper (such as in an Adobe Acrobat document).

>> **Don't use services that allow you to buy followers or run automated tasks to collect likes, followers, or shares.** Instagram considers such tactics marketing spam and will shut down accounts to curb the problem.

>> **Post photos and videos that are appropriate for a general audience.** Instagram doesn't allow nudity except in specific cases. In addition, don't post graphic photos or videos.

>> **Follow the law.** This point should be self-evident. If it isn't, perhaps you should follow Obi-Wan Kenobi's advice and go home to rethink your life.

Sharing on Other Social Media Sites

It's easy to share photos and videos on Instagram as well as from Instagram to Facebook, Twitter, and Tumblr. We describe how do those tasks in Chapter 4 (for photos) and Chapter 5 (for videos).

Of course, many other social-networking sites are available. In this section, you learn how to create a link that you can embed into other social network posts or email messages.

Copying and pasting a link to another social network

Instagram's capability to share directly with other social networks is limited to Facebook, Twitter, and Tumblr. But other networks, especially business networks such as LinkedIn, are also worthy of your Instagram posts.

Fortunately, Instagram makes it easy for you to get a web address (URL) link to your post that you can copy and paste to other social networks. Here's how to do that on a smartphone or tablet:

1. **On the Instagram home screen, tap your profile icon, in the lower-right corner.**

   The Profile screen appears.

2. **Swipe up and down in your Profile screen, if necessary, to find the posted photo or video you want to link to.**

3. **Tap the photo thumbnail or video frame.**

   The Post screen appears. If you tapped a video frame, the video plays in the Post screen automatically.

4. **Tap the menu icon (three dots), which appears at the top right.**

   The menu shown in Figure 7-1 appears.

5. **Tap Copy Link.**

   A message appears for a few seconds, telling you that the link has been copied to the clipboard. Now you can paste the link into a post on another social-networking website or in an email message, as shown in the next section.

To view the post before you send it, click or tap the photo or video. On a smartphone or tablet, you see the original Instagram post. On a computer, you see the post on the Instagram website in a separate browser tab.

FIGURE 7-1:
The Post menu
on an iPhone or
iPad (left) and the
Share menu on
an Android
smartphone or
tablet (right).

Embedding your photo or video on a web page

If you want to share photos or videos on a web page or in a blog post, you can embed them from the Instagram website on your computer.

When you embed a photo or video, you can click or tap the photo or video to open the original post in the Instagram app on your smartphone or tablet.

If you're using a web browser on your computer, the original Instagram post will appear in a separate browser tab. (You may need to log into Instagram to view the post.) When you finish viewing the original post, close the tab to return to the web page you were viewing.

To embed a photo or video, do the following:

1. **On your computer, log into the Instagram website if you haven't done so already.**

2. **Click the profile icon (silhouette of a person), in the upper-right corner.**

   The Profile screen appears.

3. **Click the photo or video you want to share.**

   The screen displays your photo or video and caption, as well as any comments and likes.

4. **Click the menu icon (three dots), at the top right of the image, and then click Embed (see Figure 7-2).**

   If you decide that you don't want to embed your code, close the window by clicking anywhere outside the pop-up window or by pressing the Esc key.

Go to post
Share
Copy Link
Embed
Cancel

FIGURE 7-2:
You can embed your photo or video here.

5. **If you don't want a caption included with the photo or video, deselect (clear) the Include Caption check box.**

6. **Click the Copy Embed Code button.**

Now you can use your favorite website design program to paste the embedded code in a blog post or on a web page.

REMEMBER

When you embed one of your Instagram photos or videos on a website or in a blog post, anyone who has access to that website or blog post will be able to see your photo or video.

Garnering Comments

After you post a photo or video, any of your followers can comment on it. In this section, we describe two tried-and-true methods to encourage your followers to respond: Include a caption and mention your followers.

Including a caption

A caption adds context to your photo or video and lets people know what they're seeing. If you don't add a caption, your viewers might be confused, and that reflects badly on your business. For example, if you show a photo of your new product but you don't tell viewers what it is and why it's helpful, they may think you don't know what you're doing and you'll be left wondering why you're not getting any attention.

After you create a post and edit your photo or video, you add the caption in the New Post screen.

Do you need more details? Bookmark this page and flip to the section on enriching photos in Chapter 4. The information about adding captions to photos applies also to videos.

Instagram truncates all captions after about three lines of text. If there's more text to read, a More link appears at the end of the truncated text. To read the entire caption, you have to tap or click the link.

TIP

How much text should be in your caption? It's generally a good idea to communicate too much rather than too little, so consider writing one to three short paragraphs. Make sure that the first few lines are enticing enough that your viewer will want to tap or click the More link and read your entire caption.

Mentioning your followers

When one of your followers posts a photo or video, you can leave a like by tapping or clicking the heart icon to the right of the photo or video, or by double-tapping the photo or video.

After you mention someone in a comment, that person will receive a notification in his or her feed. And perhaps the person you complimented will be more interested in both finding your latest posts and commenting on them. That, in turn, increases your profile's visibility to other Instagram users when they search for new and interesting profiles.

Reviewing Your Comments

When you get a comment or a like, a notification appears in your feed. You can see how many comments and likes you have for a post by tapping the profile icon in the lower-right corner of the Instagram home screen, swiping until you see the thumbnail of the photo or video you posted, and then tapping the image.

Now you see

>> The Photo screen if your post contains only one photo

>> The Post screen if your post contains more than one photo

>> The Video screen if your post contains a video

Likes and comments appear below the photo or video. Tap one of the comments or tap the comment icon (cartoon bubble) below the photo or video to open the Comments screen shown in Figure 7-3.

Any responses to a comment appear below the original comment so you can see the conversation thread.

If you want to like the comment without replying to it, tap the like icon (white heart) to the right of the comment. After you tap the icon, the heart turns red and one more like appears for the comment. Return to the Photo, Post, or Video screen by tapping the back icon (<) in the upper-left corner.

REMEMBER

If you want to view all your notifications, tap the heart icon at the bottom of the Post, Photo, or Video screen. Then tap the You tab at the top of the Notifications screen if the tab isn't already active. You'll see as many as 100 of your most recent notifications as you swipe in the list. You can view a user's profile by tapping the username in a notification (the username is in bold).

FIGURE 7-3:
Your caption appears at the top of the Comments.

Deciding to respond or delete

You can reply to a comment in two ways, depending on whether you're using the iPhone or iPad, an Android smartphone or tablet, or a computer running Windows.

iPhone, iPad, and Windows users

If you're using an iPhone, an iPad, or a Windows PC, you can reply to a comment by tapping (or clicking) Reply below the comment.

If you want to delete a comment, you can use the comment options. iPhone and iPad users tap and hold down on the comment and then swipe left to display the options shown in Figure 7-4. Windows users should move the mouse pointer over the comment and then click the menu icon (three dots) to the right of the comment.

There are three options, from left to right:

>> **Pin:** Pin the comment to the top of your post so everyone sees it.

>> **Exclamation mark:** Report the commenter to Instagram. (You find out more about reporting commenters later in this chapter.) If you delete your own comment, the exclamation mark doesn't appear in the menu. You can report only one commenter at a time.

>> **Trash can:** Delete the comment.

WARNING

After you delete a comment, a red bar appears at the top of the Comments screen so you can undo the deletion. If you don't tap the bar within five seconds, the comment is deleted permanently.

If you want to close the comment menu without making any changes, tap and hold down on the comment to the left of the menu and swipe to the right. Windows users should click Cancel in the menu.

FIGURE 7-4:
The comment options push the comment to the left.

When you reply to the commenter by tapping Reply, a comment area appears, with the username of the commenter entered automatically. Now you can type your reply and then tap (or click) Post to the right of the comment area.

Have you changed your mind about writing a reply? Tap (or click) the back icon (<) in the upper-left corner of the screen and you'll return to the Photo screen.

Android smartphone and tablet users

Android smartphone and tablet users can reply to a comment by tapping Reply below the comment. The comment area appears with the commenter's username entered automatically. After you type your comment, tap Post to the right of the comment area or tap the blue Send key on the keyboard.

If you want to delete one or more comments — either your comments or someone else's comments — tap the comment(s). A blue menu bar appears at the top of the screen (see Figure 7-5) that contains the following icons you can tap:

>> **X:** Close the menu bar without making any changes.

>> **Pin:** Pin the comment to the top of your post.

>> **Exclamation point (!):** Report the commenter. (You learn more about reporting commenters later in this chapter.) If you tap more than one comment or you delete your own comment, the exclamation mark doesn't appear in the menu. You can report only one commenter at a time.

>> **Trash can:** Delete the comment(s).

WARNING

After you delete a comment, a red bar appears at the top of the Comments screen so you can undo the deletion. If you don't tap the bar within five seconds, the comment is deleted permanently.

You can close the menu bar by tapping all the selected comments to deselect them.

Mac and website users

Mac users can use only the Instagram website. If you're using a Mac, another computer, or another device to access the website, you can delete only comments written by someone else — not your own comments.

FIGURE 7-5:
The number of selected comments appears in the blue bar.

Here's how to delete a comment:

1. **Click or tap on the profile icon in the upper-right corner of the web page.**

2. **Scroll or swipe until you see the thumbnail of the photo or video that contains the comments.**

3. **Click or tap the thumbnail.**

    The list of comments appears.

4. **Click or tap the menu icon (three dots) to the right of the comment, and then tap Delete.**

    The comment disappears from the list.

Reporting Commenters When All Else Fails

Instagram asks that you resolve disputes between you and another person who posts a photo, video, or comment that you think may violate Instagram's Community Guidelines. For example, if someone's comment contains inaccurate information about you, you can post a comment or send a private Instagram Direct message and ask the commenter to remove the comment.

If the commenter won't cooperate or the comment is clearly a violation of the Community Guidelines (such as a threat of violence), Instagram strongly recommends that you don't escalate the situation yourself. Instead, report the user to Instagram and have Instagram staffers review the situation.

WARNING

If you refuse to heed Instagram's warning and decide to attack the commenter with nasty comments of your own, you may find yourself in trouble if the commenter reports you for harassment.

Reporting a commenter

Before you report a commenter, review the latest Community Guidelines at `https://help.instagram.com/477434105621119/?helpref=hc_fnav`. If you still believe the commenter must be reported to Instagram for further action, you can use Instagram's built-in reporting tools.

REMEMBER

You can report a user only from your iPhone, iPad, Android smartphone or tablet, or the Windows app. You can't report a user from the Instagram website.

Reporting from an iPhone, an iPad, or the Windows app

If you're reading comments on your iPhone, iPad, or in the Windows app and you come across a comment that violates the Community Guidelines, tap (or click) and hold down on the comment in the list and then swipe (or drag) to the left.

The gray report button appears to the right of the comment. Tap (or click) the button to open the menu at the bottom of the screen, tap (or click) Report This Comment, and then select the It's Spam option.

If you select It's Spam, the menu closes and the comment disappears from the Comments screen so you can continue to read comments. When you tap (or click) It's Inappropriate, the Report screen opens. You can decide how to report the comment and take any additional steps or get more information. For example, if you choose I Just Don't Like It, the Blocking People page appears so you can learn how to block commenters.

Reporting from an Android smartphone or tablet

When you see a comment on your Android smartphone or tablet that you think violates the Community Guidelines, tap and hold down on the comment in the list.

The comment gets a light blue background, and a blue bar at the top of the screen tells you that the comment is selected. Tap the exclamation point to open the menu, tap Report This Comment, and then tap It's Spam or It's Inappropriate.

If you tap It's Spam, the menu closes and the comment disappears. Now you can get back to reading other comments. If you tap It's Inappropriate, the Report Comment screen opens so you can decide how to report the comment and take any additional steps or get more information. For example, if you tap This Comment Shouldn't Be on Instagram, you see a list of reasons that you can choose from, such as nudity or sexual activity.

Blocking a commenter

If a commenter is obnoxious, that alone isn't a reason to report the commenter to Instagram but you can block the commenter. Then you no longer have to read anything from that user again. As on other networking sites such as Facebook and LinkedIn, Instagram doesn't tell users that they've been blocked.

REMEMBER

You can block a user only in the Instagram app on your smartphone or tablet. You block a user on his or her profile page, not from the Comments screen.

Here's how to block a user:

1. **In the comments below the photo or from the Comments screen, tap the username of the commenter.**

   The username is the first text you see in the comment and is in bold text.

2. **In the commenter's profile page, tap the three dots in the upper-right corner of the screen.**

   The menu shown in Figure 7-6 appears.

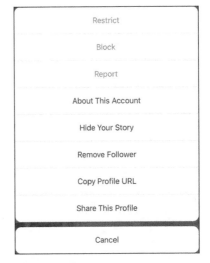

FIGURE 7-6:
Use this menu to block someone from commenting.

3. **Tap Block.**

4. **In the Block Account window, tap Block.**

Tap or click the < icon to return to the Comments screen. The blocked user's comments no longer appear on the screen. To unblock someone, follow the same steps, except tap Unblock in Step 3.

IN THIS CHAPTER

» **Sending photos or videos privately**

» **Recording and sending a voice message**

» **Messaging with a group**

» **Chatting live with other Instagram users**

» **Managing the direct messages in your inbox**

Chapter **8**

Direct Messaging with Ease

osting photos and videos to your profile is just one of many ways to share your content and promote your business. You can also use the Instagram Direct service to send a private message to a single follower or a group of 2 to 32 followers. Businesses often find that direct messages are a great way to connect with customers to share more information, set up appointments, or answer questions.

This chapter tells you all about how to share a direct message with your friends and fans. Because anyone can follow you (unless your account is private), direct messaging is Instagram's way of letting you connect with one person or a group of people in a private setting.

In this chapter, we start by showing you how to send a simple text message by using Instagram Direct. Then we get more advanced with sending photos, videos, GIFs, and voice messages, and show you how to reply to the direct messages you receive. Next, you discover how to use the live chat feature in Instagram Direct. Finally, we show you how to delete or mute the messages you've sent and received so your inbox doesn't get overwhelmed.

Starting a New Direct Message

If you want to start your conversation with a text message, Instagram makes it easy. Follow these steps:

1. **If the Direct screen isn't open, tap or click the Instagram Direct icon (paper airplane) in the upper-right corner of your home screen (see Figure 8-1).**

   This is also where you receive new messages. A red circle with the number of messages waiting for you is shown on top of the Direct icon. Your new messages are revealed when you tap the number.

2. **Tap or click the pencil in a square icon, as shown in Figure 8-2.**

   The New Message screen appears.

© glwheeler76

FIGURE 8-1:
The Instagram Direct icon is located at the top right of your home screen.

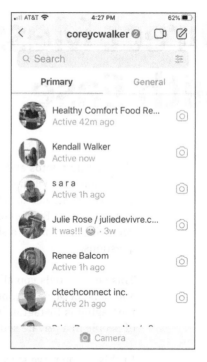

FIGURE 8-2:
Create a message by tapping the pencil in the upper right.

3. **Search for a name by typing in the Search box or scroll in the list to find the recipients, and then tap or click their usernames.**

   A blue check mark appears to the right of each recipient name after you tap or click it, as shown in Figure 8-3.

4. **On the iPhone, tap or click Chat to display the message box.**

   On Android, the message box appears at the bottom of the screen after you select one or more recipients.

5. **Start typing in the message box (see Figure 8-4), and then tap Send.**

6. **Return to the Direct screen by tapping or clicking the < icon at the top of the screen.**

   The message you just sent appears at the top of the list. Each message entry in the list displays the recipient's or group's name, followed by whether the recipient is active now or when they were last active.

   View your message on the screen by tapping the entry.

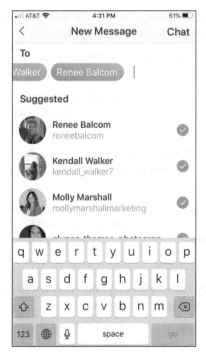

FIGURE 8-3:
Select the message recipients.

FIGURE 8-4:
Type a message in the Message box at the bottom of the page.

7. **Return to the Instagram home screen by tapping or clicking the < icon.**

TIP

You can unsend a message by holding down on the message. Then tap Unsend (iPhone) or Unsend Message (Android). The message has now been erased from the conversation (but it may have been seen if the contact is quick to read messages).

Sending Photos and Videos Privately

Sometimes it's helpful to send a potential client a product photo or brief video through Instagram rather than a text message. You can even customize the photo or video with words, filters, GIFs, and more.

1. **At the bottom of the main Direct screen, tap or click Camera, as shown in Figure 8-5.**

If you need to get to the Direct screen, first tap or click the Direct icon from the Instagram home screen or window.

2. **Take a photo by tapping or clicking the white button (see Figure 8-6), or film a video by holding down on the white button.**

You can instead choose a photo or video from your camera roll by tapping the small square at the lower left and then tapping the photo or video.

The switch cameras icon at the lower-right enables you to switch between the front and rear cameras, if necessary. If you're unhappy with what you shot, tap the X in the upper right to delete the photo or video and try again.

3. **If you want to layer text on top of your photo or video, tap or click the text icon (Aa). Type your message (as shown in Figure 8-7), and then tap Done.**

Photos and videos here have all the same custom capabilities as they do in Instagram stories. For more information about how to add filters, GIFs, polls and more, refer to Chapter 15.

4. **Tap Send To > at the lower right.**

5. **Select your recipients by scrolling through the recipient list and then tapping Send next to one or more usernames.**

The photo is sent fairly quickly and *Done* appears in a blue bar at the bottom of the screen. An Undo button appears for a few seconds before changing to

Sent; you can tap Undo if you sent an image by accident. You can also send your photo to be shown on your Instagram story or to your Close Friends Only, as shown in Figure 8-8.

TIP

You can search for a recipient by tapping the Search box above the list and typing your search terms. As you type, the usernames that most closely match your terms appear in the results list. When you find the name of the recipients you're looking for, tap or click their names in the list.

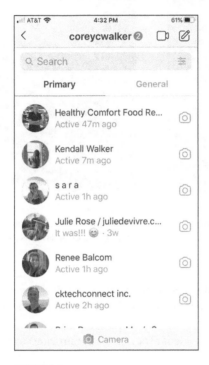

FIGURE 8-5:
Tap Camera at the bottom of the main Direct page.

FIGURE 8-6:
Tap or hold down the white button to take a photo or video, respectively.

6. **Tap Done.**

The Direct screen appears, with the message you sent to the recipient at the top of the conversation list.

FIGURE 8-7:
Add text to your photo by tapping the Aa.

FIGURE 8-8:
Send a message to your close friends by tapping the Close Friends icon.

WARNING

Direct messages are private, and Instagram means it — you can't do several things with a direct message that you can do with a public message:

>> You can't share photos or videos sent with Instagram Direct to other social networking websites.

>> Any hashtags or locations you add to your private message aren't searchable in Instagram.

>> Your messages won't appear in the feed screen or in your profile. You can, however, send a photo or video filmed in Instagram Direct to your Instagram story.

Do photos and videos last forever or do they disappear? The answer is: It depends. If you send a photo or video using the method outlined previously, the photo or video remains viewable in the recipient's message indefinitely. However, if you would like to send a disappearing photo or video, follow these instructions:

1. **Tap or click the Instagram Direct icon, which appears in the upper-right corner of your home screen.**

2. **Type in the Search field to locate the contact you want or scroll through your existing messages to find the person. Tap the person's name.**

   If you had a previous conversation with the contact, the old message thread appears. Otherwise, you'll see a blank screen with the contact's name at the top and a message bar at the bottom.

3. **Tap the blue camera icon at the bottom of the screen.**

4. **Take a photo by tapping or clicking the white button, or film a video by holding down on the white button (refer to Figure 8-6).**

   To switch between the front and rear cameras, tap the switch cameras icon. To delete the photo or video and try again, tap the X.

   TIP

   If you'd rather use a photo or video you took previously, you can choose one from your camera roll. Tap the small square at the lower left, and then tap the photo or video, as shown in Figure 8-9. You can also choose multiple photos or videos at once by tapping Select Multiple, tapping each thumbnail you want, and tapping Next at the bottom of the screen.

5. **If you want to layer text on top of your photo or video, tap or click the text (Aa) icon. Type your message, and then tap Done.**

   Photos and videos here have all the same custom capabilities as they do in Instagram stories. For more information about how to add filters, GIFs, polls, and more, refer to Chapter 15.

6. **Decide how you want the photo to be viewed by choosing View Once, Allow Replay, or Keep in Chat, as shown in Figure 8-10.**

   View Once allows one view and then it disappears. Allow Replay allows one view and one replay, and then it disappears. Keep in Chat keeps the photo or video in the message thread indefinitely.

7. **Tap the Send button.**

   You can also tap the Send to Others button if you want to send to your Instagram story, close friends only, or other contacts.

FIGURE 8-9:
Choose photos or videos from your camera roll.

FIGURE 8-10:
Choose how you would like your message to be viewed.

Sharing GIFs

Sometimes all you need to communicate a message is a fun GIF. Instagram imports hundreds of available GIFs via Giphy for you to use in Instagram Direct. To send a GIF in a message, follow these steps:

1. **Tap or click the Instagram Direct icon.**

2. **Type in the Search feature (or scroll through your recent messages list) to locate the contact you want and tap his or her name to reveal the message screen.**

3. **iPhone only: Tap the black + button in the right corner of the Message bar at the bottom of the screen.**

   On an Android device, the gif icon appears on the message bar automatically.

   A smiley face GIF button appears, as shown in Figure 8-11.

4. **Tap the GIF button to see suggested GIFs, as shown in Figure 8-12.**

   You can also use the Search Giphy bar to search for specific GIFs.

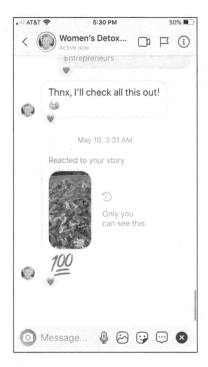

FIGURE 8-11:
On an iPhone, reveal the GIF button by tapping the black + button in the Message box.

FIGURE 8-12:
Select from the suggested GIFs or can search for other GIFs.

5. **Tap the GIF you like best.**

   The GIF is sent automatically, so be careful what you tap!

Using Voice Messages

Tired of typing, or have a lot to say and prefer to leave a quick voice message? Instagram has a solution! To send a voice message, follow these steps:

1. **Tap or click the Instagram Direct icon.**

2. **Type in the Search bar (or scroll through your recent messages list) to locate the contact and then tap his or her name to reveal the message screen.**

3. **To record your message (up to one minute), press and hold down on the microphone icon located in the right corner of the Message bar (as shown in Figure 8-13).**

WARNING

When recording a voice message, the message will be sent automatically when you release the icon button. If you want to delete the message and rerecord it, slide your finger to the trash can on the left; then hold down on the microphone again to rerecord. You can unsend a sent recording by holding down on the recorded message and tapping Unsend.

Creating a New Group Message

If you'd like to send a private message to two or more people at once, you can create a group conversation. This feature is useful if

FIGURE 8-13:
Press and hold the microphone icon while recording your voice message.

you have a group of clients who have subscribed to your program or you'd like to share a sale to VIP customers. To create a new group conversation:

1. **Tap or click the Instagram Direct icon.**

2. **Tap the pencil icon at the upper right.**

3. **Type names in the Search field (or scroll through the list) to locate the contacts you want and tap their names.**

   The names appear in blue at the top of the screen, and can be deleted by tapping them again.

4. **Tap Chat.**

5. **Android only: Send an initial message to the group.**

   Android users must send a message before naming the group. You send a message to the group in the same way you send a message to an individual.

6. **Enter the name of the group, as shown in Figure 8-14.**

   This group is saved after you name it. You can send other messages to the same group later by looking for it in the Search box, or scrolling through your sent messages.

   TIP

   You can rename your group name later by tapping the group name and entering a new name. The members of the group can see this name, so choose wisely!

7. **Type a message, take a photo or video, or send a GIF or a voice message to the group.**

   Instructions for sending each of these message types are the same for a single message or a group message and were outlined previously in the chapter.

FIGURE 8-14:
Enter the name of the group to save it for future messages.

If you need to include more group members later, tap the group name (iPhone or Android) or the *i* icon (iPhone), tap Add People, search and select the contacts you'd like to add, and then tap Next (iPhone) or Done (Android). The new group members are added to your thread and can see the entire previous conversation except for any disappearing photos or videos.

Replying to a Direct Message

If you've had a previous conversation with one or more recipients, you can tap the individual or group name in the Direct screen to view your past conversation(s) and write a new message to start a new conversation. The Message screen appears and you see all the text, photos, and videos you sent previously to that recipient or group.

Swipe or scroll to view your entire conversation. You can also type a new message, as described earlier in this chapter.

If you're already having a private message conversation in Instagram Direct, you can respond by sending a photo to one or more of your followers. Here's how:

1. **Tap or click the Instagram Direct icon.**

   The Direct screen appears with the most recent direct message conversations appearing at the top.

2. **Tap or click the camera icon to the right of the username in the list.**

   The Camera screen appears with the front camera active. In the Windows app, your webcam becomes active so you can take a photo of yourself. You may be prompted to enable access to your camera or microphone or both.

3. **Take a photo by tapping or clicking the white shutter button, or take a video by holding down on the button.**

   You can switch between the front and back camera on your iPhone, iPad, Android smartphone, or Android tablet by tapping the switch cameras icon.

4. **Tap Send.**

Using Live Chat in Direct Messages

Sometimes it's nice to carry on a conversation face-to-face, even if it's not in person. You can live chat with up to six people using Instagram Direct. To use video chat on Instagram:

1. **Tap or click the Instagram Direct icon.**

2. **Locate the contact or group you want, and then tap the name to reveal the message screen.**

   To locate the contact or group, type in the Search field or scroll through your recent messages list.

3. **Tap the movie camera icon at the top right.**

   As shown in Figure 8-15, the contact or group is notified that you're requesting a live chat and can choose to answer or dismiss the call.

FIGURE 8-15:
Live Chat contacts can choose whether to answer or dismiss the call.

WARNING

Anyone you've direct messaged with previously can request a live chat. If you don't want them to have this capability, on iPhone you can mute video chat by scrolling to the person's name, swiping left, and then tapping Mute; then tap Mute Video Chat. On Android, you hold down on the person's name and choose Mute Video Chats from the pop-up list of options.

If you've already started a chat with one or more people, you can add more people (up to six) to an ongoing conversation.

To add more people to your video chat, follow these steps:

1. **While still in your video chat, simply swipe up to add another contact.**

   You see your list of recently messaged contacts. You can also use Search to find other contacts.

2. **When you've located your contact, tap Add next to the person's username.**

   The contact receives a notification that you'd like to video chat, and he or she can pick up the chat, ignore it, or decline it.

Navigating Your Inbox

If you've been following the instructions in this chapter, you likely have several message threads piling up in your inbox. You may have even discovered some contacts you'd rather not hear from anymore.

New messages are indicated by a number in a red circle next to the Direct icon at the top of your home screen, as shown in Figure 8-16. By tapping the Direct icon, you are taken to the Messages screen, where you can tap a new message to view it.

When you've finished viewing the message, you can

>> Let it sit in your inbox indefinitely.

>> Reply to the message with text, a photo, a video, a GIF, or a heart.

FIGURE 8-16:
The number in the red circle tells you the number of new direct messages you've received.

>> Delete the message by swiping left, tapping More, and then tapping Delete (iPhone), or by holding down on the account name and choosing Delete (Android). See Figure 8-17.

>> Mute the conversation so you no longer receive notifications from the person messaging you on Instagram Direct by swiping left and tapping More and then tapping Mute (iPhone) or holding down on the account name and choosing Mute (Android). When you unmute someone, you can still access the messages the person sent during the muted period by opening the conversation in the DM.

>> Move the message to and from the Primary and General sections.

>> *iPhone only:* Flag the message to remember to view it later by tapping the message and then tapping the flag at the top right.

>> *iPhone only:* Mark the message as Unread so it's highlighted in bold again by swiping left and tapping Unread.

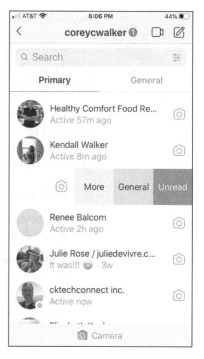

FIGURE 8-17:
Deleting a message on an iPhone.

That's really all there is to it! The Instagram Direct inbox is fairly simple to navigate, with limited options for handling your message after it's viewed.

The message search capabilities of Instagram Direct are slim. At this point, you can search for messages based on the contact's or group's name. Unlike an email inbox, you can't filter a search by subject, keywords, or date.

To search for a conversation by username or group name, follow these steps:

1. Tap or click the Instagram Direct icon.

2. Type in the Search field (or scroll through your recent messages list) to locate the contact or group you want, and then tap the name.

   You see your previous conversation and can choose to reply if you'd like.

Getting Rid of Unwanted Messages

Instagram is a huge platform with millions of users, which can result in messages from a variety of sources. There's a good chance you'll receive a message from someone that you'd rather not hear from.

Initially, if the user isn't someone you are following or have messaged with previously, Instagram funnels the person into a different section called General. You see the initial request to speak with you with a blue link that indicates the number of requests waiting. When you tap the blue link, a new page appears revealing the usernames of the people who would like to contact you. You now have the following choices to make (as shown in Figure 8-18):

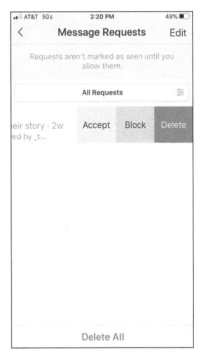

FIGURE 8-18:
Your message requests.

>> Swipe left and tap Accept to allow a communication, tap Block to refuse any further communication requests, or tap Delete to delete the message.

>> If you have several messages that you don't want to communicate with, tap the Delete All link at the bottom. All the messages in your Message Requests inbox will be deleted.

You may have started a conversation with someone, only to find out later that the person is sending inappropriate messages. To report an inappropriate message, follow these steps:

1. **Inside the conversation thread, tap and hold down on the individual comment that was inappropriate.**

A Report button appears above the message.

2. **Tap the Report button and follow the instructions.**

The message and username is sent to Instagram and the user is reported. The user is not notified that you're the person who reported them.

Chapter **9**

Wielding the Power of the Hashtag

You're starting to create cool content and have followed many people, but for some reason, your photos are garnering only a few likes. Want a solution to this problem? It's hashtags. Hashtags give your posts more reach by making them searchable to anyone, not just those in your immediate network. In fact, a study by Simply Measured (www.simplymeasured.com) found that adding just one hashtag to Instagram posts yielded an average 12.6 percent increase in engagement (likes and comments).

In this chapter, you learn how to place hashtags and discover the best practices of using hashtags. You also find out how to research hashtags that apply to your business and create branded hashtags for your Instagram account. If you're interested in learning about hashtags for Instagram stories, we suggest getting the basics about hashtags here first and then reading Chapters 14 and 15.

Investigating Hashtags

To get started, we discuss what hashtags are and why it's important to use them on Instagram. Hashtags always start with the # sign (found on the bottom right of your mobile phone keyboard when typing, or by pressing Shift-3 on a desktop computer keyboard) followed by a word, a phrase, a number, or an emoji with no spaces, such as #sundayvibes or #instamood.

REMEMBER

Characters such as $ and % as well as periods and underscores do not work in hashtags.

To add a hashtag to your photo or video, follow these instructions:

1. **Take or upload a photo or video. Tap Next.**

2. **Add a filter if you want. Tap Next.**

3. **Type or copy and paste your caption in the Write a Caption field.**

4. **Add hashtags using one of the following methods:**

   - Before you share your post: *Type or cut and paste up to 30 hashtags after your text in the caption, as shown in Figure 9-1, left, and then tap Share at the top right of the screen.*

   - After you've shared your post: *Tap the Comment bubble, and type or cut and paste up to 30 hashtags in the comment field, as shown in Figure 9-1, right. Tap Post.*

TIP

No functional difference exists between placing your hashtags in the caption or in the comments. Which method you use is your personal preference.

After you add a hashtag to your caption or comment, the hashtag becomes a searchable link that takes you to a page of all the posts using that hashtag (a hashtag hub) when tapped.

Hashtags are added to a hashtag hub chronologically, based on when the photo was posted, not when the hashtag posts. Going back days later and adding hashtags to a post will not bump your post back up in the hashtag hub.

People search hashtags to find content for a variety of reasons, such as to find a product, to learn how to do something, to follow a brand, or even to watch videos of a certain theme. We go over how to search hashtags later, in the "Researching the Right Hashtags" section.

FIGURE 9-1:
Hashtags can go in the caption (left) or below the caption in the comments (right).

TIP

If you have a private account, only users who are your approved followers will see your posts, even with a hashtag. If you're trying to get a wider audience, set your account to public so anyone can search for your content via hashtags.

Following hashtag best practices

Hashtags seem simple enough, right? But there's more to them than meets the eye, and any serious Instagrammer will tell you to follow certain do's and don'ts when using hashtags. In this section, we detail best practices for using hashtags.

Placing hashtags so you don't annoy people

If you're familiar with using hashtags on Facebook or Twitter, you're probably used to putting a couple of hashtags directly in your post. On Instagram, however, you can use up to 30 hashtags in a caption. Use one of the following tactics to keep your captions uncluttered:

TIP

>> **Type hashtags after the text in your caption. Refer to Figure 9-1, left.**

Some people type period, return, period, return several times to move the hashtags farther down out of the way of the caption text.

» **Place hashtags in the comment directly below your caption.** Refer to Figure 9-1, right.

WARNING

If you use more than 30 hashtags in a caption or a comment on your post, Instagram will not post the accompanying photo or video. Make sure to count all hashtags you use, especially if you use one or two in your caption and then a full list in a comment below to ensure that your photo or video will post.

Popular hashtags and when to use them

Believe it or not, hashtags, just like students in high school, can be popular and not so popular. There are good reasons to use some of both hashtag types. In addition, you should avoid some hashtags.

Here are some popular hashtags:

» #beautiful

» #cute

» #fashion

» #happy

» #instagood

» #love

» #me

» #photooftheday

» #picoftheday

» #selfie

» #tbt

Although these hashtags are seen by a large population on the hashtag hub (but probably not your target audience), the post may be shown for only a few moments. Those hashtags are used by millions of people daily, so they're quickly replaced by the next post using that hashtag.

When Instagram's algorithm detects a popular post (with quick engagement), it appears in the Top Posts section at the top of the hashtag hub (see Figure 9-2). These posts stay up longer. Top Posts is a coveted position because it is the first thing anyone sees when searching a hashtag. It's also a badge of honor because the best performing posts are shown there.

The popular hashtags should be used only if they apply to your post. Throwing a bunch of hashtags that don't apply to your photo or video may get it seen briefly, but it's a bad practice because people searching that hashtag won't find what they're looking for and might be ticked off that you used it.

Many hashtags are available, and many will perform much better for you than popular hashtags because they're more specific to your business. For instance, a solar company might choose #solar, #solarenergy, #solar-panels, #renewableenergy, #poweredbythe-sun, #savemoneyandenergy, #renewables, #sunpowered, and #saynotofossilfuels.

One effective tactic is to mix hashtags that receive a lot of traffic with hashtags that get little traffic. With this method, your post is seen briefly right away by many people searching for the popular hashtags. Meanwhile, your less popular hashtags are seen by fewer (yet more targeted) people for a longer time and have a better chance of making it into Top Posts. Your post may even stay there for a few days! We discuss how to research hashtags later in the section, "Researching the Right Hashtags."

TIP

You should avoid some popular hashtags, such as any that encourage following (#follow, #follow4follow, #followforfollow, #followforlikes, #followme). People who have no interest in your business will end up following and then unfollowing you. It's a big waste of time. Hashtags that reference sexual activity or body parts are generally blocked too, and don't normally belong on a business post anyway.

Storing hashtags for later

If you plan on using hashtags regularly, typing them into your phone by hand will quickly become tedious. Following are a few work-arounds for this problem:

>> **Notes:** The Notes app is preloaded on iPhones, and similar apps like ColorNote or Evernote are available for download on Android phones. Create a new note for different categories or products, and then list up to

30 hashtags, as shown in Figure 9-3, left. Before you tap Share on your post, go over to your note and copy the desired hashtags. Tap Share and open a comment to paste the hashtags.

>> **Email:** Another easy solution is to email yourself lists of hashtags. Simply open a new email, use the hashtag category in the Subject line, and then type up to 30 hashtags, as shown in Figure 9-3, middle. Create several emails with different hashtag lists, and then store them in a special email folder to retrieve and cut and paste quickly and easily.

>> **Third-party social media apps:** Many social media management apps such as Agorapulse, Buffer, Planoly, Later, and Tailwind (see Figure 9-3, right) also include hashtag saving. You can upload your content, schedule it, get hashtag suggestions, save hashtag lists for later, and measure analytics. Unlike the Notes app or email, most of these apps are not free.

FIGURE 9-3:
Store hashtags in a notes app (left), an email message (middle), or a third-party app like Tailwind.

© Tailwind

TIP

If you regularly string together the same hashtags, use predictive text on your phone to populate a set of hashtags. That way, you won't need to store them in a separate location.

Tracking hashtag analytics

If you'd like in-depth reporting about which hashtags are performing best for you, many apps can help. The three most popular apps for hashtag analytics follow:

>> **Iconosquare** (`https://pro.iconosquare.com`): This all-in-one app can not only monitor hashtag performance but also serve as your content management system to store, schedule, and post content. For hashtags specifically, you can see how each hashtag you use affects engagement (as shown in Figure 9-4); discover your most influential posts by hashtag; view the most influential people using a particular hashtag; and see the location of most of the people who are viewing a hashtag. Iconosquare tracks Instagram for only hashtags (but has many other Facebook functions) and starts at $29/month for a Pro account billed annually.

FIGURE 9-4: Iconosquare offers several ways to track hashtag analytics.

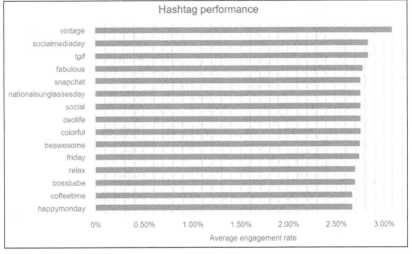

>> **Sprout Social** (`https://sproutsocial.com`): Sprout Social's Instagram integration includes scheduling, engagement tools, and access to rich analytics. Using Sprout's all-in-one platform you can plan content and post to your Instagram profile, respond to comments on your posts, and monitor and engage with people. You can also see your outbound hashtag performance, which rates your most used hashtags and your most engaged hashtags, as shown in Figure 9-5. Finally, you can search hashtags to see campaign results for contests that collect user-generated content tagged with your branded hashtag. Sprout Social is a robust solution and starts at $99/month.

>> **Tailwind:** Tailwind is a content management system tailored to Instagram and Pinterest only. It provides many ways to track hashtags, including the following: daily activity, engagement, and trends (see Figure 9-6); popular topics and hashtags related to your brand; which photos are getting the most likes and comments by hashtag; where hashtags are working better

geographically; and suggestions for related hashtags to use. Unfortunately, these features are available only at the Enterprise level (price not listed), which may be more than you want to spend if you're a small-business owner.

Instagram Outbound Hashtag Performance
Review your hashtag usage during the reporting period and contrast them with hashtags that drew the most engagement.

Most Used Hashtags		Top Hashtags by Lifetime Engagements	
#coffee	33	#coffee	85
#sproutcoffee	11	#sproutcoffee	29
#latte	10	#latte	29
#coffeeart	9	#coffeeart	27
#coffeepics	9	#coffeepics	27
#foodie	9	#foodie	27
#SproutCoffee	5	#sproutsocial	13
#cafe	5	#ilovecoffee	10
#coffeelove	5	#espresso	8
#smallbiz	5	#coffeeislife	7

FIGURE 9-5:
Sprout Social can display your most used and most engaged hashtags.

© Sprout Social

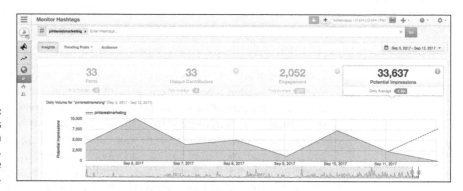

FIGURE 9-6:
Tailwind offers several in-depth hashtag analytics, but only at the Enterprise level.

As you can see, hashtag analytics apps are available, but they often require an investment. Start using Instagram and decide how closely you'll be monitoring hashtags, and then decide whether an analytic app is worth the expense.

Researching the Right Hashtags

You've been given the best practices about where to put, store, and analyze hashtags, but how can you find the right ones? In this section, we discuss several ways to research hashtags for your posts, including checking out the competition, finding related hashtags, and looking at influencer hashtags.

Checking out the competition

If you're looking for robust competitive hashtag analysis, the apps mentioned in the preceding section offer tools to dive into the competition's hashtags for a price. You can also search hashtags quickly using Instagram itself as detailed next.

Follow these steps to research your competitors' hashtags:

1. **Create a list of your top competitors, including their Instagram username, in Excel or another spreadsheet program.**

   Create a spreadsheet with columns for competitor names and hashtags. You can also include product or service categories if that makes sense for your business. See Figure 9-7 for an example. (This process is detailed in Chapter 6 in the section about watching your competition.)

2. **Log in to your Instagram account on your desktop by going to** www.instagram.com/username **and entering your username and password.**

   You must access Instagram on your desktop computer because you can't copy and paste your competitor's hashtags from your mobile device.

3. **Refer to your competitor list and type a username in the Search box at the top of the Instagram screen.**

4. **Click one of the competitor's images, and view the hashtags.**

   Copy and paste the hashtags into the Excel spreadsheet.

5. **Go through at least five images, copying and pasting any new hashtags you find.**

   Note on the spreadsheet any images that received a lot of likes. You won't be able to tell if the image's popularity is due to the image or the hashtags, but include the information just in case.

6. **Repeat Steps 3–5 for all competitors on your list.**

   Compare hashtags that they're all using, and add them to your business's hashtag list. Also note hashtags on posts in which multiple competitors received a lot of likes.

7. **Go to your Instagram mobile app and get more information about the popularity or the hashtags in your list:**

 a. Tap the magnifying glass at the bottom of your Instagram app screen, and then tap inside the Search box.

 b. On the next page that appears, tap Tags.

 c. Enter one of the hashtags from your competitor list. The hashtag you entered will appear first, with the number of posts that have used it, plus other related hashtags and how often they've been used.

 Use this information to mix some high-use and low-use hashtags, increasing the chance that your post will be seen.

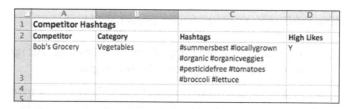

	A	B	C	D
1	Competitor Hashtags			
2	Competitor	Category	Hashtags	High Likes
3	Bob's Grocery	Vegetables	#summersbest #locallygrown #organic #organicveggies #pesticidefree #tomatoes #broccoli #lettuce	Y
4				
5				

Manual tracking is not an exact science, but it will expose you to new hashtags. And you might find a hashtag that propels the views to your account.

Picking up on similar hashtags

You might also want to find similar hashtags for your business. One easy method using Instagram mobile is to tap the magnifying glass at the bottom of your Instagram profile, type a hashtag in the Search field at the top of the screen, and then tap Search. Other similar hashtags will appear.

An additional free resource for related hashtags is RiteTag, at www.ritetag.com. (Some extra functionality requires a paid account.) With RiteTag, shown in Figure 9-8, you enter a hashtag, and it generates other suggested hashtags that work well on Instagram. It separates the hashtags into "get seen now" hashtags, which are seen quickly (and go away quickly), and hashtags that stay longer and are seen over time. RiteTag is a handy tool!

Whether you use Instagram's hashtag suggestions or RiteTag's, make sure you store the results. You can use a simple Excel spreadsheet or one of the methods described earlier, in the "Storing hashtags for later" section.

FIGURE 9-8:
RiteTag suggests
hashtags for you
based on the
hashtag you
entered.

Discovering what the cool kids are doing (influencer hashtags)

Another way to find great hashtags is to research what the influencers for your industry are using. Influencers are key people that your target audience follows and whose opinions are highly regarded. Most industries have a few key people who are popular and widely followed. If you don't know who those people are, follow these steps to find them:

1. **Choose one of the hashtags that you or a competitor uses that is specific to your business.**

   For example, choose #sacramentorestaurant instead of #restaurant.

2. **Do a Google search of that hashtag.**

   For example, in Figure 9-9, we typed *#sacramentorestaurant on instagram.*

3. **Click through to the posts that appear on Instagram. If a username is frequently featured:**

   a. *Note the username, and check to see how the number of likes and how many followers the account has.*

   b. *If the username seems like a good influencer for your industry, write down some of the other hashtags the account is using to reach your audience. Add these hashtags to your saved hashtag lists.*

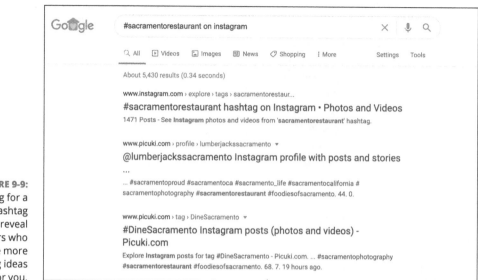

FIGURE 9-9:
Searching for a
popular hashtag
can reveal
influencers who
may have more
hashtag ideas
for you.

Creating a Branded Hashtag

Surely you've seen the hashtag #YesWeCan, or #ShareaCoke, right? These are examples of branded hashtags. A branded hashtag may start as a campaign slogan and then morph over to easily become a branded hashtag. But sometimes it's not that simple, and you'll need to do more research before launching a branded hashtag.

Here are the steps for creating a branded hashtag for your business:

1. Start by making a list of all hashtags that relate to your brand, including any slogans you use regularly.

2. Search that hashtag on Twitter and Instagram to make sure it's not already being used by someone else or for something unsavory.

3. Share the hashtag with several people to see ensure that it makes sense and the letters don't run together to form new words. For instance, the ill-fated hashtag for Kids Exchange, a consignment store for kids' clothes, was #kidsexchange, which could be misread as "kid sex change."

4. Use the hashtag on your Instagram posts and bio (and other social media), Power Point presentations, flyers, ads, and packaging to get people accustomed to seeing it and using it to tag their posts about your product or service.

Branded hashtags offer an easy way for followers to search for their favorite brands on Instagram. After you have true fans, they'll start using your hashtag on their posts, to showcase your product or service in their post or simply to interact with you. Be sure to check your branded hashtag often so you can respond and react to posts that include it!

In the next two sections, you discover best practices for using a hashtag for a promotion or contest, and how to gather user-generated content through hashtags.

Hashtag your promotion or contest

If you're launching a promotion or contest, it's important to use a unique hashtag so you can easily follow the activity of users interacting with you. (See Chapter 12 for details on setting up an Instagram contest from start to finish.)

If you already have a branded hashtag for your business, you should choose a new hashtag for this promotion or contest only. Follow the guidelines just mentioned for creating a branded hashtag, but make it specific to this contest. If your branded hashtag has already gone viral, you could just add contest to the end of it, such as #JustDoItContest, to capitalize on your already known brand.

Start using the hashtag on all posts, material, and websites related to the promotion or contest. Give followers instructions for using the hashtag in their posts, as shown in Figure 9-10.

After your promotion or contest is underway, check the hashtag often (by tapping it) to monitor the conversation or gather contest entries or both. Another simple way to view hashtags is to tap the magnifying glass at the bottom of your Instagram mobile app, and then type the hashtag in the Search box. A page with just those hashtags will appear, as shown in Figure 9-11, for you to view, respond to, and collect as contest entries.

Gathering user-generated content

When you're running a promotion or contest, you might ask followers to submit a piece of their own content to enter the contest. In Figure 9-10, for example, @jenns_trends tells her followers to take a photo during her live conference session and upload the image by Monday.

© Jenn Herman

FIGURE 9-10:
@jenns_trends tells followers that they can enter her contest by using the hashtags #LearnFromJenn and #SMMW17 in their entry posts.

FIGURE 9-11:
Search results for the hashtag #learnfromjenn.

User-generated content paired with your promotion or contest hashtag is an excellent way to expand the reach of your promotion or contest. The followers who submit content are now spreading the hashtag among their followers. Depending on the size of your brand or how viral the contest, this method can increase your reach exponentially.

Check the hashtag by tapping the magnifying glass at the bottom of your Instagram mobile app, and then typing the hashtag in the Search area. Refer to Figure 9-11 for an example of what the results look like.

Most other all-in-one content-management systems we describe, such as Sprout Social, Iconosquare, and Tailwind, also enable you to search for your hashtags to view submitted content. Finally, after you find the user-generated content via your hashtag, repost it or notify the winner or both! If your initial instructions did not include a phrase about the follower granting permission to use the image as a condition of submitting it, make sure you contact the person to get permission to repost. For official language about contest submissions and permissions, refer to Chapter 12's section on defining rules or conditions.

4

Extending Your Reach with Ads

Create a winning Instagram ad for your business.

Test your ad and get insights about its popularity on Instagram and Facebook.

Produce a winning Instagram contest to bring fun to your followers.

Mix your Instagram profile into your social marketing recipe.

Chapter **10**

Planning a Winning Ad

With over a billion people using Instagram each month and 90 percent of those following a business on Instagram, advertising on Instagram is a no-brainer. The demographics are shifting older too — Instagram is no longer just a playground for teens and Gen Y. If you're seeking Gen X or even some Baby Boomer customers, Instagram is quickly becoming a hotspot for them too.

In this chapter, we discuss choosing an ad type, the design elements needed for a good Instagram post, and selecting your target audience, which may include those Baby Boomers!

REMEMBER

You must have your Instagram account set up as a business profile to create ads. For more information about this easy (and free) upgrade, refer to Chapter 2.

INSTAGRAM DEMOGRAPHICS

According to a 2020 social media study by Statista, key usage demographics by age range are as follows:

- 13-17 years: 7 percent
- 18-24 years: 29 percent
- 25-34 years: 34 percent
- 35-44 years: 16 percent
- 45-54 years: 8 percent
- 55+ years: 6 percent

As you can see, Instagram is still a strong platform for younger audiences, but the numbers for older adults (with more money to spend) are increasing rapidly. The gender demographics have evened out with women making up 51 percent and men making up 49 percent of users. The US boasts the highest user base, but countries like India and Brazil are rapidly catching up. The international market will likely exceed US usage very soon.

The reasons for using Instagram for your advertising platform are even better:

- Demographics are highly targetable via Facebook's extensive shared database.
- The cost of entry is low. You can run a successful ad campaign for less than $20 if you use the right creative and targeting strategy!
- You can reach a new set of customers who haven't discovered your profile yet.
- It's the perfect tool to drive traffic to your website, opt-in piece, or other link of your choice.

Selecting the Right Ad Type

Six types of Instagram ads are available:

>> **Photo:** A stunning simple square or landscape photo with a call-to-action link.

>> **Video:** Up to two minutes of square or landscape video, including sound and call-to-action link.

>> **Carousel:** Two to ten photos or videos or both that users can swipe through to get in-depth information. Includes one call-to-action link for the entire sequence.

>> **Stories:** Photos or videos in this special, popular section of Instagram to complement other content in your regular feed.

>> **Collection:** Includes four products under one main image or video that opens to full-screen when someone interacts with your ad.

>> **Explore Ads:** Ads can be used separately or blended together to create a well-rounded campaign that delights different audience preferences. A huge advantage of Instagram ads is that they allow call-to-action links directly below the image. All ads display *Sponsored* in the top-right corner of the image to let users know that they are seeing a paid ad.

TIP

Normally, the only link available to you on Instagram is in the bio on your profile page. Having a call-to-action link below the image or video is a big deal!

Photo ad

A *photo ad,* like the one in Figure 10-1, is the simplest ad type, using only one photo or image in square or landscape format. Photo (and video) ads offer three destinations to choose from when you create them in the Instagram app: Your Profile, Your Website, and Your Direct Messages. Your Website is the only destination that includes a call-to-action link.

For the Your Website destination, your call-to-action link choices are as follows:

>> Learn More

>> Shop Now

>> Watch More

>> Contact Us

>> Book Now

>> Sign Up

FIGURE 10-1:
This photo ad has a Learn More call-to-action link that links to the company's website.

Each option allows you to link to a website.

If you use Facebook Ads Manager to create your Instagram photo (or video) ad, many more objectives are available: brand awareness, reach, traffic, engagement, app installs, video views, lead generation, messages, catalog sales, and store traffic. Depending on the objective of your ad, you may need to use Ads Manager for a more targeted approach.

We walk through creating the ad in Instagram's mobile app and Facebook in the next chapter.

Video ad

A *video ad* enables you to boost your message with the power of an up to 120-second video. Video is now mainstream and can capture your audience's attention in a stronger way than a still photo can. Tell a quick story, show how to use your product, ask your audience a question — you can engage with your audience in so many ways through video.

Video ads provide the same destinations and call-to-action links described in the preceding section, "Photo ads." Figure 10-2 shows an example of a video ad with a Sign Up call-to-action link. If recording video is new to you, refer to Chapter 5 to learn how to film, edit, and post videos on Instagram.

© soverve

FIGURE 10-2:
This video ad has a Sign Up call-to-action link that links to the company's website.

Carousel ad

You use a carousel ad to tell a visual story with two to ten still images or videos or both. Instead of relying on one image or video, the carousel allows your audience to be walked through an event, with step-by-step instructions, demonstrations of your product, before-and-after presentations, or even one long, scrolling panoramic image.

When you create a carousel ad, you can select the order in which the images or videos are shown. If you don't need them to follow a particular order, you can tell Instagram to arrange them to show the highest performing image or video first.

TIP

Always choose an engaging image or video as your first piece of content in a carousel. Users likely won't bother scrolling through the carousel if the main image in the feed doesn't appeal to them.

A carousel ad is square and allows only one caption and comment feed for the entire sequence (not separate captions and comments for each photo). In the newsfeed, users briefly see a black oval with 1/# (where # is the number of images or videos in the carousel) in the top right of your carousel. They also see blue dots at the bottom of the image that represent the number of images or videos in the carousel, as shown in Figure 10-3. This way, they know to scroll left to see the entire carousel.

You can't create a carousel ad in the Instagram mobile app. This type of ad is available only in Facebook Ads Manager.

The ad objectives for carousel ads are brand awareness, reach, traffic, app installs, engagement, conversions, video views, product catalog sales, store traffic, and lead generation.

Stories ad

The only way to create a Stories ad is by using Facebook's Ads Manager. Unfortunately, you can't create a Stories ad with the Instagram mobile app.

FIGURE 10-3:
The *1/5* in the top-right corner of the image and the five dots below the image tell you that this carousel ad has five images or videos.

You can use photos or videos in a Stories ad, but they must be in vertical format (versus the more common square in the newsfeed), with a suggested size of 1,080 x 1,920 pixels. This size offers the best resolution and fit to the screen. (However, if necessary, Instagram will resize your image to fit the screen.) Other dimensions may stretch or cut off parts of your photo or video.

Stories ads offer a large variety of call-to-action links such as these (and many more):

>> No Button

>> Sign Up

>> Subscribe

>> Watch More

>> Learn More

When users swipe up on the call-to-action link, they go to a website you chose when setting up the ad. Figure 10-4 shows an example of a Stories ad with a Learn More call to action.

Collection ad

The collection format provides a unique user experience that allows viewers to purchase your products and services from Instagram. The ad is shown in the newsfeed and features four products under a main image or video that opens full-screen when someone interacts with your ad.

Using an Effective Ad Strategy

Now that you have learned about the different ad types available, it's time to get down to the nitty-gritty of designing the ad, from size specs to audience types and more.

Design requirements

The design requirements vary for each ad type we discussed previously in the chapter. In this section, we outline all the specs you need to create an ad in the correct size.

For photo, video, carousel, and collection ads, use the following specs:

» **Image ratio:** 1:1 (square), 1.91:1 (landscape), 4:5 (vertical). Carousel ads accommodate only square images and videos. Collection ads accommodate only square or landscape images and videos.

» **Image size minimum:** 500 x 500 pixels (square), 600 x 315 pixels (landscape), 600 x 750 pixels (vertical).

» **Image size maximum:** No maximum resolution.

» **Caption text:** 125 characters recommended, up to 300 characters. Ninety characters and below recommended for Collection ads.

- >> **Video length:** 120 seconds.
- >> **File type:** .png or .jpg for photos, and .mp4 or .mov for videos.
- >> **File size max:** 30MB for photos, 4GB for videos.

Some of the specs for Instagram Stories ads are different:

- >> **Image ratio:** 4:5 (vertical only) or 9:16 for photos
- >> **Image size minimum:** 600 x 1,067 pixels
- >> **Image size maximum:** 1,080 x 1,920 pixels
- >> **Video length:** 120 seconds
- >> **File type:** .png or .jpg for photos, .mp4 or .mov for videos
- >> **File size max:** 30MB for photos, 4GB for videos

TIP

Video ads that are 15 seconds or less automatically play for the full duration. Ads that are longer than 15 seconds are split into separate cards. Instagram automatically displays 1, 2, or 3 cards for the ad. A Keep Watching option appears on the last card, which the viewer can tap if desired.

Selecting your target audience

A wide variety of options are available to target your perfect audience. You have basic choices such as location and age, but you can also get specific and use people's interests, page likes, and more. Here are some of the many options available to you:

- >> Location
- >> Gender
- >> Age range
- >> Languages
- >> Interests (health, guinea pigs, video games, floral design, specific Facebook pages, like Trader Joe's or 24 Hour Fitness, you name it)
- >> Employers
- >> Homeowner or renter
- >> Single, married, divorced, widowed, in a relationship
- >> Children or no children
- >> Connections (whether they are fans of your page, use your app, and so forth)

>> Custom audiences (advanced feature that looks at people you already know using information you provide to Facebook to build a targeted audience)

>> Lookalike audiences (subset of a custom audience that creates a new targeted audience that is similar to your existing custom audience)

Jot down a wider target audience using your ideal location, gender, and age first, and then write ideas for a narrower audience using more specific interests and demographics.

When building the ad in Facebook's Ads Manager, you can see whether your selections are too broad or specific by checking a meter that changes as you add or subtract characteristics. It will also give you an estimated daily reach based on your targeting selections and your budget, as shown in Figure 10-5.

If you find the audience is too broad, try adding a specific interest. If your audience is too narrow, there may not be enough people to see the ad. In this case, eliminate interests that are extremely niche to help your ad's daily reach.

Chapter 11 details how to create the audience in Facebook Ads Manager.

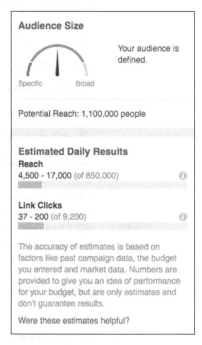

Audience Size

Your audience is defined.

Specific   Broad

Potential Reach: 1,100,000 people

Estimated Daily Results
Reach
4,500 - 17,000 (of 850,000)

Link Clicks
37 - 200 (of 9,200)

The accuracy of estimates is based on factors like past campaign data, the budget you entered and market data. Numbers are provided to give you an idea of performance for your budget, but are only estimates and don't guarantee results.

Were these estimates helpful?

FIGURE 10-5:
The meter displays the ad's estimated daily reach based on the demographics, interests, and budget you select.

Choosing ad images wisely

If you've been cruising around on Instagram for a while, you've surely noticed accounts that are simply amazing. The best accounts normally stick to a theme, use consistent colors or filters, and style their images in a certain way to create a unique brand look.

After you have your page's brand determined, it's important to choose an image for your ad that best represents your overall look. It should be obvious that the ad belongs with the rest of your images (or videos). In this section, we go over several ways to choose the best images for your ad.

REMEMBER

Your ad will likely go to people who have never seen your profile page before. Choose a strong image that draws people into your account so they want to keep seeing more.

Use people

Using people in your ad helps to make a connection with your audience. Studies have found that candid photos versus perfectly staged photos perform better. And photos where the person is not looking at the camera, like the photo in Figure 10-6, perform the best. The theory is that it's easier for your audience to imagine themselves as that person if they are not posing for the camera.

Choose a pop of color

Your image should look like it belongs with the rest of your profile, but you also want your image to stand out and stop the scroll. A great way to achieve this is by incorporating a pop of bright color, as shown in Figure 10-7. The eye can't help but get drawn toward a bright image and stop at least briefly to find out what it is.

Create a mood

Creating a mood with your photo helps your audience picture themselves in the situation. Images that convey trust, security, and coziness tend to work best. (See Figure 10-8.) If these terms don't fit with your brand, choose a word that does, and try to find an image that expresses that feeling.

FIGURE 10-6:
Using people in your ad helps to forge a connection with your audience.

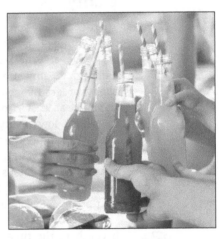

FIGURE 10-7:
A pop of bright color will get your ad noticed.

Lighting

There is nothing worse than a photo that is too dark, has weird shadows, or is washed out, as shown in Figure 10-9. Luckily, even photos that weren't taken in the best circumstances can often be fixed — and you don't have to be a Photoshop expert! For more in-depth coverage of great editing tools, refer to Chapter 4. If you can't get the image to look just right, choose an image with better lighting for your ad, and save that image for your regular feed.

FIGURE 10-8:
The smile of this doctor conveys warmth and trust.

FIGURE 10-9:
Photos with bad lighting should never be used as an ad.

Clarity

There is actually something worse than bad lighting — photos that are blurry or grainy are the worst. Unlike bad lighting, it's almost impossible to fix a blurry or grainy photo. Your images should be at least 72 dpi for online use. Choosing a low quality image for an ad sets a bad impression right from the start. It leaves your audience wondering what other details might get overlooked if they work with you or buy your product. See Figure 10-10.

FIGURE 10-10:
Blurry or grainy photos are almost impossible to fix. Never use them in an ad.

TIP

If you have the time and resources to do a photo shoot, creating a custom image that fits your brand is best. If that isn't possible, check out stock photo companies such as iStock (www.istockphoto.com) or Adobe Stock (https://stock.adobe.com), which offer affordable royalty-free images at a reasonable rate.

A caption can speak (less than) 1,000 words

Although you can usually squeeze in 2,200 characters in a normal Instagram caption, Instagram ads require that you keep your captions short and sweet with a 300-character limit. Because only the first two to three lines are shown — people have to click the More link to see the rest — it's best to put your most important message at the beginning.

Here are some other tips to create a winning ad caption:

- » **Don't go in for the sale right away.** This audience is likely new to you. Let them get to know you by offering something of value to them for free, such as a checklist, email program, or sample product.

- » **Ask questions.** Create more engagement by asking your audience a question, and they will feel more inclined to comment.

- » **Tell them to tag a friend.** Another good engagement tip is to tell people to "Tag a friend who might like to see this, win this, wear this, and so on." When paired with a great image, your target audience will start sharing away!

- » **Provide details.** If the image doesn't instantly explain what your product or service is, use the caption to create deeper context with the image.

- » **Use only a few hashtags.** Although up to 30 hashtags in a comment below the initial caption are often used for a regular post, we don't recommend that many for an ad. Choose 1 to 3 hashtags that get to the heart of your message and place them in the caption. This is a great time to use a specialty hashtag created just for your brand.

- » **Include a call to action.** Last, but certainly not least, always include a call to action (CTA). This is the number-one thing you want people to do when they see your ad. Phrases such as *Tap the Learn More button for a free download* or *Sign up this week for our bonus offer* tell your audience exactly what they should do next to continue a relationship with you. Don't forget this crucial piece of the puzzle!

Chapter **11**

Creating an Effective Instagram Ad

fter you decide what type of ad will work best for you, it's time to find out how to create the ad. In this chapter, we walk through creating an Instagram ad directly through Instagram's mobile app and from Facebook Ads Manager. If you're planning on running the same creative campaign on Facebook, it's helpful to understand Facebook Ads Manager so your Instagram and Facebook campaigns are synced.

TIP

Facebook optimizes campaigns run on both platforms. Whichever platform is performing better (based on the objective you set) will get more ads shown.

We also cover the important topics of testing your ads and measuring the results. By making simple tweaks based on the data uncovered through testing and measuring, you can make a huge difference in the effectiveness of ongoing and new campaigns.

Using the Instagram Mobile App to Create an Ad

You can create photo ads and video ads by using the Instagram mobile app. If you want to create carousel or stories ads, you must use Facebook Ads Manager or Instagram's API (an area that developers use and that is beyond the scope of this book).

Here are the steps for creating a photo or video ad using the Instagram mobile app:

1. **Post your photo or video to Instagram as you normally would for a general post, with a caption, hashtags, and a location, as shown in Figure 11-1.**

2. **Tap the blue Promote button.**

    A new page appears, asking where you would like to send people for the promotion. If it's your first time doing this, the initial page will have a message about ads and a Create Promotion button that you'll need to tap first.

3. **Choose the destination by tapping the circle next to Your Profile, Your Website, or Your Direct Messages, as shown in Figure 11-2, and then tap Next (iOS) or the arrow (Android).**

4. **Determine your audience:**

    *   *Let Instagram choose an audience for you by selecting Automatic, the default.*

    *   *Create your own audience (which we recommend) by tapping the arrow to the right of Create Your Own. On the Create Audience page, name your audience, and choose a location, interests, gender, and age ranges. Then tap Done (iOS) or the check mark (Android).*

5. **After you have defined your audience, tap Next (iOS) or the arrow (Android).**

6. **Use the sliding scales to determine your daily budget and duration, and then tap Next.**

7. **Review your promotion, and then tap Create Promotion to get the promotion started.**

    If you have not set up a payment option yet, you will be directed to do so before you can tap the Create Promotion button.

That's it — pretty easy, right?

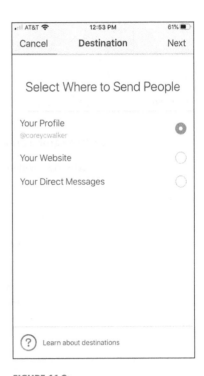

FIGURE 11-1:
Tap the blue Promote button to start the ad process.

FIGURE 11-2:
Choose the destination for your ad, and then follow the prompts to finish the ad.

Using Facebook to Create an Ad

You can create photo, video, or carousel Instagram ads through the Facebook Ads Manager. Note that you must have a Facebook business page and an ad account to run ads on Instagram.

Creating the campaign

To create a photo, video, or carousel Instagram ad by using Ads Manager, follow these steps:

1. **Go to the Ads Manager page using one of these methods:**

   - *Type www.facebook.com/adsmanager.*

   - *Go to your Facebook business page and click the Ad Center link on the left side of the page. Then click All Ads. Scroll to the bottom of the All Ads page and click the Ads Manager link.*

   The Ads Manager page appears, as shown in Figure 11-3.

FIGURE 11-3:
The main Ads
Manager page.

2. **Click the green Create button in the upper left to start the campaign.**

   The screen shown in Figure 11-4 appears.

| Create New Campaign | Use Existing Campaign | ✕ |

Choose a Campaign Objective
Learn More

Awareness	Consideration	Conversion
◯ Brand awareness	◯ Traffic	◯ Conversions
◯ Reach	◯ Engagement	◯ Catalog sales
	◯ App installs	◯ Store traffic
	◯ Video views	
	◯ Lead generation	
	◯ Messages	

Cancel   Continue

FIGURE 11-4:
You can create
a new campaign
or use an
existing one.

3. **Choose one of the following: Create New Campaign or Use Existing Campaign.**

   To follow along with the example, tap Create New Campaign.

4. **If you chose Create New Campaign, do the following:**

   a. *Choose a Campaign Objective and tap Continue.* To follow along with our example, choose Traffic for the objective.

   b. *Enter a New Campaign name, as shown in Figure 11-5, and then tap Next.*

   At this point, your campaign draft is saved. You can keep going by following the instructions in the next section, "Creating the ad set." Or come back to the draft later by hovering your cursor over the campaign's name on the Ads Manager main page and clicking Edit.

5. **If you chose Use Existing Campaign, click the Choose a Campaign field, and then select the existing campaign you'd like to use. Then do one of the following:**

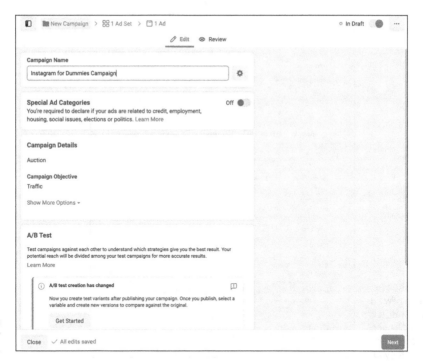

FIGURE 11-5:
Enter a new
campaign name.

- *If you want to create a new ad set: Choose Create Ad Set, name the ad set, and click Continue.* Then continue to the next section, "Creating the ad set."

- *If you want to use an existing ad set: Choose Use an Existing Ad Set, tap the Choose an Ad Set field, choose the name of the ad set you want to use from the drop-down menu, and click Continue.* The Ad Setup page appears. Skip the "Creating the ad set" section, and go directly to "Creating the ad."

Creating the ad set

After you have created a new campaign or chosen an existing campaign, you'll land on the New Ad Set page. Follow these instructions to create your new ad set.

1. **In the Ad Set Name field, enter a new Ad Set Name, as shown in Figure 11-6.**

   If you're continuing from an existing campaign, you already entered an ad set name and it will appear in the Ad Set Name field.

2. **Scroll down and tap the button corresponding to where you want to send traffic.**

   You can send users to a website, an app, Messenger, or WhatsApp. To follow along with the example, choose Website.

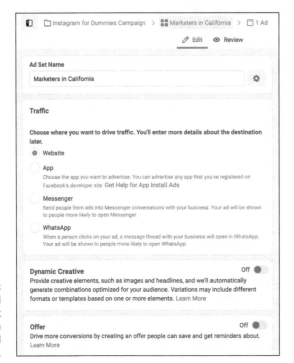

FIGURE 11-6:
Enter a new ad
set name if it
hasn't been
pre-populated
for you.

3. **Leave Dynamic Creative and Offer set to the default (off).**

4. **Scroll down, and under Budget & Schedule (see Figure 11-7), choose Daily Budget or Lifetime Budget and then choose how much you would like to spend either daily or for the entire campaign.**

5. **Choose a start date. And unless you'd like this ad to be shown indefinitely, select the Set an End Date option, and enter the end date.**

6. **In the Audience area, choose Create New Audience or Use Saved Audience.**

   To follow along with the example, choose Create New Audience. Ignore the Custom Audiences area because that option is beyond the scope of this book.

7. **Scroll down, and click the edit icon (pencil) in the Locations section to access the following options (see Figure 11-8):**

   a. *Choose whether you want to include people who live in that location, have recently been there, or have traveled there.* Most often you want people who live there, but sometimes you might want to target people who have been there recently, such as a promotion to bring them back to the location.

   b. *Type the cities, states, or countries you want to target in the Search Locations field.* You can click the down arrow to the right of an entry to display a drop-down and slider. Then choose a 10- to 50-mile radius around the city, depending how far from the city's center you want to target.

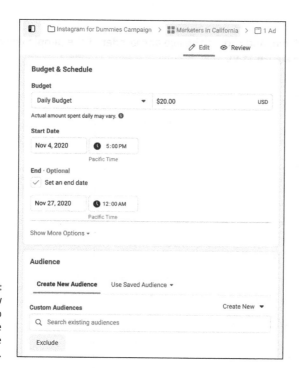

FIGURE 11-7:
Choose how much you want to spend and the schedule for the ad set.

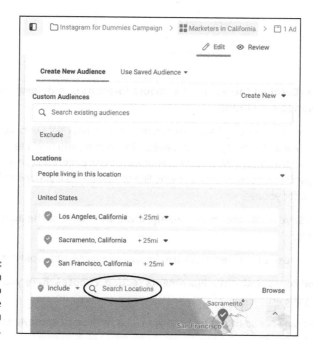

FIGURE 11-8:
Use the Search Locations field to type the location(s) you want to target.

8. Scroll down, and choose the age and gender of the people you're targeting (see Figure 11-9).

FIGURE 11-9:
Choose other demographics, such as age and gender.

9. In the Detailed Targeting area, choose interests or employers of people related to your brand.

You can also list other Facebook business pages that relate to or compete with yours. For instance, if you own a weight-loss center, you might target people who like the Weight Watchers Facebook business page. You can also exclude people with certain interests or who like certain pages if you think they'd be a bad fit for your ad.

10. Click Save Audience. In the pop-up, enter the name of the audience and save it.

You can use this audience again in future campaigns and avoid the setup process.

11. Scroll down, and in the Placements section, choose where you want to run your ad:

- *To run your ad throughout Instagram and Facebook: Choose Automatic Placements.*

- *To run your ad only on Instagram: Choose Manual Placements and deselect everything except Instagram, as shown in Figure 11-10.*

FIGURE 11-10:
Deselect all
options except
Instagram if you
want to run an
Instagram-only
campaign.

12. Scroll down, and in the Optimization
for Delivery drop-down menu,
choose Link Clicks.

Leave all other fields at their default
settings.

13. Click Next.

The New Ad page appears. Continue to
the next section, "Creating the ad."

Creating the ad

After you've completed the Ad Set page or
if you're using an existing ad set, you are
taken to the New Ad page to create your
ad. Follow these instructions:

1. In the Ad Name field, enter the name
of the ad.

2. Under Identity, check to see that the
correct Facebook page and
Instagram page are selected, as
shown in Figure 11-11.

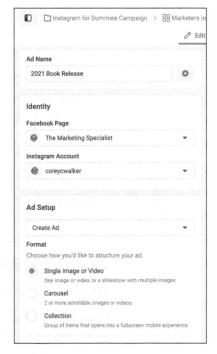

FIGURE 11-11:
Select the account on which you want to
run the ad.

If they're not correct, use the drop-down menus to switch to the correct accounts.

3. **In the Ad Setup section, decide whether to create an ad or use an existing post (the Creative Hub Mockup option is beyond the scope of this book) and do the following:**

To create an ad:

a. *Choose Create Ad from the drop-down menu.*

b. *Choose whether you would like to create a carousel, single image, single video, slide show, or collection.*

c. *Depending on which option you chose, upload an image, a video, or multiple images and videos to the Ad Creative section.*

d. *Enter your primary text, choose your destination (Website, Facebook Event, or Phone Call), and enter the website or phone number in which you'd like to link the ad.*

e. *Check the preview on the right, and then click Publish to process the ad.*

To use an existing post (from your Facebook or Instagram business page):

a. *Select Use Existing Post.*

b. *Click the Select Post button under the Ad Creative area.* A new page appears with posts to choose from.

c. *Select the post you want to use, and click Continue, which brings you back to the New Ad page.*

d. *If the ad is okay, click Publish to submit the ad.* If you need to make any changes, you must edit it on your Facebook or Instagram business page.

TIP

If you don't have an Instagram account yet (maybe you're doing your homework first by reading this book), you can use your Facebook business page and it will represent you on Instagram using your Facebook business page name.

Running an Instagram Stories ad in Ads Manager

Instagram stories can be created only in Facebook Ads Manager, not in the mobile app. To run a Stories ad using Facebook Ads Manager, do the following:

1. **Complete all the steps in the "Creating the campaign" section (you can use an existing campaign or create a new one). Then complete Steps 1-10 in the "Creating the ad set" section.**

2. **In the Placements section, select Manual Placements. In the Platforms section, deselect all but Instagram, as shown in Figure 11-12.**

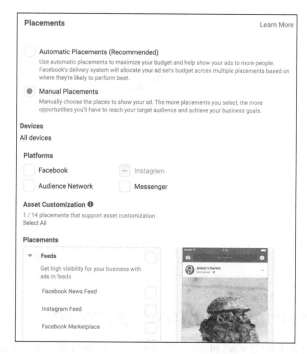

3. **In the second Placements section, below Asset Customization, click the down arrow to the left of Stories, and then deselect everything except Instagram Stories, as shown in Figure 11-13.**

4. **Scroll down to the Optimization & Delivery section and choose Link Clicks.**

    Leave all other fields at their default settings.

5. **Click Next.**

    The New Ad page appears. Follow the instructions in the preceding section, "Creating the ad."

TIP

Because stories are vertical, the recommended image size is 1,080 x 1,920 pixels for an image, or filming in the vertical format on your phone for video.

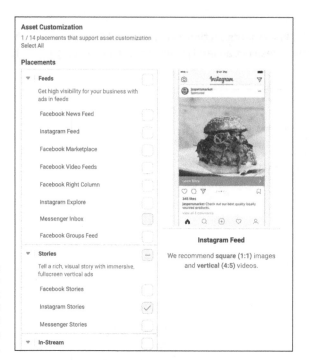

FIGURE 11-13:
Deselect every
option except
Instagram Stories
in the second
Placements
section.

Monitoring your Instagram ad

After you finish your ad placement, be sure to monitor your Instagram notifications and engage with your audience!

You'll start seeing many more notifications than you normally would — don't ignore them. Tap the heart at the bottom of your screen to see all notifications, and then tap the image from your ad to access your ad's post. From there, you can respond to comments and questions.

TIP

It may be tempting to tap the heart icon to simply like a comment, but it's best to add a short comment. Doing so makes a difference to the people receiving a personal acknowledgment from you, and it may lead to further conversation about how you or your product might help them.

A/B Testing

After you have designed your first ad and created that perfect caption, you may want to consider A/B testing. In *A/B testing*, you schedule two or more ads, switching one of the ad elements to test which version performs better. In this way, you can hone in on what your audience prefers. Marketers often choose a small budget and time frame to A/B test, and then spend more money and time on the winner of the test.

Here are some examples of A/B tests:

» Use the same image in two ads, switching out the caption. This could be a complete switch, or you could switch only hashtags, or switch only the call to action, or switch between asking a question and telling users to tag a friend.

» Use different images in two ads, keeping the same caption.

» Use the same image and caption, switching the call-to-action ad link from, say, Learn More to Sign Up or Shop Now.

» Use the same image, caption, and call-to-action link, switching your audience to test who responds to the ad more frequently.

Anything that can be swapped out can be tested, but be sure you know the type of results you're looking for. The goal of the test is simply to find the best converting image, caption, call to action, or audience so you can put your ad budget toward the winner.

TIP

Run the test during the same time period with a similar audience if you're testing the ad image, caption, or call-to-action link to prevent seasonality from affecting your results.

You can run the A/B test by scheduling the two ads separately in the Instagram mobile app and then monitoring the results.

Facebook offers ways to A/B test your Instagram ads via the Facebook Ads Manager.

1. **Go to the main Facebook Ads Manager screen by typing** www.facebook. com/adsmanager **in the URL bar, and select the campaign you want to test by clicking the box to the left of the campaign name.**

    Note the campaign must be published (not in draft) for you to do this.

2. **Click the A/B Test button above the campaign name.**

    A pop-up appears that allows you to choose different variables to test, as shown in Figure 11-14.

3. **Choose a variable from the drop-down list, and then click Next.**

    A pop-up shows that Facebook has created two new campaigns to test. In the example in Figure 11-15, age and gender are being tested against the previously saved audience.

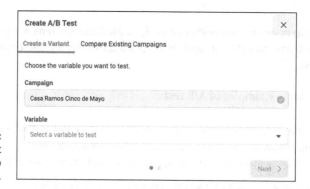

FIGURE 11-14:
You can split-test
your ad in two
ways.

FIGURE 11-15:
Facebook will
create two
campaigns to
test.

WARNING

Note that this is a live test that will cost you money.

4. **Scroll down to Test Settings, and set the Total Lifetime Budget, as shown in Figure 11-16.**

    The budget will be split between the two campaigns.

5. **Set the Test Schedule.**

    Remember, this is a test to see the best option for running your complete campaign, so it should be briefer than a normal ad campaign.

Create A/B Test   ✕

Test Settings
Edit or review your settings before publishing your test

Test Name

Audience Test - Casa Ramos Cinco de Mayo

Total Lifetime Budget

$200.00   USD

Budget is split 50/50 between ad sets in this test.

Test Schedule

Start

Oct 11, 2020   🕐 12:00 AM

End

Oct 15, 2020   🕐 12:00 AM
Pacific Time

Determining the Winner
Pick how you want to determine the winning version of your test.

Key Metric

Cost per Result ▾

Estimated Test Power

⚫   ‹ Previous   **Create Test**

FIGURE 11-16:
Set the total
lifetime budget
and test
schedule.

6. **Use the drop-down menu to choose the key metric you will use to determine the winner of the split test.**

7. **To begin testing, click Create Test.**

    Final test results can be found in the Experiments section of Ads Manager under Results.

Measuring Your Ad Results

After you've created and placed an ad, the next task is to measure your ad results. Many businesses overlook this step, but you're smarter than they are! Tracking the effectiveness of a campaign sets you up for future success and saves you money and loads of time. Why would you want to keep running an ad that barely converts to a sale when you could be running a winner?

In this section, you discover how to measure your ad results using Instagram and Facebook Ads Manager.

Viewing Insights via Instagram

Insights include data from your posts about impressions, reach, likes, comments, and more. They are easy to receive via the mobile app. Follow these steps to access them:

1. On your Instagram profile page, tap the Insights button below your bio description.

2. Scroll down to the Promotions area, as shown in Figure 11-17.

3. Tap the See All link to see some of your results (Figure 11-18, left) and then tap the gray View Insights link below the promotion thumbnail to see more information (Figure 11-18, right).

   The Promotion Insights page lets displays the number of likes, comments, and saves received as well as interactions, discovery, and impressions. You also see how much time has elapsed, how much money you've spent, and the demographics of your audience.

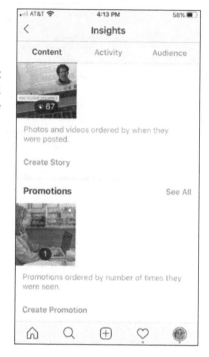

FIGURE 11-17:
The Promotions area of Instagram shows only active campaigns in this area.

TIP

Now that you've collected this data, store it in a spreadsheet so you can compare it to one of your typical post's results as well as future campaigns. This data is important to use for comparison if you plan on A/B testing other images, captions, text, audiences, or even ad types.

Viewing Insights via Facebook Ads Manager

Ads Manager provides more data on your Instagram ad than Instagram's mobile app. And you can see campaign results in Facebook Ads Manager whether you created the ad in Facebook or in Instagram. If you're tracking results closely, Facebook Ads Manager is the better bet because it shows more information about the money you spent and the cost per result. It also allows you to export the data to a .csv or .xls file.

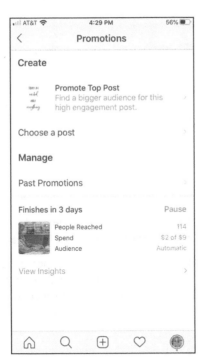

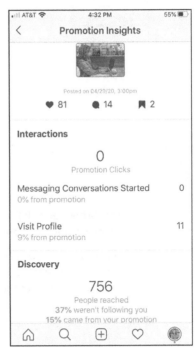

FIGURE 11-18:
The Promotions page (left) shows information about your promotion, and the Promotions Insights page (right) shows further details about your promotion's performance.

Follow these steps to view your results in Facebook Ads Manager:

1. **Go to the Ads Manager page using one of these methods:**

   - *Type www.facebook.com/adsmanager.*

   - *Go to your Facebook business page and click the Ad Center link on the left side of the page. Then click All Ads. Scroll to the bottom of the All Ads page and click the Ads Manager link.*

   All current and completed ads appear on the dashboard.

2. **View a summary of the results by looking to the right of your campaign name (refer to Figure 11-3).**

   Scroll right to see everything!

3. **Drill down into the campaign by hovering your cursor over the campaign name and clicking View Charts when it appears.**

   Figure 11-19 shows the Charts screen.

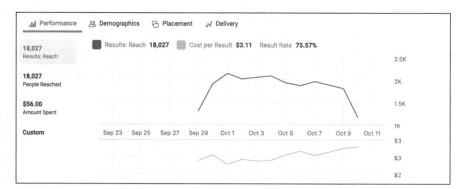

FIGURE 11-19:
Click View Charts
under your
campaign name
to see more
campaign results.

4. **Toggle between all four Chart screen options (Performance, Demographics, Placement, and Delivery) to get the information you need.**

    That's all there is to it! Check your web traffic and any other conversions taking place on your website. Include this information with your other Instagram campaign results data so they're part of your final data analysis.

IN THIS CHAPTER

» Understanding the benefits of contests on Instagram

» Learning the rules and regulations for contests

» Following the steps to a rewarding contest

» Executing a contest successfully

» Finalizing the contest

Chapter **12**

Creating a Winning Contest

N ow that you're comfortable with using Instagram, it's time to focus on increasing your audience and creating more results for your business. One of the most effective ways to do this on Instagram is by running contests.

In this chapter, we explain how Instagram contests can be valuable to your business. We also show you the steps to follow to create a successful Instagram contest from start to finish.

Exploring the Benefits of Hosting Instagram Contests

Contests are common on social media, and you've likely seen many of them in your own social media feeds. So many businesses use contests because they know how valuable they are.

Instagram has some of the highest levels of engagement of any social media platform. And running contests or promotions on the platform can drastically increase that engagement for your business. Instagram contests typically require entrants to both like and comment on a photo, thereby increasing engagement on the post.

This increased engagement benefits you: When your followers interact with more of your content, your posts appear higher in their feeds due to the Instagram algorithm.

TECHNICAL STUFF

Instagram employs an algorithm that sorts through all content created by each person that a user follows. This content is then re-sorted in the user's feed, with the content the user is most likely to engage with near the top of the user's feed. Multiple components affect the algorithm, including how often a user interacts with an account's content, the type of content the user typically interacts with, the time the user spends on Instagram, and a piece's popularity with other users.

We talk more about contest entry requirements later in this chapter. Here, we describe ways that different requirements can benefit your business.

Contests on Instagram often require entrants to follow the account, which increases your followers. In addition, some contests require participants to take a photo and upload it to their account. Each participant sharing content about the company provides reach to new audiences. The company also gets access to a variety of user-generated content that it can repurpose. (For more on user-generated content, see Chapter 9.)

Finally, Instagram contests are simple to implement and administer. This allows you to get many positive results without an overwhelming commitment or cost, increasing your return on investment.

Following the Rules and Restrictions for Running Contests

When running a contest, you need to be aware of several federal and state rules and regulations, far beyond Instagram's requirements. We recommend that you investigate local and national regulations regarding contests, giveaways, promotions, and lotteries before running any contest on social media.

For example, in California, contest and sweepstake laws are defined in CA Bus & Prof Code § 17539. An Internet search for your state's contest or sweepstake laws will help you find the proper rules and regulations. In the US, the Federal Trade

Commission (FTC) regulates disclosure of endorsements (www.ftc.gov/tips-advice/business-center/guidance/ftcs-endorsement-guides-what-people-are-asking) and the Federal Communications Commission (FCC) regulates the broadcasting of contests (www.fcc.gov/consumers/guides/broadcasting-contests-lotteries-and-solicitation-funds and www.fcc.gov/general/broadcast-contests).

While these laws and regulations will give you good guidance, they may be updated or revised at any time. It is always in your best interest to review legal counsel for the most accurate legal advice related to running contests.

Each social media platform has its own rules and restrictions for running contests, and Instagram is no exception. Here, we outline the specific details you need to be aware of for Instagram contests.

WARNING

Although these rules apply at the time this book was published, they can evolve at any point. Read about the current regulations for Instagram contests and promotions at https://help.instagram.com/179379842258600.

Listing the official contest rules

Instagram requires that you include the official contest rules in your contest post. These official rules of entry typically include the requirements to enter, the date and time (include the time zone) the contest ends, how winners will be chosen and notified, and any restrictions for entry.

You can simply list these rules of entry directly in your post caption on Instagram. Figure 12-1 is an example of how to format your contest caption to include this information.

If you have more detailed contest rules and terms of entry, or legal disclaimers for your entry requirements, you can include a reference to a website link or a notification to click the link in your profile for full contest rules. Figure 12-2 provides an example of what these more detailed rules and terms of entry might look like.

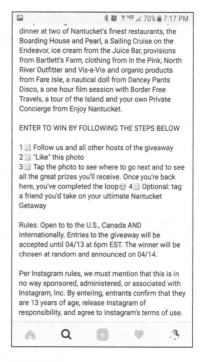

dinner at two of Nantucket's finest restaurants, the Boarding House and Pearl, a Sailing Cruise on the Endeavor, ice cream from the Juice Bar, provisions from Bartlett's Farm, clothing from In the Pink, North River Outfitter and Vis-a-Vis and organic products from Fare Isle, a nautical doll from Dancey Pants Disco, a one hour film session with Border Free Travels, a tour of the Island and your own Private Concierge from Enjoy Nantucket.

ENTER TO WIN BY FOLLOWING THE STEPS BELOW

1 ☐ Follow us and all other hosts of the giveaway
2 ☐ "Like" this photo
3 ☐ Tap the photo to see where to go next and to see all the great prizes you'll receive. Once you're back here, you've completed the loop😊 4 ☐ Optional: tag a friend you'd take on your ultimate Nantucket Getaway

Rules: Open to to the U.S., Canada AND internationally. Entries to the giveaway will be accepted until 04/13 at 6pm EST. The winner will be chosen at random and announced on 04/14.

Per Instagram rules, we must mention that this is in no way sponsored, administered, or associated with Instagram, Inc. By entering, entrants confirm that they are 13 years of age, release Instagram of responsibility, and agree to Instagram's terms of use.

FIGURE 12-1:
Include your contest rules and terms of entry directly in the post caption.

FIGURE 12-2:
Detailed contest
rules may be
referenced as a
link to a website
or a source for
information.

Releasing Instagram of any involvement

Instagram requires that you include a short paragraph in each contest post that relieves it of any involvement or participation in the contest.

Here is a sample of the verbiage to include, which you can change as needed: "Per Instagram rules, this promotion is in no way sponsored, administered, or associated with Instagram, Inc. By entering, entrants confirm that they are 13+ years of age, release Instagram of responsibility, and agree to Instagram's terms of use."

Planning a Successful Contest

No one wants to put time and energy into something that falls flat on its face or doesn't drive results.

A successful contest on Instagram has the following 11 key components:

» State your contest goals.

» Choose a prize.

>> Establish entry requirements.

>> Define rules or conditions.

>> Determine the contest's length.

>> Figure out the promotion schedule.

>> Choose a hashtag.

>> Design the contest's images.

>> Craft post captions.

>> Decide how winners will be chosen and notified.

>> Outline who will respond to contest engagement.

We cover them all in this section so that you'll have the information you need to run a rewarding contest.

Stating your contest goals

Your Instagram contest needs to be designed to serve your business in some way. To successfully execute a contest, you first need to know what you want as a result from the contest.

Businesses typically run a contest for one or more of the following reasons:

>> Increase engagement on their posts

>> Add followers to their Instagram account

>> Increase visits to their website as well as opt-ins or signups for something

>> Gain user-generated content that they can repurpose

It's best to choose one key goal for a single contest, but some companies choose several. For example, more followers might be their primary goal, with increasing engagement as a secondary goal.

After you know why you're running your contest, you're ready to move on with planning.

Choosing a prize

To get people to participate, you have to provide something of value that they would like to win. Prizes can range from low value to extremely high value, depending on your resources and goals.

TIP

Your prize should always be related to your business! Giving away an iPad or other generic prize doesn't attract your ideal audience and creates unnecessary interest in your contest. Instead, choose one or your own products or services that would appeal to your target audience.

Your prize should be commensurate with the level of participation to enter. For example, if the prize is valued at $10, a simple "like a photo" contest is appropriate. By comparison, asking people to take a photo, post it to their account, and use your hashtag to promote you requires a considerable amount of work and effort, so the prize should be significantly more valuable.

You also need to decide how many winners will be awarded. Will more than one person win the same prize? Or will one winner get the grand prize and one or more additional winners receive a smaller prize? If you want to offer different levels of prizes, you need to determine what they are.

Establishing entry requirements

To be entered into the contest, participants have to do something. Some of the most common entry requirements follow:

>> Following your account

>> Liking the photo you posted

>> Mentioning one or more people in the comments

>> Posting a photo with a specific hashtag

>> Filling out a form on your website

You may even choose to have them complete two or three of these requirements as a full entry into the contest. Figure 12-3 shows one contest that requires multiple components to enter.

TIP

It's best to limit the number of criteria for entry to two or three steps. The more complicated you make the entry process, the fewer participants.

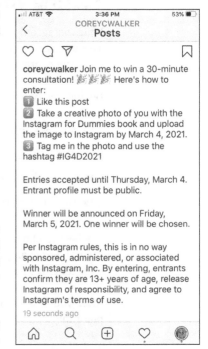

FIGURE 12-3:
A contest may include multiple criteria to submit a complete entry.

Defining the rules or conditions

We mentioned Instagram's contest rules, as well as the need to follow any local, state, and federal regulations. You also need to determine your own rules for entry.

Add any criteria related to age restrictions, geographical restrictions, content to be shared in photographs, and limits to quantities awarded in the contest.

Determining the contest's length

You have many things to consider when determining the length of your contest. The first factor is how many days or weeks the contest will run. Typically, for the best performance, contests that are longer than 3 days and less than 2 weeks are best.

For contests that require entrants to post a photo or create content, it's best to let the contest run longer in order to give them time to create and upload their entries.

Knowing your contest duration, you then need to determine the exact day and time the contest will both begin and end so that you can include this in your contest details and your planning calendar.

Figuring out the promotion schedule

Now that you know how long the contest will run and when it will start and end, you need to determine how often you will promote the contest on Instagram.

You always want to promote the contest on the first day and then again on the last day to remind people to enter before time runs out. Depending on the length of the contest, however, you might want to promote the contest also one or more times throughout to keep momentum and to reach more people.

Choosing a hashtag

It's advantageous to use a unique hashtag for each contest because it helps you track the contest on Instagram and allows your audience to easily participate.

When every participant uses the same hashtag to identify his or her post or entry, you can view the submissions in the hashtag search gallery on Instagram by tapping the hashtag in your contest announcement post or by using the Search feature on the Explore page.

Having a unique hashtag for each contest also allows you to monitor participation in each contest and compare those contests to determine which ones perform best or drive the best engagement.

Choosing the right hashtag may take a little time. When selecting your contest hashtag, consider the following:

» The hashtag should be unique to the individual contest.

» The hashtag should be related to your brand or the specific topic of the contest or both.

» The hashtag can be longer than usual to add distinguishing context.

Figure 12-4 shows two examples of unique hashtags that different accounts utilized in their contests. You can see how each one used a hashtag related to the contest theme.

TIP

Include your contest hashtag as a text overlay on the images promoting the contest. Doing so will make the post image stand out on Instagram and build awareness of the contest.

Designing contest images

To promote your contest on Instagram in accordance with the schedule you determined in the previous steps, you need to create at least one image to post as the contest notification. You can create more than one image to keep the momentum going and content fresh in the Instagram feed.

The images should be related to the contest's theme. For example, if you're creating a back-to-school contest, your post image might be school supplies or an apple on a teacher's desk. The images should set the tone for the theme and the purpose of the contest, as shown in Figure 12-5.

One of the images may also include an example or preview of the prize. For example, if the prize is a box of your products, a well-staged photo of the box and its components will get your audience excited for what they could win and help encourage them to participate.

FIGURE 12-5:
Your images should match the theme of your contest.

REMEMBER

You can also include a text box or text details on your image to highlight the contest or provide contest details. In Figure 12-4, the @Petco contest post includes details about the dates, the prize, and the contest hashtag.

Crafting post captions for the contest

Your post caption should let people know you are running a contest and also get them excited about the contest and encourage them to participate. Write a post caption for each post of the contest in advance. This enables you to share a cohesive message throughout the contest and ensures that you don't omit necessary or important information.

TIP

If you plan to run contests frequently, draft a caption template for contest posts and save it on your mobile device. This way, you can open it each time you plan to run a contest, and update the information for the current contest details.

Your caption should include the following:

>> A statement that you are running a contest

>> Prize details

>> Your contest entry requirements

>> Legal disclosures

We talk about the legal disclosure requirements previously in this chapter. You want to include all those details in your post captions.

Refer to Figures 12-1 and 12-3 for great examples of incorporating all these details into a contest caption.

Deciding how winners will be chosen and notified

How you will determine winners depends on how the contest was structured and how the entries were submitted. The two most common ways to choose a winner are using judges and through random selection.

If your plan is to have someone judge the entries to determine a winner, you need to clearly state the winning criteria. For example, if you require entrants to submit photos of their pets with your product, two obvious criteria are that the photo must include both a pet and your product. Additional criteria may include creativity, unique animals, or content that is most closely aligned with your brand theme and styling.

After you decide how the winners will be chosen, outline how you will notify them. It's best to notify the winners directly and privately first. You can do this by sending them a direct message on Instagram (see Chapter 8 for details on direct messaging). Or if they submitted entries by including an email address, you can email their notification. You might also post a comment on their original post on their Instagram account, if that's an option.

After you notify the winners privately, you might want to post something on your Instagram account, announcing the winners of the contest. This step isn't necessary and many brands do not do this. For smaller brands, however, the transparency of announcing winners can build trust with your audience that you are actually awarding prizes to real people.

Outlining who will respond to contest engagement

If you're the only one managing your Instagram account, all contest management will fall on you. If you have more than one person on your team, though, clearly outline who is responsible for reviewing and responding to contest engagement.

Throughout the contest, people will request clarification about entry requirements, ask about the prize, or otherwise want more information on the contest. Someone on your team must be able to respond to these questions quickly and accurately.

You also need someone to monitor the entrants and ensure that they are valid entries. Depending on the entrant requirements you established, this task might include the following:

>> Monitoring your post for comments and usernames listed in the comments

>> Monitoring the contest hashtag for post entries made on participants' accounts

>> Verifying that each entrant is, in fact, following your account

Monitoring and validating are time-consuming. Be sure to factor in enough time to review entrants before announcing a winner.

Executing a Winning Contest

Now that you have everything in place to run the contest successfully, it's time to execute it.

If you've completed all the preparatory steps outlined in this chapter, the contest execution will be fairly smooth. However, things can always pop up or go unexpectedly, so be prepared to be flexible throughout the contest period.

The first thing to do is to post your first contest announcement image and caption, based on the timeline you established for the contest. After that post goes up on Instagram, actively cross-promote the contest to your audience. Share the contest image to other social media sites for your business and encourage those followers to join you on Instagram to enter the contest. Send an email to your email list, informing the recipients about the contest and asking them to submit their entry on Instagram. If you have a physical business location, encourage your customers who come in to participate as well.

As the contest gets going, ensure that you are monitoring and readily responding to comments and questions.

In accordance with the contest time frame you established, post subsequent contest posts and reminders to your Instagram account throughout the duration of the contest. Post your final contest post on the last day of the contest and get ready to wrap it up!

Following Up

After the contest has reached the end date and time, you need to close out the contest, announce the winners, and review the entire contest.

TIP

After the contest is officially closed, go back to your contest posts on Instagram and edit the caption to add "Contest Closed" or a similar statement at the top of the caption. This ensures that anyone reading your post after the contest entry period understands that the contest is over and won't attempt to participate.

Now that you have all your entrants, you need to select a winner. Whether you're selecting a randomly generated winner or having the entries judged, choose your individual winner, multiple winner, or winners for different prize levels.

Next, you have to notify the winners. Follow the plan you put in place to notify them directly first. Then make a public post on your profile, if you choose to do so, announcing the winners.

If you must deliver prizes to the winners, coordinate the delivery with them. Do so through private messaging or email communications.

TIP

If you're shipping winners a physical package, send them the tracking number of the package so that they can confirm when it will arrive.

After the contest is completed, review your contest analytics. Some of the information to review and measure follows:

>> Number of new followers on your Instagram account

>> Number of people who participated

>> Number of likes and comments on your contest posts

>> Amount of traffic generated to your website during the contest period

>> Number of conversions through opt-ins or sales during the contest or as a result of the contest

To determine what contest strategies and tactics performed best for you and your business, compare the results from multiple contests. Each time you run a contest, track the analytics just mentioned and compare them to previous contests.

See if the following factors contributed to an increase in participation or conversions:

>> Duration of the contest

>> Number of posts promoting the contest

>> Prize

>> Types of images promoting the contest

Contests on Instagram can provide big benefits when executed properly. Remember, though, that time and repeated contests are necessary to deliver significant results. This is why it helps to plan and to track each contest.

Chapter **13**

Connecting Your Marketing Dots

I f you've read any of the previous chapters, you've already discovered many expert tips for using Instagram for your business. However, most people who have success with Instagram don't use it in a vacuum. It's important to know where and how to place Instagram in your total marketing mix to get the best results. In this chapter, we discuss incorporating Instagram with your other social media, website, and offline activities, as well as how to monitor your Instagram stats to ensure that you're on the right track.

Incorporating Instagram in Your Marketing Mix

Let's face it, Instagram *is* awesome, right? We sure think so. But it should be just one of many tactics in your marketing plan. Businesses that are truly successful use Instagram as part of their overall mix, not as their entire focus.

Here are some other marketing avenues to consider:

>> Facebook, Twitter, LinkedIn, Pinterest, SnapChat, TikTok, and YouTube

>> Email and blogs

>> Webinars

>> SEO

>> Google Ads

>> Review sites such as Yelp, Angie's List, and TripAdvisor

>> Industry forums, conferences, speaking engagements, and events

>> Local events (chamber, rotary, neighborhood)

>> One-on-one appointments

>> Direct mail and telesales

That list is not all encompassing, but we hope it gets you brainstorming. Your industry or company may offer more ways to market your business. The most important point is to choose the best vehicles for the audience you're trying to reach. Instagram may be the perfect target, but you can get Instagram traffic from other places, online and offline. Let's get started!

Connecting Instagram to Other Social Networks

An easy way to get more Instagram content views is to connect your other social networks to your Instagram account. Currently, the US-based networks that you can link to Instagram are Facebook, Twitter, and Tumblr. Adding linked accounts is a snap:

1. **From your Instagram profile page, tap the three lines located at the top right of your screen.**

2. **Tap Settings, Account.**

3. **Scroll down and tap Linked Accounts (see Figure 13-1).**

4. **To add Facebook, tap the Facebook link.**

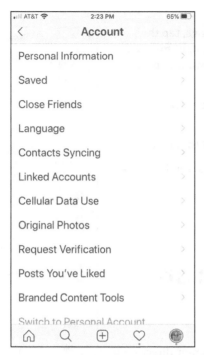

FIGURE 13-1:
Access Linked
Accounts from
the Account page
(left), and then
use the Linked
Accounts page to
connect
Instagram with
Facebook,
Twitter, or Tumblr
(right).

Account

Personal Information

Saved

Close Friends

Language

Contacts Syncing

Linked Accounts

Cellular Data Use

Original Photos

Request Verification

Posts You've Liked

Branded Content Tools

Switch to Personal Account

Linked Accounts

Facebook   The Marketing Spe...

Twitter

Tumblr

新浪微博

Ameba

ミクシィ

VKontakte

OK.ru

5. **Authorize Instagram to share photos on your Facebook page.**

You're automatically redirected back to the Share To page in Instagram. You
can then tell Instagram if you'd like to automatically share your Instagram
stories or posts to Facebook or any other connected profiles or pages you
manage by toggling the button from gray to blue. You can unlink your account
from Facebook at any time by tapping Unlink Account.

6. **Repeat this process for all other networks that you want to link to
Instagram.**

7. **To return to your profile page, tap your profile picture at the bottom
right of the screen.**

After you save the Linked Accounts settings, you won't need to touch that area
again unless you want to add another social network or unlink an account. You can
now share an image or video that you post on Instagram directly to the other networks you set up. Here's how:

1. **Upload your image or video along with a caption as you would for a
normal post.**

2. **If you would like to tag people or add a location, do that next.**

3. **At the bottom of the page, tap the slider to move it to the right for each network to which you want to post your Instagram post.**

    The tab for each selected network turns blue. See Figure 13-2.

4. **Tap Share at the top of the screen.**

    The post goes to Instagram and any other network you selected.

That's it!

Including Instagram on Your Website

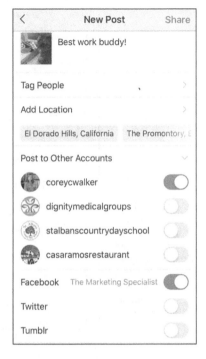

FIGURE 13-2:
Share your Instagram post to other platforms by tapping the appropriate social network tab.

You can incorporate Instagram directly on your website in several ways. The main three tactics we discuss are as follows:

» Linking a button on your website to Instagram

» Allowing users to share your articles or blog posts on their social media accounts

» Embedding your Instagram feed on your website

TIP

Exact instructions for adding these items to your website may differ depending on how your website was built. If you did not build your website, ask your webmaster for help if needed.

Linking your website to your Instagram page

If you have a website, all your business's social networks should be linked to your website so your prospective customers can easily find and follow you on Instagram, Facebook, and more. See Figure 13-3 for an example. Most website builders, such as Wix, SquareSpace, and GoDaddy, offer a variety of social media icons that you can easily drop in. For Instagram specifically, you need to link the icon to your Instagram web address: `http://www.instagram.com/yourusername`.

If your website was not built on a website builder platform, you can still add a link to Instagram. Here's how:

1. **Do a Google search for an Instagram icon available for downloading.**

   Many are available for free.

2. **Download the icon that best fits your website's design, and save it to your computer.**

3. **Go to your website's content management system or backend.**

FIGURE 13-3:
Add links to your social media profile on your website.

   Details for this process are beyond the scope of the book. Consult your webmaster for help if needed.

4. **Add the Instagram social media icon to your page as you would for any other image.**

5. **Link the Instagram icon to** http://www.instagram.com/yourusername.

That's all there is to it. Repeat the process for all active business social media accounts.

TIP

Make sure you size the social media icons correctly (all the same size, not too large or small) before you upload them to your site. The standard size for social media icons is 32 x 32 pixels.

Allowing others to share your content via Instagram

You've likely noticed and used social media share buttons, which typically appear at the top or bottom of a web article or blog, as shown in Figure 13-4. Share buttons enable you to share that content via your Facebook, Twitter, LinkedIn, Pinterest, and several other social networks — except Instagram. Unfortunately, Instagram's current terms of service do not allow you to add a Share This button on your website.

FIGURE 13-4:
Social media share buttons for a variety of networks are available at the bottom of this web article.

We still encourage you to add your other social networks to further your content reach. Most website builders have share button widgets so you can easily share your content. If you have a custom website, here are some websites that work similarly and offer share button solutions at no or low monthly costs:

>> AddThis, at www.addthis.com

>> AddToAny, at www.addtoany.com

>> ShareThis, at www.sharethis.com

Embedding your Instagram feed on your website

Looking to entice your website viewers to check out your Instagram profile? Add your Instagram feed to one of your website's pages, as shown in Figure 13-5. Users click an individual image to be taken to that image on your Instagram profile. It's a great way to tempt people to go to your account.

TIP

Before you embed your Instagram feed on your website, think through your strategy. Would you rather have your audience stay on your website or go over to Instagram? Make sure you aren't luring them away from the place you want them to be!

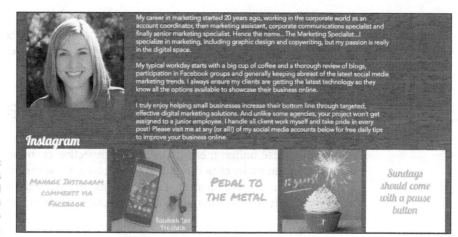

FIGURE 13-5:
This website has
its Instagram feed
embedded on
one of its web
pages.

Similar to the social media icons discussed earlier in this section, many website builder companies offer widgets or apps to easily insert your Instagram feed on your website. Follow their instructions for adding the Instagram feed widget. You'll need to know your Instagram web address for this task (http://www.instagram.com/yourusername).

If you have a custom or WordPress website, you can add the Instagram feed by using one of several widgets, such as the following:

>> Juicer, at www.juicer.io

>> POWr, at www.powr.io/plugins/instagram-feed

>> SnapWidget, at https://snapwidget.com/

All three have free options for smaller accounts and follow similar directions:

1. **Sign up on their website by providing an email and password.**

2. **Choose Instagram as the social media network.**

3. **Sign in to your Instagram account and allow the app to access your account.**

4. **Provide your Instagram account's web address:** http://www.instagram.com/yourusername.

5. **Click Embed in Your Site (or something similar, such as Generate Embed Code) to generate the embed code.**

6. **Copy and paste the embed code on the backend of your website on the web page where you would like the feed to appear.**

If you're unfamiliar with your website's HTML code, provide the embed code to your webmaster to copy and paste in the correct spot on your website.

Promoting Instagram on Printed Materials

It's handy to use online methods to send prospective customers to Instagram because they can easily click through to your profile. However, it's still important to advertise your account on printed materials, as shown in Figure 13-6. You never know when a flyer or brochure might be someone's ticket to visiting your Instagram account.

FIGURE 13-6:
The bottom of this flyer shows several ways to contact the business, including through Instagram.

Use the official Instagram icon (a high-resolution icon is available for free download at `https://en.instagram-brand.com/assets/icons` along with *@yourusername* on printed items such as the following:

>> Business cards

>> Postcards

>> Flyers

>> Brochures

>> Posters

>> In-store signage

Make sure any social media icons you use are high-resolution files that will print correctly. Never use blurry or pixelated icons. If you need help creating your print materials, hire an experienced graphic designer.

Incorporate the Instagram logo and your username as often as you can to remind potential customers to find you there. In the next section, we discuss how you can integrate Instagram into your promotions, both online *and* offline.

Incorporating Instagram into an Event or Promotion

If you have an upcoming event or promotion, Instagram can be a fabulous way to advertise. Before going too far into this section, we recommend you read Chapter 12 thoroughly first. All the legal details and do's and don'ts for Instagram contests are covered there.

After you know the ins and outs of running a contest on Instagram, it's time to look at it from a slightly different angle. Sometimes you can use Instagram as a supplement to other marketing tactics such as email marketing or direct mail to promote your event or promotion.

Here are some ways you can use Instagram to increase attendance at an event:

>> Create an official event hashtag for consistent use throughout the event's promotion and the event itself. (See Chapter 9 for details on using hashtags.)

>> Create custom graphics with text overlays announcing the event, and provide the details in the caption, as shown in Figure 13-7. Use the link in your profile bio as a link to more information or registration. Tell people to comment if they are participating, and tag a friend who might also like to participate.

>> Post photos or videos of certain aspects of the event, such as speakers, special guests, and fun activities, as shown in Figure 13-8.

FIGURE 13-7:
Custom graphics with text overlays can be helpful when announcing an event on Instagram.

- » Post behind-the-scenes photos or videos of event prep, such as putting together hundreds of swag bags, setting up decorations, or late-night pizza sessions after burning the midnight oil.

- » Post posters, purchase space on a billboard, or hire a van advertised with your event to drive around town. Have clear instructions asking people to take a photo of the ad and upload it to their Instagram account using the event hashtag.

- » Use an influencer in your industry to help spread the word about your event. Be prepared to pay for this!

- » Ask people to post a photo or video that relates to your event (user-generated content) using the event hashtag for a chance to win free tickets to the event.

TIP

To increase the reach of your event posts, use Instagram ads. You can target a specific audience rather than just those who are currently following you. For more information about Instagram planning and creating ads, read Chapters 10 and 11, respectively.

FIGURE 13-8:
Posting photos highlighting a certain feature of an event can get people excited about attending.

At the event, use signs like those in Figure 13-9, asking people to upload photos of the event using the event hashtag. Repost their photos, making sure you appropriately tag them and give them photo credit.

You should also designate or hire an official photographer to ensure that you get quality photos of all major aspects of the event. Posting these photos at the beginning of the event can generate more attendees on-the-fly if your event accepts last-minute walk-ins. Post more photos the following week to keep the buzz going about your brand. And if you hold the event annually, you can use those photos also to promote the event the next year.

Aside from events, Instagram can be used to promote a promotion, such as a flash sale at your store or product giveaway:

» Similar to promoting an event, post custom graphics with text overlays announcing the promotion and provide details in the caption, as shown in Figure 13-10. The link in your bio can link to more information or a sales page.

» Ask Instagram followers to repost your promotion post and tag you in exchange for a reduction in the price of the product or service.

» Create an Instagram-exclusive deal in which you provide a discount or coupon code only to people who view the deal on Instagram. This approach provides an easy way to track people who are coming from this network versus others.

FIGURE 13-9:
Include signs with your event hashtag to encourage people to post photos during the event.

FIGURE 13-10:
Custom graphics with text overlays can call attention to your promotion.

» Message new followers of your page with a free gift or discount on your products or services.

» Ask Instagram followers to post a photo or video of your product, tagging you and using the specified hashtag, to receive a gift or product discount.

» Use an influencer in your industry or someone your audience would recognize, to promote your sale. Have that person offer a unique discount code so you can track the tactic's effectiveness.

» Use Instagram Stories to offer 24-hour-only specials, as shown in Figure 13-11. Post a notice in your store, in your email newsletters, and on your website to let your customers know about these flash specials.

FIGURE 13-11:
Instagram Stories are the perfect place to post 24-hour specials because the story automatically disappears after 24 hours.

Monitoring Your Instagram Stats

Any good marketer knows that analytics are a huge key to your marketing success. By monitoring follower growth, engagement (likes, mentions, and comments), website clicks, and branded hashtag growth, you can track what's working and do more of it. And you can stop doing the tactics that aren't working too! If you have an Instagram business profile, Instagram offers basic and easy to access insights through the mobile app. In addition, several third-party apps allow you to dig a little deeper than what Instagram offers. We go over both types in this section.

Using Instagram's native analytics

As mentioned, Instagram offers several insights to track your Instagram success by using the mobile app. To begin, tap the Insights button located below your bio on your Instagram profile page on your phone, as shown in Figure 13-12. When you do, the Insights page shown in Figure 13-13 appears.

FIGURE 13-12:
The Instagram Insights button is below your bio on your profile page.

FIGURE 13-13:
The Insights page displays results from the past week for your Instagram business account.

On the Insights page, you see the following tabs, which contain data about your account:

>> **Content:** The content you've posted for the last seven days including reach for each post, story, or promotion

>> **Activity:** Overall reach (number of unique accounts that saw your account), impressions, and interactions for the last seven days on your account

>> **Audience:** Your follower count, growth, demographics, and most active times of the day for posting

Depending on your Instagram goals, you may choose to track some or all of these analytics. Some easy metrics to track are follower growth, impressions growth, and which posts and stories are getting the best engagement. A simple Excel spreadsheet updated weekly, like the one in Figure 13-14, may be all you need to notice trends and make adjustments to your tactics and post styles.

FIGURE 13-14:
This Excel
spreadsheet
shows key
metrics that are
being tracked.

Week	Followers	Impressions	Best Post	B. Post Impressions	B. Post Likes	B. Post Comments	Best Story	Story Impressions	Story Messages	Notes
Feb 1-6, 2021	5,667	4,555	Sunflower girl	800	189	13	Dancing sunflower	98	5	
Feb 7-13, 2021	5,779	4,676	Computer screen	855	226	17	BTS of graphic design	108	3	
Feb 14-20, 2021	5,876	4,546	25% sale promo	998	211	14	25% off Boomerang	122	8	#beautysale
Feb. 21-27, 2021	6,005	4,699	Selfie w/dog	1,233	315	22	Dog begging	202	13	

In the next section, we discuss various third-party applications that can be used to track your Instagram data.

Best third-party apps for Instagram analytics

Instagram's Insights are a great tool for providing an overall view of how your account and posts are performing. However, a number of other analytics tools can help you dive deeper for more in-depth data. In this section, we discuss two popular third-party analytics apps: Iconosquare and Sprout Social.

Iconosquare

If you are into Instagram more than any other social media network, Iconosquare might be a great fit for you. Iconosquare offers analytics and content management for Instagram only. Its strong suit is analytics, but it is also a robust content management system that enables you to research hashtags, upload content, schedule content, and sort your content later by topic.

The analytics area, which is shown in Figure 13-15, is where you can see detailed data about your Instagram account. Iconosquare offers all the standard data that Instagram Insights offers, plus the following:

>> Daily gained and lost followers

>> Comparisons about your post's real-time performance versus previous posts

>> Performance on each of your hashtags and various other ways to see data about what areas of the world are using your hashtags and at what time

>> Performance based on the filter used

>> Comparison of your performance versus your competitors' performance

You can also handpick which data you'd like exported into a report, which can be a huge timesaver versus creating your own spreadsheet.

FIGURE 13-15:
Iconosquare offers more options than Instagram Insights for data analysis, such as hashtag tracking and competitor comparisons.

Iconosquare is a paid subscription app, with costs ranging from $29/month for basic functions (which you can get free on Instagram Insights) to $59/month and up for more advanced functions for marketing teams. To get information on current offerings and pricing, visit `https://pro.iconosquare.com/`.

Sprout Social

If you want one app to do everything — including content creation and management, scheduling, analytics, and reporting for most of the major social media networks — Sprout Social has you covered. The Sprout Social dashboard is shown in Figure 13-16.

Sprout Social offers the following services (and more) for Instagram, Facebook, Twitter, LinkedIn, and YouTube:

>> Plan, schedule, and post messages

>> Store content for later use

>> Edit images with filters or text overlays

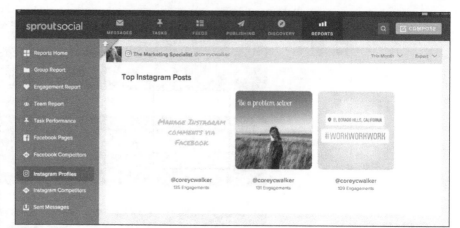

FIGURE 13-16:
The Sprout
Social dashboard
offers easy-to-
understand
reporting for
Instagram and
most other social
media networks.

» Suggest optimal send times

» Track post performance by likes, shares, and comments

» Track campaign URLs for referral traffic and conversions

» Watch Instagram follower growth

» Compare Instagram profiles with competitors

» Identify key influencers for your brand

» Track and report hashtags

» Unlimited exports of reports and PDFs

Sprout Social starts at $99/month, which does not include all features. For full pricing and detailed information about which analytics offerings are included in each pricing tier, visit https://sproutsocial.com.

TIP

Before investing in a monthly or yearly analytics package for any of the third-party apps, research which data you think you'll need. Third-party apps have a lot of extra bells and whistles, but if you aren't going to use them, you're wasting money. We suggest that you use the free analytics provided by the Instagram app first to see whether they give you enough data to evaluate your results, and then decide whether you need more information from a paid app.

5

Using Instagram Stories as Another Avenue

Chapter **14**

Sharing with Instagram Stories

Throughout this book, we discuss many features in Instagram's original newsfeed. But did you know that the Instagram mobile app also has a completely different section called Instagram stories?

Instagram stories were introduced in the latter half of 2016 in an attempt to get more users to post content. The lure was that the content disappears within 24 hours, allowing those who had been meticulously curating their semi-permanent Instagram feed to hang loose a bit. Users now have a place on Instagram where they can be more spontaneous by, say, taking a quick behind-the-scenes photo or shooting a 15-second video explaining something they did that day.

In this chapter, you learn all about Instagram stories and discover which type of content is best. In the next chapter, you find out about enhancements you can add to your stories.

Instagram stories are a great complement to your regular Instagram feed, so don't skip out on this chapter!

Checking Out Instagram Stories

Before you start creating your own story, it's helpful to learn about how Instagram stories started and watch a few stories others have created.

It's no secret that Instagram stories are a copycat of Snapchat's stories; Instagram didn't even bother to change the name! Snapchat was garnering a lot of growth and success with its stories, particularly in the teens and twenties demographic. Instagram (and its daddy, Facebook) took the feature that most people liked best about Snapchat — stories — and built it into Instagram. The addition of stories and their fun filters (although not as robust as Snapchat's) added to Instagram's explosive growth.

Now that we have the short history of Instagram stories out of the way, let's talk about where to find them. Instagram stories are located in a bar at the top of your newsfeed and are represented by a multicolored ring around the profile picture of the story's creator, as shown in Figure 14-1, left. Tap the profile picture, and the story opens full-screen. Unlike on a regular posts, you can't like or comment publicly. You can, however, send a direct message, as shown in Figure 14-1, right.

FIGURE 14-1:
View stories by tapping a profile picture at the top of your newsfeed (left). Stories open up full-screen on your phone (right).

© Satin Web Solutions (left)

New stories (personalized for you) are shown first. By scrolling left, you can see all stories that the people you follow have published in the last 24 hours. The post vanishes 24 hours after it was posted.

Instagram always takes you to the content you haven't seen in that person's story. For instance, if you watched two out of five stories by someone, Instagram would play the third story in the sequence when you came back within the 24-hour window of the post. Each person's story has white dashes at the top that indicate the number of stories for that person that day.

Here's how you navigate between stories:

» To skip an individual story, tap on the right of the screen.

» To skip an entire profile's stories sequence, swipe left.

» To go to the previous story, swipe right.

» To see the previous story, tap the left side of the screen.

» To pause a story, tap and hold down on the screen.

Getting Started

Instagram stories are a fun little add-on to Instagram and there are tons of features to explore! In this section, find out about the nuts and bolts of creating a basic story either within the app or by taking and then uploading a photo or video. In the next chapter, you discover the more advanced features: text, stickers, hashtags, filters, and more.

Creating an Instagram story in the app

Creating an Instagram story in the app is simple: You can take photos or record a 15-second video. We go into more detail about adding stickers, hashtags, and filters in the next chapter.

To get started creating a photo or video story, follow these steps:

1. **From your newsfeed (home screen), swipe right or tap the camera icon at the top left of the screen.**

   You can also tap your profile picture with the blue plus sign in the row of stories at the top of your screen.

2. **Take a photo or a video:**

- *To take a photo, hold the phone up vertically and tap the white circle (refer to Figure 14-2).*

- *To take a video, hold down on the white circle.* A colorful bar outlines the circle to help you know when your 15 seconds (the maximum time) is up.

 If you want the phone in selfie mode (camera facing you versus away from you), tap the two arrows located to the right of the white circle before you tap the white circle.

3. **To retake the photo or video, tap the X at the top left of the screen, choose Discard in the pop-up box, and repeat Step 2.**

4. **To add a photo filter to your photo or video, swipe right or left on the photo until you reach the filter option you want.**

5. **If you'd like to save the photo or video, tap the save icon (down arrow and line).**

 You can then access it from your camera roll to email, text, or post on other social media.

 You have another opportunity to save the photo or video later, after it posts, which we discuss in the "Saving Your Story" section of this chapter.

FIGURE 14-2:
Tap or hold down on the white circle to take a photo or video, respectively.

TIP

If you'd like to save all your stories automatically every time, tap the gear icon (settings) on the stories screen, slide Save to Camera Roll (iOS) or Save to Gallery (Android) to the right, and then tap Done.

6. **Make the story available:**

- *To make the story available to all your followers, tap Your Story at the bottom of the screen.* It will post at the top of your followers' newsfeed.

- *To send the story as a direct message (DM) that disappears after the person views it, tap Send To. When the screen shown in Figure 14-3 appears, select the people to whom you want to send the DM, and then tap Send.* For details about sending DMs, skip to the section in this chapter titled "Using Direct Messages to Send a Story."

TIP

To film a video without the hassle of holding down the button the entire time, use the Hands-Free setting. In the icon list on the left side of the screen, tap the down arrow and then tap Hands-Free. You can then record video by tapping the white circle with the colorful box inside. Filming will stop automatically after 15 seconds.

When you use the Boomerang setting, Instagram takes a burst of photos and stitches them together to create a mini video that then plays forward and backward — like a boomerang.

Uploading a photo or video from your camera roll

Sometimes, you may prefer to upload a photo or video stored on your camera roll instead of capturing it in the Instagram app.

TIP

In the past, Instagram stories would load only photos or videos taken in the last 24 hours. Luckily, that has changed, and you can now access your entire camera roll. When you swipe up or tap the small photo icon to load a photo or video, you see photos from the last 24 hours first. If you keep scrolling up, you'll see your entire camera roll, and can load older items by tapping them.

FIGURE 14-3:
Send your story as a disappearing message to an individual user or a group.

Follow these steps to upload a photo or video to Instagram stories:

1. **Swipe right from the newsfeed or tap the camera icon at the top of the newsfeed to access Instagram stories.**

2. **Swipe up from the bottom of the screen or tap the box with a small photo thumbnail at the bottom left.**

    Thumbnails of all available photos and videos are displayed on the screen, as shown in Figure 14-4.

3. **Tap the photo or video you'd like to post.**

REMEMBER

If you upload an image that is more than 24 hours old, the date of that image posts as a sticker on the story. You can drag the date to the trash can to remove it from the story. What's more, if you upload a video that is more than 15 seconds long, Instagram divides your video every 15 seconds and uploads the videos as multiple stories.

4. **To add a photo filter to your photo or video, swipe right until you reach the filter option you want.**

5. **To post your story, tap Your Story. To send it as a direct message to an individual or a group, tap Send To and then tap Send to the right of the name of the recipient or group.**

See Step 6 in the preceding section for details on direct messages.

FIGURE 14-4:
Swipe up from the bottom of the Instagram stories screen to see photos in your camera roll.

Adding a Text Post

When Instagram stories released, only photos or videos could be used as a backdrop for text. After several clever Instagrammers came up with work-arounds for a solid-colored background for a text post, Instagram finally built that functionality into the app. Now you can easily select a color background, and then type a text message overlay to your followers. Here's how:

1. **Swipe right from the newsfeed or tap the camera icon at the top of the newsfeed to access Instagram stories.**

2. **Tap the Aa icon on the left side of the screen, as shown in Figure 14-5.**

3. **Tap where the screen reads *Tap to type*, and enter your text.**

4. **To change your text's color:**

   - *iOS: Tap the color wheel at the top of the screen and then tap a color below your text.*

   - *Android: Tap Next, tap the text you typed, tap the color wheel, and then tap a color below your text.*

TIP

Scroll left for more text colors, or tap the eye dropper circle at the left side of the row to sample a specific color. Change the justification from left, center, or right by tapping the four lines at the upper left of the screen (available only with certain fonts).

5. **To change the background color of the screen, tap the colored circle repeatedly until you see the background color (or color gradient) you want.**

   The circle appears at the bottom of the screen on an iPhone and at the top of the screen on an Android phone.

6. **To choose another font, swipe back and forth between the font icons above the keyboard until you see the font you want, and then tap that font.**

7. **Tap Next.**

8. **To post your story, tap Your Story or Close Friends; to send your story as a direct message to an individual or group, tap Send To and then tap Send to the right of the name of the recipient or group.**

FIGURE 14-5:
Tap the Aa icon to create a text-only post.

Saving Your Story

Sometimes stories are so good, you can't bear the thought of them disappearing forever. Well, you're in luck. You can save them to enjoy later and to repost on other social media networks in the following three ways:

>> **Save before you post your story.** After you create or upload a photo or video, tap the save icon (down arrow and line), located at the top center of the screen (see Figure 14-6). You must do this before you tap Your Story or Next.

>> **Save after you've posted your story (within the 24-hour window).** Go to the newsfeed or your profile page and tap your profile picture. If you have an active story, it will appear. Tap the right side of the screen until you see the story you want to save. Tap the three small dots at the bottom right of the screen, and then tap Save (see Figure 14-7).

>> Automatically save all your stories to your camera roll. Tap the gear icon (settings) at the top left of the Story page. On the Story Controls screen, slide Save to Camera Roll to the right, and then tap Done.

FIGURE 14-6:
You can save your story before you post it.

FIGURE 14-7:
You can save your story after you've posted it as well.

Using Direct Messages to Send a Story

Would you prefer to send a quick message to a client, prospective client, colleague, or group of people instead of posting in the general stories area for your entire following to see? A direct message (DM) is the answer.

Follow these steps to send a story via a direct message:

1. **Create your story in the app or upload a photo or video.**

Directions for both are in the beginning of this section.

2. **Tap Send To at the bottom right of your screen.**

The Share screen appears.

3. **Select the individual to send the story to by tapping Send to the right of the person's username, as shown in Figure 14-8.**

You can still add the story for all your followers to view by tapping Your Story on this new page instead of sending it via DM.

Alternatively, you can create a group and then send them a direct message with your story:

1. **Create your story in the app or upload a photo or video.**

2. **Tap Send To.**

3. **In the Close Friends Only entry at the top of the list, tap Create List (iOS) or Edit (Android).**

4. **On the Close Friends screen, tap Get Started.**

5. **Next to each username you'd like to add to the group, tap the circle (iOS) or Add (Android), as shown in Figure 14-9.**

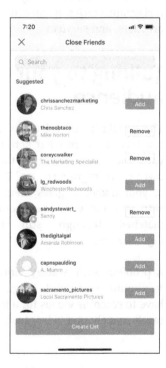

FIGURE 14-8:
Send a direct message to individuals.

FIGURE 14-9:
You can also send a direct message to a group.

6. **Tap Create List at the bottom of the screen to create the new group.**

   The group is then available for you, preselected on the next page.

7. **Tap Share.**

Determining the Best Content to Share

Instagram stories was designed to be a looser, less perfect area of Instagram. Many Instagrammers agonize over choosing the right photo or caption for their newsfeed so their aesthetic is maintained flawlessly. Instagram stories allows those users to offer a less polished version of themselves or their business. In this section, we detail some of the common ways businesses use Instagram stories to promote their brand, products, and services.

© @martinholsinger

FIGURE 14-10:
@martinholsinger talks to his target audience of residential contractors through Instagram stories videos.

Talking to your audience

The popularity of video has surged in the last few years, so what better way to grab your audience's attention than talking to them via Instagram stories? Talking directly to your audience gives them a familiarity with you and your business that can't be matched through still images. See Figure 14-10.

A problem with a story video is that the maximum 15-second length means you have to combine videos for a longer conversation, and all the stops and starts can result in a choppy video. Instagram helps you with this problem by allowing you to record a 60-second video, which Instagram then splices into 15-second clips. The result is a story video that flows more smoothly, with little disruption between each clip.

Providing before-and-after and series shots

Stories are meant to be played in a series continuously, so before-and-after images or a series of photos work well to draw in followers. Using *before* and *after* labels or using small bits of text on a series can encourage followers to stick with your story until the end.

Hairstylists, home decorators, stagers, remodelers, plastic surgeons, makeup artists, and landscapers have a great time creating before-and-after images in Instagram stories, as you can see in Figure 14-11.

FIGURE 14-11: @egglestondesigns uses before-and-after shots to show her home staging skills.

© Eggleston Designs

Products and services can also be showcased in a creative series that keeps followers on a path to see what's next. See the example shown in Figure 14-12.

Whether using before-and-after photos or a series, add a graphic or video at the end, giving followers a call to action based on the information you've shared.

Peeking behind the scenes

Because many Instagrammers are involved in launches, events, conferences, podcasts, and other exciting activities, behind-the-scenes stories are a great way to let your audience in on how the magic really happens.

Whether it's showing the types of equipment used (see Figure 14-13), hanging decorations for an exclusive party, or interviewing speakers backstage before a conference starts, followers love to get to know more about how your business works through behind-the-scenes stories.

Showing your travels

There's something so interesting about traveling to other places via Instagram stories. You can watch someone sipping coffee in Vienna, and then in the next moment see another person at a convention in Minnesota.

Business people will often chronicle their travel to conferences or meetings, or showcase the luxury vacation they earned by working hard at their business all year, as shown in Figure 14-14.

© Brian Fanzo

FIGURE 14-13:
@isocialfanz shows his followers the equipment he uses to record his Instagram stories.

FIGURE 14-14:
@coreycwalker shows her followers her conference travel to Cape Cod.

Advertising Your Story

Although we always encourage engagement as a way to increase your following and new customers, sometimes it's not enough. Or maybe you want to tell your target audience right away about a promotion or an event you're planning. That's when advertising your stories makes perfect sense.

You can run a campaign solely on Instagram stories or use it to complement a campaign you're running via the newsfeed. Just like an Instagram ad on the newsfeed, you can choose a target audience that is not following you already. For more information about the specs of an Instagram Stories ad and the available action links, see Chapter 10.

An Instagram Stories ad is labeled *Sponsored* at the top left and has an action link (*Learn more* in Figure 14-15) at the bottom of the page. Users swipe up on the action link to go to the website you've chosen.

At this time, you can advertise on Instagram stories only through Facebook Ads Manager, not through the Instagram mobile app. We detail exact steps for creating an Instagram Stories ad in Chapter 11.

FIGURE 14-15: Instagram Stories ads have a call to action at the bottom of the screen.

Chapter **15**

Making Your Story More Fun

n Chapter 14, we show you how to create and share a basic Instagram story. However, there is so much more you can add to your stories to make them come alive and get seen by more people!

Instagram stories has rolled out a number of additions to enhance the stories you create. In this chapter, we discuss how to create your own graphics; add text, username tags, stickers, hashtags, geolocation tags, and website links; use face filters, Boomerang, Layout, and SuperZoom; and shoot a Hands-Free video.

In addition, you find out how to use Instagram LIVE, including how to prepare for, promote, save, and repurpose your broadcast.

Creating Graphics for Stories

If you enjoy posting graphics versus photos, you'll be happy to hear that you can use graphics in Instagram stories. Create your graphic in Illustrator or Photoshop, making sure the graphic is 1,080 pixels wide x 1,920 pixels high. Export the graphic as a .jpg, and email it to yourself.

Next, open the email app on your phone, and download it to your camera roll. Then upload the graphic to Instagram stories in the same way you upload a photo. (For details on uploading to stories, see Chapter 14.)

TIP

You can use other apps or services in addition to email to get your graphics. For example, you can use Apple's AirDrop if you're copying from a Mac or an iPad to your iPhone. Or copy and paste your graphics to Dropbox and then access them in the Dropbox desktop or mobile app.

If you don't have Illustrator or Photoshop, we recommend using Adobe Spark Post for Graphics (https://spark.adobe.com/) to create your graphics. It's much simpler for someone without design experience to use. Adobe Spark Post for Graphics is available on your phone (which saves the step of emailing the graphic) and includes Instagram stories templates, which you can alter. You can also create your own design.

To create an Instagram story graphic on your phone using Adobe Spark, follow these instructions:

1. **Download the Adobe Spark Post for Graphics app from the App Store or the Google Play Store and create a username and password.**

   You can also log in through Facebook or Google. The app is free, but you have to pay a $9.99 monthly premium fee if you want all the features.

2. **Choose a design:**

   - *Tap a category at the top of the screen, such as Lifestyle, Business, School, or Travel, as shown in Figure 15-1. Make a selection in the list of designs in that category that appear.*

   - *Tap a design in the Featured section. If a design has a yellow flag, you can use it only with a paid account.*

3. **Tap Remix This Template.**

   The screen shown in Figure 15-2 appears.

4. **Change the design by tapping the options below the image:**

   - **Add:** Add an image, a video, a text, an icon, a sticker, or a logo by tapping the appropriate option in the menu. The options you see depend on your selection.

   - **Colors:** In the Colors section, you can change the color scheme of your image and text. Several color palettes are available, and you can also create your own palette. To change to a built-in color palette, simply tap a new palette. Tap Done to save the palette to your design.

FIGURE 15-1:
Adobe Spark offers categories and featured designs that you can alter.

FIGURE 15-2:
Customize a template design's photo, layout, and more.

- **Animation:** Select how you want to animate your image. After you select a filter or an animation, tap Done.

- **Layout:** Alter the layout of your image by changing the grid. (This change will typically prompt you to upload more photos, depending on the layout you select.) Tap the grid you like, and then tap Done. To add more photos, tap Add and following the instructions detailed earlier in this section about adding photos.

- **Brand:** Premium (paid) customers can use the Brand section to add their own fonts and filters to a design.

- **Resize:** Resize your design according to its use. You can choose correct sizing for a Facebook ad, Instagram, Instagram stories, YouTube, and more. Tap the size you want, and then tap Done.

5. **When you're satisfied with your graphic, tap the share icon (up arrow in a box) in the upper-right corner of the screen. Then choose Save Image or Save Video to save the graphic to your camera roll.**

Do not tap the Instagram icon. Selecting that will send the graphic to your main Instagram newsfeed, not to Instagram stories.

6. **Upload the graphic just as you would upload a photo to Instagram stories.**

For details on uploading a photo to stories, see Chapter 9.

When you create an image in Adobe Spark, it saves the image in My Posts. For future images, it may be easier to use My Posts to alter one of your own designs if you normally stick to similar colors, styles, and fonts for your brand. The editing features and sharing process are the same as using one of Adobe Spark's templates.

Canva (www.canva.com) and Easil (https://about.easil.com) are other popular apps that allow you to create graphics based on their templates.

Adding Text and Username Tags

Adding text to your photo or video can add context (and often humor) to your story. You can also tag another user using text. Follow these steps to add text or username tags:

1. **Take a photo or video in Instagram stories, or upload a photo or video there.**

2. **Tap the Aa icon at the top right of your screen, as shown in Figure 15-3, left.**

A new screen with a keyboard appears.

3. **Type your word or phrase (emojis work here too), as shown in Figure 15-3, right.**

You can change the text color, size, and font:

- *To change the text color from white (the default), tap the multicolored circle at the top of the screen. Then, in the row of colors just above the keyboard, tap a colored circle. Scroll left or right to reveal more color choices or tap and hold down on a color circle to reveal another color selection palette.*

- *To change the type size, find the slider on the left side of the page and move it up or down.*

- *To change the font, tap the font style. Scroll left or right to reveal more font choices.*

TIP

If you change the text color, you can change the font by tapping the font icon (*A* in a circle) at the top of the screen.

REMEMBER

Certain colors and features, such as text boxes and highlight effects, don't work with all fonts.

Stickers   Text   Slider   Colors

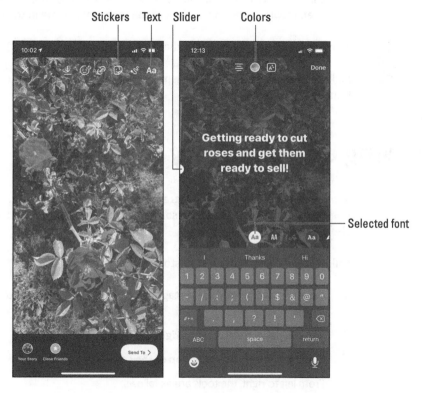

Selected font

FIGURE 15-3:
To add text, tap Aa in the top-right of the screen (left) and then use the keyboard (right).

4. **If you want to tag someone, type @*username* and select the person from the suggested profiles.**

   The person will be notified that you tagged him or her in your story.

5. **Tap Done.**

6. **(Optional) Make further changes:**

   - *Move the text by tapping and holding down on the text and then sliding it to its new position.*

   - *Change the type size by placing two fingers on the text and sliding your fingers apart or together.*

   - *Change the angle of the text by placing two fingers on the text and twisting left or right.*

7. **Share the story by tapping Your Story or Close Friends; save it by tapping the down arrow and line icon; or send it as a DM by tapping Send To and then tapping Send to the right of the recipient's name in the list.**

TIP

To create block text (white text that has a color boxed behind it), tap the A at the top of the keyboard screen (labeled in Figure 15-3, right). Tapping the A again makes the background transparent, and tapping again removes the transparency.

Drawing on Your Story

Another popular feature of Instagram stories is the drawing tool. You can use your finger to draw arrows, to circle something, to write words, or to draw anything else you'd like!

Follow these steps to draw on a story:

1. **Take a photo or video in Instagram stories, or upload a photo or video there.**

2. **Tap the pen icon at the top right of the screen.**

3. **Tap a drawing tool, at the top of the screen.**

   From left to right, the tools are as follows:

   - *Magic marker:* Draws like a fat magic marker.

   - *Arrow:* Draws like a fat magic marker and adds an arrow where you stop drawing.

   - *Highlighter:* Draws like a highlighter and is slightly transparent.

   - *Neon:* Draws like a neon light with an outline of the color you select.

   - *Eraser:* Erases anything you draw. Use your finger to rub across the drawing to erase. Erasing will not affect your photo or video.

4. **Start drawing! You can use your finger or a stylus.**

   See what each drawing tool's line looks like in Figure 15-4. You can change the color or line width as follows:

   - *To change the color of any drawing tool (except the eraser), tap a colored circle (at the bottom of the screen).*

   - *To change the line width, tap the half circle at the left side of the screen, and move the slider up or down.*

5. **When you have finished drawing, tap Done (iOS) or the check mark (Android) at the top right of the screen.**

   You can still go back and erase or add to your drawing by tapping the pen tool again.

6. **Share the story by tapping Your Story or Close Friends; save it by tapping the save icon (down arrow and line); or send it as a DM by tapping Send To and then tapping Send to the right of the recipient's name in the list.**

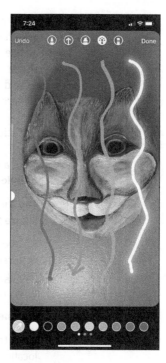

FIGURE 15-4:
You can draw with a magic marker, an arrow, a highlighter, and neon.

TIP

When you have text that is hard to read over a busy photo or video, make the text stand out by scribbling behind it. Or, if you'd like to create a solid color background that covers the entire screen, take a photo of anything, tap the drawing tool, select a color, and then tap and hold down anywhere on the screen.

Stickers and Tags

The sticker page is available after you take or upload a photo or video. Simply tap the square smiley face at the top of the screen (refer to Figure 15-3). Stickers are an easy way to add color and fun to your photos or videos. Instagram changes its stickers based on the day or holiday, such as the sticker with the time the photo was taken in Figure 15-5.

The sticker page is also where you can find location geotags, the temperature and time for your location, hashtags, and photo stickers.

Instagram also includes interactive stickers, such as ones where you can ask your viewers to take a poll, answer a question, and use a slider to tell you how much they like your photo or video. (We go into more detail about adding hashtag stickers and GIF stickers in Chapter 16.)

To add a sticker, simply follow these steps:

1. **Take a photo or video in Instagram stories, or upload a photo or video there.**

2. **Tap the icon for stickers (labeled in Figure 15-3, left).**

   A screen with stickers appears. Scroll to view featured stickers, standard stickers (including geotags, hashtags, selfie photos, the temperature, and the time), and a wide variety of emojis.

3. **Tap the sticker you want to add.**

   If you tapped the location sticker, tap one of the locations presented to you. That location is added as a geotag to your story, and your story is added to all other stories currently using that geotag. This is a great way to get your story seen by local people who don't necessarily follow you. See Figure 15-6 (left).

FIGURE 15-5:
You can choose from a variety of stickers.

4. **Adjust the position, size, or angle of the sticker as desired:**

   - *Move the sticker by tapping and holding down on the sticker and then sliding it.*

   - *Change the size by placing two fingers on the sticker and then sliding your fingers apart or together.*

   - *Change the angle of the sticker by placing two fingers on the sticker and then twisting left or right.*

5. **Share the story by tapping Your Story or Close Friends; save it by tapping the save icon (down arrow and line); or send it as a DM by tapping Send To and then tapping Send to the right of the recipient's name.**

Adding a Link to Your Website

A popular feature available only to business profiles with 10,000 or more followers is adding a link to your website. This important addition offers a direct way for businesses to send people to their website to get more information, register for events, or make a purchase. To add a website link:

1. **Take a photo or video in Instagram stories, or upload a photo or video there.**

2. **Tap the chain link icon (see Figure 15-7, left) at the top of your story.**

   The More Options page appears (see Figure 15-7, middle).

3. **Tap Web Link.**

4. **Type your website destination (see Figure 15-7, right.)**

5. **Tap Done (iOS) or the blue check mark (Android).**

Your followers will see a *See More* link at the bottom of your story, indicating a website link. Make sure you add a call to action either verbally during your video or by adding *Swipe Up to See More* overlay text to a still image.

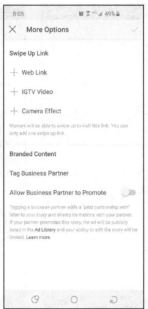

FIGURE 15-7:
To add a link, tap the chain link at the top of your story (left), tap Web Link (middle), and then type your website destination link (right).

Instagram doesn't track links on stories. To capture the analytics on your website clicks, use a URL shortener such as Bitly (`https://bitly.com`) or Rebrandly (`www.rebrandly.com`), and then access metrics via its dashboard.

TIP

Making Funny Faces with Face Filters

A *face filter* is an app that applies a filter over your face using the camera, making you look, for example, like a dog, an alien, or a rock star. Instagram stories didn't offer face filters when it launched, so a lot of people continued using Snapchat for that feature, or created Snaps with filters and then loaded them to Instagram stories. Now, Instagram users can rejoice at the fact that their favorite feature of Snapchat is available on Instagram!

Here's how it works:

1. **Open Instagram stories by swiping right or using the camera icon at the top of the newsfeed.**

2. **Put the camera in selfie mode by tapping the camera switch icon in the lower-right corner of the screen.**

   Filters appear at the bottom of the screen. Scroll to the left to see all available filters.

3. **To apply a filter, as shown in Figure 15-8, swipe left or right until the filter appears in the center of the screen.**

   Instagram applies the filter automatically. You can remove the filter by tapping the X above the filter.

4. **Take a photo by tapping the white button, or record a video by holding down the white button.**

   You can use filters in the Normal, Boomerang, or Hands-Free camera settings.

REMEMBER

5. **To try again, tap the X at the top left of the page and go back to Step 4.**

6. **Share your story by tapping Your Story or Close Friends; save it by tapping the down arrow and line icon; or send it as a DM by tapping Send To and then tapping Send to the right of the recipient's name.**

TIP

Can't find a filter that suits you? To see a list of more filters, scroll left in the row of filters until you reach the end of the row and tap Browse Effects. Then select a new effect from the Effect Gallery screen.

FIGURE 15-8:
Instagram stories offer fun face filters that alter your appearance, add graphics that show how you're feeling, and so much more.

Using Boomerang to Keep Fans Coming Back

Boomerang is a feature that takes a burst of photos and creates a looping backward and forward video clip from them. An action such as twirling a pencil or blowing a bubble becomes more exciting when played in a loop!

Follow these steps to use Boomerang:

1. **Open Instagram stories by swiping right or using the camera icon at the top of the newsfeed.**

2. **Tap the Boomerang icon (infinity symbol), as shown in Figure 15-9.**

3. **To switch from forward-facing video mode to selfie video mode and back, tap the camera switch icon in the lower-right corner of the screen.**

   You can also use Boomerang with one of the face filters, as described in the preceding section.

4. **Tap the white circle with the Boomerang logo (infinity symbol).**

   You don't need to hold down the white button as you would for video. The app is actually taking several pictures in a rapid burst.

5. **Trim the photos in your Boomerang and add effects by tapping the infinity symbol at the top of the screen.**

6. **If you're not satisfied with your Boomerang and want to try again, tap X at the top left and go back to Step 3.**

7. **Share the Boomerang story by tapping Your Story or Close Friends; save it by tapping the down arrow and line icon; or send it as a DM by tapping Send To and then tapping Send to the right of the recipient's name.**

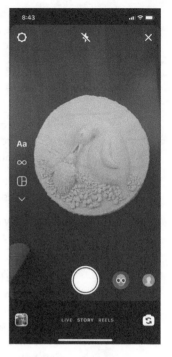

FIGURE 15-9:
The Boomerang icon is on the left side of the screen.

TIP

Boomerang works best when recording movement. To try it out, film someone doing a cartwheel, making funny faces in the camera, or dancing!

Creating a Collage with Layout

The Layout feature enables you to add two to six photos in different frames to your story. Here's how:

1. **Open Instagram stories by swiping right or by using the camera icon at the top of the newsfeed.**

2. **Tap the Layout icon (frame outline) on the left side of the screen.**

3. **Slide through the six available layouts above the Layout title until you find the one you like.**

The camera view appears in the top or top-left frame, depending on the layout you're using. To switch from forward-facing video mode to selfie video mode and back, tap the camera switch icon in the lower-right corner of the screen.

4. **Take your first photo by tapping the white circle with the Layout logo (frame outline).**

   The photo appears in the top or top-left frame, and now the live camera is located in the right, middle, or top-right frame, depending on your layout. See Figure 15-10.

5. **If you're not satisfied with your layout and want to try again, tap X at the upper left and repeat, starting at Step 4 or at Step 3 if you want to try a different layout.**

6. **Share the Layout Story by tapping Your Story or Close Friends; save it by tapping the down arrow and line icon; or send it as a DM by tapping Send To and then tapping Send to the right of the recipient's name.**

FIGURE 15-10:
The photo is in the upper-left quadrant, and the live camera is in the upper-right quadrant.

Using SuperZoom for Drama

SuperZoom enables you to add ten dramatic effects to your photos. The stories camera zooms in on whatever you're filming and then adds music or graphics or both to enhance the drama. Follow these steps to create a SuperZoom story:

1. **Open Instagram stories by swiping right or using the camera icon at the top of the newsfeed.**

2. **Tap the down arrow on the left side of the screen.**

3. **Tap SuperZoom to view the SuperZoom screen, as shown in Figure 15-11.**

4. **Slide through the ten available effects below the photo until you find the one you like.**

   To switch from forward-facing video mode to selfie video mode and back, tap the camera switch icon in the lower-right corner of the screen.

5. To add the effect, tap the white circle with the SuperZoom logo (circle inside other circles).

6. If you're not satisfied with your SuperZoom and you want to try again, tap X at the upper left and repeat, starting at Step 4 or at Step 3 if you want to try a different effect.

7. Share the SuperZoom story by tapping Your Story or Close Friends; save it by tapping the down arrow; or send it as a DM by tapping Send To and then tapping Send to the right of the recipient's name.

Using Hands-Free to Make Life Easier

FIGURE 15-11: The SuperZoom screen.

To film a video without the hassle of holding down the button the entire time, use the Hands-Free setting. Tap the down arrow on the left side of the screen and then tap Hands-Free. You can then record video by tapping the white circle with the colorful circle inside. Tap the white circle again to stop. If you don't tap it again, Hands-Free will keep filming a longer video, but it will allow only four 15-second segments to post as a "stitched together" video.

Using Reels to Stand Out

The Instagram Reels feature, which rolled out to the majority of users in August 2020, is a response to the popularity of TikTok and a way to create similar content in the Instagram platform.

Reels, like Instagram stories, are built into the existing Instagram interface. You can even access the reels camera from the Story screen. Reels

>> Are short-form video content, in full 9:16 portrait mode

>> Are 15 or 30 seconds long

>> Can be filmed directly in the reels camera or uploaded from your camera roll on your mobile device

>> Can be filmed as one full take or a series of takes stitched together

>> Can be uploaded only on mobile devices

First you learn more about reels, and then you discover how you can use them for your business.

Finding and watching reels

Chances are you've seen reels on Instagram already, even if you didn't realize it. Reels can be uploaded to stories, your feed, a reels gallery on your profile, and even the Explore page. They're pretty much everywhere!

You can recognize a reels video by the icon in the lower-left corner of the video when scrolling through your feed or in the upper-right corner when looking at someone's Instagram profile, as shown in Figure 15-12.

If a reels video has been uploaded to the feed of someone you follow, you'll see the video in your home feed and also on the person's profile. What's more, if the person didn't share the reels video to the feed, a Reels tab on the profile will display uploaded videos, as shown in Figure 15-13.

FIGURE 15-12:
The Instagram Reel has a Reels icon in the post.

In addition to seeing the reels of people you follow or accounts you visit, you can find new reels in the Explore page. At the top of the Explore page, a reels video will be selected for you. As you scroll through the Explore feed, you'll see more reels videos interspersed as vertical videos and labeled as reels, as shown in Figure 15-14.

After you view one video from the Explore feed or from your home feed, you can swipe up to scroll through more videos in reels and find fun new content from other creators.

Creating a reel

Now that you know where to find reels and have checked out a few, you probably want to get started creating your own! Here's what you need to know to get started:

© John Kapos/@perfectionchocolates

FIGURE 15-13:
Instagram Reels have a tab on the account profile page.

1. **Open Instagram stories by swiping right or by tapping the camera icon at the top of the newsfeed.**

2. **Slide the Story setting to the left, changing it to Reels.**

3. **Change settings by tapping the appropriate icon, as shown in Figure 15-15:**

   - *Length:* Choose a 15- or 30-second length for your reel.

   - *Audio:* Search for an audio file to add to your reel. This feature is available only on personal and creator accounts.

   - *Speed:* Open a menu and select from one of five speed settings. The default is 1x.

   - *Effects:* Open the filters and make your selection. Scroll to the left to see all available filters.

   - *Timer:* Open the Timer window to set the timer for hands-free recording.

     To add effects to your clips, you have to select them before you record. You can't go back and add or edit clips for these four features after you've recorded them.

4. **Record your clip by tapping and holding down on the Reels logo.**

   You can record up to 15 seconds. As you record, a red bar appears across the top of the screen indicating your progress. If you record multiple clips, you'll notice a white line indicating the start of each new clip.

5. **Trim the clip as needed:**

   a. *To replay the clip, tap the left arrow icon.*

   b. *Trim the clip by clicking the clip icon (scissors) and then clicking the left and right bars at the bottom of the screen.*

c. *When you're finished, click Trim in the upper-right corner to return to the editing screen.*

In the editing screen, you can also delete the entire clip by tapping the trash can icon.

You can also upload videos from your camera roll. The platform supports only videos, not images. To access your camera roll, tap the video icon in the lower-left corner of the screen. Then tap the video you want to record in the camera roll screen. If you upload a video longer than 15 seconds or longer than the amount of time left in your current reels video, the uploaded video will be trimmed to the allowed time. Select the portion of the video to upload and tap the upload icon (check mark) in the lower-right corner of the screen (iOS), or tap Add in the upper-right corner of the screen (Android) to add it to your reels creation.

6. **Replay and edit the clip as needed.**

Replay the reel by tapping the right-arrow icon at the bottom of the screen (refer to Figure 15-15). You can add stickers, text, and doodles much like you do in Instagram stories. When you're finished, tap the right-arrow icon.

7. **Enhance your reel as follows:**

- *Change the cover photo:* Tap the cover thumbnail image and then select a frame from the reel. You can also add an image from your camera roll (iOS) or gallery (Android).

- *Write a caption:* Tap in the box and then type your caption. As with a feed post, you can write up to 2,200 characters and 30 hashtags.

- *Share to your feed:* By default, Instagram shares your reel to your feed. If you don't want to do this, swipe the Also Share to Feed slider to the left.

TIP

If you're not ready to share the post publicly, tap Save as Draft at the bottom of the screen to save the video file so you can edit it later. To access a saved draft, open your Instagram profile and tap the Reels icon directly above the grid of posts, and then tap Drafts. In the Reels Drafts screen, tap the thumbnail image for the video.

FIGURE 15-14:
Instagram Reels are discoverable in the Explore feed.

8. **To share your reel, do the following:**

- *To share your reel to Instagram Reels, tap Share (see Figure 15-16).*

- *To share your reel to a story, tap the Stories tab, and then tap Share to the right of Your Story in the list, as shown in Figure 15-17.* Instagram uploads the reel to the story as-is. You can't add stickers, tags, or anything else to the story.

What's the catch?

If you're going to embrace Reels and create them for your Instagram account, you should be aware of the following nuances:

>> A progress bar isn't visible when viewing a reels video, so you won't know how long it is. But with a maximum of 30 seconds, this limitation shouldn't be a problem.

>> You can pause a reel video, but you can't rewind or fast-forward it. You have to let it play out, at which point it loops again.

>> For videos you've created, you can't edit the caption after uploading the video. You have to delete the video and re-upload (assuming you saved the video) and make the changes you wanted.

>> The preview in the reels video is only a line of text. You have to tap More to scroll the entire caption. This isn't ideal for long captions or calls to action.

>> Insights are not available for reels. The video thumbnail displays the total view counts but not insights for likes, comments, clicks, followers, and so on. And the Insights tab on your profile doesn't list any details about your reels video, although if the post was uploaded to your feed, that reach does count towards your account's overall reach for the week.

Some of these issues may be resolved by the time you read this.

FIGURE 15-15:
The setting icons appear on the left side of the Reels screen.

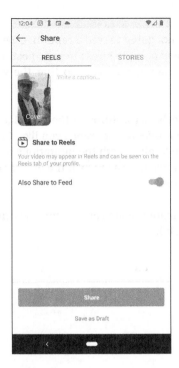

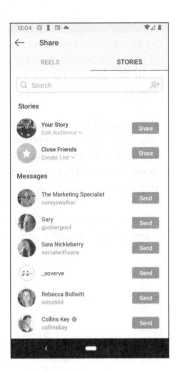

FIGURE 15-16:
The Share screen allows you to share the reel to your feed, Reels, and stories.

FIGURE 15-17:
Share your reel to your story.

Capitalizing on reels

Now that you know what you can and can't do with Instagram Reels, you may be wondering how to apply reels to your brand or business. Although many reels (and TikTok videos) feature dancing or music, business accounts don't have a music option so you have to find other ways to use these videos.

If you create tutorials or step-by-step videos for products or tips in your industry, you can create a similar style of video for reels. Or create a quick behind-the-scenes or meet-the-staff video to showcase your company. If you're in the fashion industry, you can find many fun ideas for showing off clothing combinations and styles. If you have a product that requires assembly, create a stop-motion video of someone building the product.

Most people who watch reels are not going to read a caption, especially a long one. If you have a call to action or a key point to stress in your post, make sure it's in both the audio and the text overlay of the video so that the viewer hears and sees it.

Before you jump into creating reels, scroll through the reels feed in the Explore page and look at the reels of other accounts or brands you like. Get a feel for what works and what you like. Become familiar with the limitations of reels before you commit to creating content. After you have a grasp of the process of filming, editing, and uploading videos, have fun!

To stand out on the platform, create unique content for reels that works in the scope of your brand's voice and style.

Chapter **16**

Sharing Your Stories in New Ways

n this chapter, we explain how take your stories to another level by adding personalized style and content, including various stickers, animations, doodles, and text. These features can be combined in a variety of ways to create your own unique style and message.

Jazzing Up Your Story Post Using Stickers

Instagram has many fun stickers to choose from — and they keep adding more, so there are always fun new ways to augment your content. In this section, you look at some of the more common stickers available and see how to use them in your content.

Stickers are available by tapping the sticker icon — a square smiley face — in the Story screen after you've uploaded or taken a photo or video (see Figure 16-1, left). Tapping the sticker icon opens a screen (or tray) with various sticker and emoji options, as shown in Figure 16-1, right.

FIGURE 16-1:
Tap the smiley
face sticker icon
(left) to access
story stickers
(right).

Location, mention, and hashtag stickers for search and notifications

Just as you can @mention someone on an Instagram post, tag a location in a post, or use hashtags for search, you can do much the same with your Instagram stories.

Using the location, mention, and hashtag stickers can help you appear in more searches, enable new people to find you, and let others know you're talking about them.

Location stickers

Adding a location sticker to your post lets your followers know where you are. It also allows you to show up in search results (if you're a public profile) for that location and others nearby.

When people look for locations in Instagram search, they see posts associated with that location. These search results combine both feed posts and stories in the results. When you add a location sticker, you may appear in those search results.

TIP

For more exposure, use a location tag for the smallest location possible. Don't tag a city; instead, tag a physical location or smaller area. When you tag a specific location, you increase your chances of appearing in more location results in surrounding areas or in larger location results. For example, if you use a location sticker for a specific restaurant, the map system in Instagram knows exactly where that restaurant is located. You may show up in search results for that restaurant, a park nearby, the local neighborhood, and maybe even the city as a whole (see Figure 16-2).

When you tap the location sticker to select it, a new screen appears with a list of nearby locations. You can scroll through this list and tap to select the location you want to add. If your location isn't listed, or the location isn't near you when you're adding the story, you can type in the search bar for the name of the location you want to tag. A list of related locations will appear, and you can select the correct one by tapping it (see Figure 16-3).

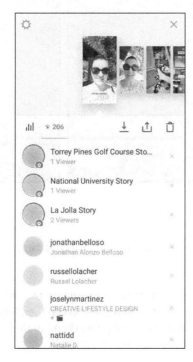

FIGURE 16-2:
Tagging a small location — in this case, National University — allowed this post to appear in multiple other search results for surrounding areas.

FIGURE 16-3:
Select your location from the list of locations or use the search bar to find the location of your choice.

After you select the location, the sticker will appear on your story. You can pinch to zoom to make it smaller or larger. You can drag it around the screen or turn it on an angle to place it where you want.

You can also tap the location sticker to change its background. Three color options are typically available for you to tap through, as shown in Figure 16-4.

FIGURE 16-4:
Tap the location sticker to choose different color and background options.

Mention stickers

If you want to tag someone in your Instagram story, you simply have to tap the @mention sticker.

Begin typing the name of the person or their username to find them. Relevant users who match that name will appear along the screen (see Figure 16-5). Keep typing until you find the person you're looking for; then tap their profile photo to select their username and add the sticker to your story.

REMEMBER

If you @mention someone, that person can share your story to his or her story.

As with location stickers, you can drag the sticker around, pinch to enlarge or shrink, and tap to change the background and color options.

You can @mention multiple people in your story. Simply add another @mention sticker for each person you want to tag.

The person or people who are tagged in your story will be notified via a direct message that you tagged them, and they'll be able to see your story.

Hashtag stickers

You can use up to 30 hashtags on a feed post on Instagram, but you're limited in terms of the number of hashtags you can use in a story post. If you use the hashtag sticker, you can add only one hashtag sticker to each individual post.

To add your hashtag sticker, choose the Hashtag sticker from the sticker screen and type your hashtag (you don't need to include the #). When you're done, tap Done in the upper-right corner. The sticker is added to your story. Just as you did with the location sticker, you can tap through to change color styles, move the sticker, and resize it.

FIGURE 16-5:
Type the name or username of a person you want to @mention with a sticker and select the user from the list of options.

You can add more hashtags to a story post by using the text box and manually typing a list of hashtags. Be aware, however, that Instagram will recognize only the first three hashtags in a text box, so don't use any more than that.

GIFs, sliders, emojis, and more

The previous three stickers are incredibly functional and help with search and exposure. But they don't do much for the fun factor or to drive engagement. Fortunately, plenty of other sticker options are available to up the fun factor!

GIF stickers

A cultural norm with social media is the use of *GIFs* (short animated pieces) to convey a thought, an emotion, or a response. Instagram is partnered with Giphy so you can add GIFs to your stories, too. Here's how to find the stickers you want:

1. **Open Instagram stories by swiping right or tapping the camera icon at the top of the newsfeed.**

2. **Click the Aa icon on the left side of the screen.**

3. **Tap the sticker icon at the top of the screen.**

4. **Tap the GIF sticker in the stickers screen.**

   The GIF sticker screen appears, as shown in Figure 16-6.

Thumbnail-sized animated GIF stickers appear above the keyboard. Swipe up and down to select the GIF sticker option from the sticker screen. A list of popular and trending GIFs appear for you to choose from. You can also search for a keyword or topic related to the GIF you want to use.

You can add multiple GIFs to a story post to add the style and context you want. Adding GIFs is a creative way to take a simple photo and make it animated and engaging.

Slider stickers

The slider sticker is designed to boost engagement and interaction with your story. Viewers can physically drag the sticker to indicate their level of participation. You'll find plenty of creative ways to utilize this sticker!

FIGURE 16-6:
Use the search bar in the GIF sticker screen to find animations related to the topic of your choice.

To add the sticker, select the slider sticker (heart eyes emoji) from the sticker screen. Then select the emoji to include as the slider mechanism. Note that multiple options are available; scroll left and right on the emojis to see more options. Next, type your question and tap Done when complete. You can drag and resize the sticker to place it anywhere on the image (see Figure 16-7).

Emojis

You have the entire emoji keyboard to utilize and add as stickers to your stories. Tap the sticker icon and scroll up on the sticker screen to reveal trendy stickers, emojis, and more.

FIGURE 16-7:
Type your question (left) and then readers can drag the smiley face (right) to answer.

Questions, polls, quizzes, chats, and more

Do you want to learn more about your followers? Or maybe share more about you? The variety of questions, polls, quizzes, and chat stickers will allow you to do that and really draw participation from your followers.

Questions sticker

The questions sticker allows you to pose a question to your audience and have them submit responses. Your question can be on any topic you choose! Responses will appear in the story insights for that post and are visible only to you.

Select the questions sticker from the sticker screen, type a question of your choice, and post the sticker to the story. Your followers will have the option to type a response in the sticker itself (see Figure 16-8, left). You can see those responses by tapping the viewers in the lower-left corner of your own story (see Figure 16-8, middle) to navigate to the post insights (see Figure 16-8, right).

FIGURE 16-8:
Use the question
sticker to
generate dialogue
and participation
with your
followers.

Poll and quiz stickers

Both the poll and quiz stickers work much the same as the questions sticker. You can create a question and provide answer options for your audience to choose from. The polls results will appear after the viewer has selected a response.

For the quiz sticker, type the question and then add answers. It defaults to two answers, but you can add more. Then tap the option that is the correct response (see Figure 16-9).

As with all stickers, pinch, drag, and move the quiz sticker where you want it in your story.

Use the countdown sticker to intrigue your followers

One of the best ways to keep your followers on top of what you have going on is to use the countdown sticker, as shown in Figure 16-10. This allows you to set a date and time for an upcoming event.

FIGURE 16-9:
Use the quiz sticker to test your followers.

People who subscribe to the sticker are automatically notified when it expires.

If you're holding a sale, having a promotion, putting on a live event, broadcasting an Instagram Live show, or doing any other type of event, you can use the countdown sticker to let people know when that event will happen.

It's best to set the timer for when an event starts, not when it ends. For example, a countdown for when a sale ends isn't helpful because the sale is already over when your followers are notified.

FIGURE 16-10:
Tap the countdown sticker to set the end date and time.

Picture in picture for the fun of it

To make things even crazier with your stories, you can take a photo with the selfie (front-facing) camera to add to your story. Select the camera icon sticker from the sticker screen.

A small window will appear in your story showing the camera is on (see Figure 16-11). Position yourself or the object in the view of the lens and tap the white shutter button below the window to take the picture. Then you can drag the photo around the screen and pinch to change the size. You can also tap on the photo to change the frame of the photo.

Deleting stickers that don't work

It's easy to add stickers, and it's just as easy to remove them if you don't like them (before you post the story). After you've added the sticker to your story, you can tap and hold the sticker. You'll see the garbage can appear at the bottom of the story screen (see Figure 16-12). Simply drag the sticker to the garbage can and it'll be removed.

FIGURE 16-11:
Add a picture-in-picture effect to your stories by using the camera sticker.

FIGURE 16-12:
Tap and hold any sticker in a story to drag it down to the trash can to remove it from your post.

Personalizing Stories with Doodles

Instagram stories have a variety of drawing tools that allow you to add freehand doodles and scribbles of your own. To access the drawing tools, tap the pen icon at the top of the story screen (see Figure 16-13).

You'll notice a variety of pen and drawing tools along the top of the screen. Each pen offers a different effect, from a simple pen/pencil to a highlighter, an eraser, and more.

On the left side of the screen, you'll notice a sizing tool. You can drag the dot up and down to make the drawing tool thicker or thinner. Along the bottom of the screen are color options. You can scroll left and right along the color option bar to access more color selections (see Figure 16-14).

FIGURE 16-13:
Select the pen icon from the story toolbar to access the drawing tools.

FIGURE 16-14:
Doodle tools offer different pen options, different thickness options, and different color options.

TIP

You can also get really creative and choose any color of the rainbow, not just the color options listed. If you tap and hold any color circle on the row of colors, the whole spectrum of colors will appear and you can drag your finger to find the perfect shade.

If you want to match something specific, you can tap the eyedropper tool next to the color palettes and then tap the specific color you want to match on your image. That color will become your pen color.

TIP

If you want to fill the screen with a transparent color, choose the standard pen tool, pick the color of your choice, and then tap and hold the screen. The color you chose will fill the entire screen as a transparent layer above the photo or video.

You can even layer various aspects to get really creative with your drawing tools. For example, upload an image to your story. Then select the pen tool and color. Tap and hold the screen to fill the screen with that color, laying it on top of the image you uploaded. Then select the Eraser tool from the drawing tools and erase the color fill to reveal the image behind it (see Figure 16-15).

FIGURE 16-15:
Combine drawing tools by overlaying a solid color on top of an image and then using the eraser tool to reveal the image behind.

When you're done with any doodle, tap the check mark to save it to your story.

TIP

While you're adding doodles, note the Undo option (iOS) or a backward-facing curved arrow (Android) at the top of the screen. Tap Undo or the arrow to undo the last doodle you created. You can keep undoing all the way back to the first one you added.

Saying More with Text

For all the fun you've had this far creating doodles and adding stickers, there's still another way to personalize your stories! You can add text boxes to your stories, too.

To access the Text option, tap the Aa icon in the top toolbar when creating your story or simply tap anywhere on the screen to open the text tool.

You can add multiple text boxes to your story and place them wherever you choose. They can be pinched to change the size and rotated as you please.

Changing your font option

The font option will default to Classic. You can change this easily to one of the other font options by simply tapping the font style above the keyboard. You'll navigate through the available options (see Figure 16-16).

FIGURE 16-16: Instagram stories offer a variety of font options for you to personalize your posts.

Figure 16-17 shows you some examples of what the different fonts look like in stories. Choose the font that best represents your style or the purpose of that story.

In addition to font choices, you can choose different colors for your fonts.

FIGURE 16-17:
Instagram stories
offer a variety of
font options to
choose from.

Certain fonts will also allow you to add background colors or to fill the text box with a color. If you see the "A**" icon, that lets you know that option is available. Tapping the "A**" icon will fill the text box with the selected color, which you can also change by tapping a color palette of the options.

Removing your text boxes

REMEMBER

Similar to stickers, text boxes can be easily removed if you decide you don't want them. Simply tap and hold to reveal the trash can icon and drag the text box onto the trash can to remove it.

TIP

Do you want to add a new story with just text? You can find the details in Chapter 15.

Chapter 17

Using Highlights to Keep Stories Longer

When you start using Instagram stories, you can keep those stories alive longer! Stories disappear after 24 hours, so it can be frustrating to know that the content you created is lost. Fortunately, highlights allow you to select certain stories that will stay active on your profile in galleries you set up.

In this chapter, we explain how to set up highlights and how to add content to them. We also talk about some of the reasons why you may want to use highlights and give you some creative ideas for highlight topics.

Getting Acquainted with Highlights

Story highlights are the series of circles directly below a person's bio on his or her Instagram profile (see Figure 17-1). A person may have only a few of these galleries or a number of them that you can scroll through.

Each highlight gallery is a collection of stories from that account. One story post or a series of story posts from various times are uploaded to each highlight.

A story disappears from the account after 24 hours, but highlights are an opportunity to keep that content on your profile for as long as you want it there.

You can customize all the highlights for your own profile with whatever topics and titles you want!

Creating a Highlight Gallery

Story highlights are available to all users. You must have active or archived stories on your profile, though, to have access to adding a highlight gallery. If you've never shared a story before, go ahead and create one! That will open up the option to add highlights to your profile.

If you do have access to highlights, you'll see the story highlights section below the bio information on your profile. If you haven't yet created a highlight, the circles will be gray and you'll see a circle with a plus sign (+) to create a new highlight easily.

FIGURE 17-1:
Story highlights are the series of circles below the bio and are a place to collect stories to live more than 24 hours.

Adding a highlight from your profile

To create a highlight from your profile, tap the plus sign (+) in the circle below your bio. A list of archived stories appears, as shown in Figure 17-2. Scroll through the list of posts and select one or more that you want to add to the highlight.

Tap Next after you've selected your posts and move on to the following instructions for naming and customizing your highlight.

Adding a highlight from an active story

If you have an active story on your profile and want to use that one to create a highlight, open the story post from your profile or feed.

At the bottom of your story post is a variety of buttons, including the highlight icon, which is a circle with a heart in the center (see Figure 17-3). Tap that icon, and then select New from the Add to Highlights screen. Proceed with the following instructions for naming and customizing your highlight.

FIGURE 17-2:
When starting a new story highlights gallery, you'll be able to choose which post(s) from your archived stories to add.

FIGURE 17-3:
When you access an active story, you'll see the highlight icon, which you tap to add the story to a highlight gallery.

Naming and customizing your highlight

Now that you've started a highlight, you need to give it a name! Here are some things to be aware of:

>> Highlight titles can be up to 16 characters in length.

>> The titles get cut off after a handful of characters (there's no set limit).

>> Keep the titles as short as possible and keep the important title info at the start of the title.

Type your highlight title and then tap Add to create the new highlight on your profile.

Setting a cover image for your highlight

After you save the highlight, tap View on Profile in the Added to Highlights box. Your new highlight appears under the connection buttons. Now you can change and improve the look of your highlight cover image by following these steps:

1. **Tap the highlight in the profile.**

2. **Tap the more icon (three dots) in the lower right of the story screen.**

3. **Tap Edit Highlight in the menu.**

4. **Tap Edit Cover in the Edit Highlight screen.**

    Drag or zoom (by pinching) to reposition your cover image, as shown in Figure 17-4.

FIGURE 17-4:
Reposition your image as needed.

After creating your highlight, you can change the cover image to a crop of any image in the highlight gallery. Begin by tapping the highlight from your profile to open the gallery. In the lower-right corner, tap the three dots icon and select Edit Highlight from the list. Then tap Edit Cover and follow the same steps to select a new image and position it for the cover image.

Creating a custom cover image

You may notice that people have specific images or logos set up for their highlights (see Figure 17-5). In this situation, they've uploaded a custom-designed image to their stories and then added it to their highlight.

Tools such as Canva (www.canva.com) offer templates for creating these types of covers, but you could also create them using Photoshop or another design tool. Simply create the background color or design you want and place your graphic or logo in the center of the image. Edit your highlight following the steps earlier to select a cover image and set this as your cover image for each individual highlight.

FIGURE 17-5:
Custom covers for highlights offer a creative and appealing way to showcase the topics of each highlight.

Adding Content to a Highlight

Now that you have your highlights set up, you'll want to keep adding content to them. Here, we walk you through the steps to add to and delete content from a highlight.

Sharing a current story

If you have an active story on your profile that you want to add to an existing highlight, you simply have to access that story from your profile and tap the high-light icon (circle with a heart) just as you would when creating a new highlight. Your story will be added to the highlight.

Finding an archived story

To add more content to an existing highlight, you can also select from older, archived stories.

The first option is to tap the highlight on your profile. In the highlight screen, tap the more icon (three dots) and then tap Edit Highlight. Next, select the Add tab (on Android devices) or the Stories tab (on iOS devices) to scroll through archived stories and select as many as you want to add to the highlight (see Figure 17-6).

Alternatively, you can go into your archived stories by tapping the three-line button on your profile screen, and then selecting the Archive tab from the menu page to view all your old stories in that feed (see Figure 17-7). Select a story from the list and tap the highlight icon at the bottom of the story to add it to a highlight.

FIGURE 17-6:
Add archived stories in the Add tab to a highlight.

FIGURE 17-7:
You can add archived stories to a highlight.

Deleting a story from a highlight

If you decide you no longer want a particular story to appear in your highlight gallery, you can easily remove it.

Select the highlight from your profile and advance through the story posts in the highlight until you arrive at the one you want to remove. Tap the more icon (three dots) in the lower right. Tap Remove from Highlight from the pop-up menu (see Figure 17-8), and confirm that you want to remove that item from the highlight.

If you want to delete a bulk number of story posts, go to Edit Highlight from the three-dot button and deselect all the story posts from the list. Tapping Done will save the changes, removing those stories from the highlight.

Coming Up with Fun Ideas for Highlights

You can use highlights for any topic that you create with your stories! It's best to group your stories into specific topics for your highlights, though.

FIGURE 17-8:
Deleting any post from a highlight is just as easy as adding a post.

For example, you may have a lot of stories of your family. But you could create one highlight for family vacations, another for holiday celebrations, and another for your pets.

TIP You can have plenty of different highlights, so feel free to use them as best suited for you. Just realize that only the four most recently used highlights appear on your profile. After that, users will have to scroll to see your other highlight galleries.

Chapter **18**

Going Live on Instagram

Q uickly after they launched, Instagram stories dramatically changed the way people used Instagram. Some users even abandoned the newsfeed and use only Instagram stories.

With the popularity of stories and the growth of Facebook Live, including a live video option in Instagram stories seemed like a natural next step.

In this chapter, you learn all about how to go live, and get tips for making your live broadcast more successful before, during, and after filming.

Getting Started with Live Videos

So, you're ready to go live, but how do you even get to it? Its location isn't obvious. Follow these steps:

1. **Open Instagram stories by swiping right or tapping the camera icon at the top of the newsfeed.**

2. **At the bottom of the screen, swipe Story to the right so you're on Live.**

   Figure 18-1 (left) shows the Instagram Live screen.

3. **If you want only certain people to view your live broadcast, tap the gear icon (settings) in the upper left, tap Hide Story From, and select the followers you want to omit.**

4. **When you're ready to start, tap the white button with the Go Live icon (broadcast symbol).**

   Instagram checks your connection, and you're on! See Figure 18-1, right. You'll begin seeing *Username* Has Joined and the number of people who have joined.

FIGURE 18-1:
Go Live on
Instagram (left);
your video is live
(right).

5. **Immediately announce the topic and purpose of the video, and then let people who are viewing the recorded video know that you'll get to the topic at hand shortly.**

   Greet as many people as possible. Say hi, calling them by their name or username. Make them feel welcome.

6. **Now that you're live, you can do the following:**

   • Turn off comments by tapping the three dots at the lower left of the screen (refer to Figure 18-1, right). The screen shown in Figure 18-2, left, appears. However, we recommend that you keep them turned on for more interaction.

   • Add a face filter by tapping the face with stars icon, which is in the lower-right corner.

- Turn the camera from the front-facing selfie camera to the rear-facing camera to showcase what you're seeing, rather than showing your face. Tap the curved double arrow in the upper left (refer to Figure 18-1, right) to change the camera view.

- Enter the name of your live broadcast by tapping Title on the left side of the screen. In the Add Title screen, tap Add a Title, type the title of your live broadcast, and then tap Add Title.

- To keep track of your time, tap the pink Live button at the top of the screen. A timer appears.

- To see the names of the people who have joined, tap the number to the right of the pink Live button. To kick people out of your Live broadcast, place an X by their name.

7. **When you're finished, tap End, and then tap End Now (iOS) or End Video (Android).**

8. **Save the live video by tapping Download Video, as shown in Figure 18-2, right.**

You must save your live broadcast immediately after recording (before you agree to share it). After it's shared, there is no option to go back and save it.

FIGURE 18-2: Turn off commenting (left), and save or share your live video (right).

Knowing When to Go Live

TIP

You can go live anytime you want. But it helps to go live when you have plenty of followers online. Choose times of day that work best for you and your followers to ensure that more people tune in to the live broadcast. You can also check the Audience section in Insights to view your followers' most active times. For more on Insights, see Chapter 11.

You may also want to broadcast when you're at an event or experiencing something in your life. Sometimes you can't plan, and it's okay to go live when the moment strikes you.

WARNING

Instagram Live has a 60-minute time limit. You'll see a 15-second timer countdown when your time is almost up, and then the live broadcast will end. If possible, plan your schedule accordingly so as not to exceed that limit.

Developing a Game Plan

TIP

Now that you know how to physically tap all the buttons to record a live broadcast, it's time to talk strategy. We recommend going on Instagram Live with forethought about what you'll be doing. Here are a few tips to help you execute the best Instagram Live possible:

» **Think of a topic that will interest your followers.** Some ideas to consider: Showcase your family life, stream your child's rehearsal, show off some of your vacation, share a holiday tradition.

» **If you plan to talk on the live broadcast, jot down several talking points, but don't memorize or look overly rehearsed.** Live broadcasts are supposed to be a bit off the cuff.

» **Think about some common questions you might get asked, and prepare your answers.** You can also ask people to submit questions beforehand.

» **If possible, do a test video on your regular camera app where you plan to do the live broadcast, and at the same time of day.** Check the lighting and the background. Make sure that you can get a decent signal in that location.

>> Promote your live broadcast ahead of time by posting about it in your Instagram stories, on Facebook, and other social media.

>> Be as interactive as possible with your followers during the broadcast.

>> Save your broadcast so you can repurpose it to other online media, and then publish your broadcast so it's available for 24 hours.

TIP

It's often helpful to have a tripod to hold your camera steady and in place while filming live. Arkon Mounts (www.arkon.com) has several tripods available for less than $50.

Alerting Your Fans

To help get more viewers to your Live video, promote it. You can do this in a variety of ways, but the most obvious route is through Instagram itself. Post a graphic or a video in your Instagram newsfeed and stories stating the topic, date, and time, as shown in Figure 18-3. If you have an email newsletter or blog, you'll want to promote it there too. Finally, reach out to your other social media networks, and post information about the Live video there, making sure to include your Instagram handle.

Instagram sends a notification to your followers (unless they've turned off this feature) to let them know you are live. Your profile pic will be labeled *Live* in the bar at the top of the newsfeed so people can jump in from there too.

FIGURE 18-3:
Post graphics on Instagram before your Live broadcast to promote it.

Acknowledging Live Followers

While you're waiting for more people to view your live video, acknowledge the people who are joining you. Use their names or usernames and thank them for participating. Introduce the topic you're sharing on the live video, and after a few minutes of welcoming guests, you can start speaking about the topic at hand.

People will likely comment while you're talking. It's nice to answer questions and comments as they arise, but sometimes it's not practical if you're trying to explain something. In this case, let them know that you're happy to take comments and questions and you'll address them at the end or when you wrap up that current thought.

Inviting a Guest onto the Live Broadcast

If being live on camera alone makes you nervous, or if you just want to include someone else in your video, Instagram allows you to invite one guest into the live show with you.

Tap the two-face icon (see Figure 18-4) in your live video to invite someone to that video. A screen will appear with a list of recommendations of people to invite into the video, or you can use the search bar to type their name.

Alternatively, someone can request to join your live video when he or she taps the same button while watching your live broadcast. You'll receive a notification that the person wants to participate, and you can choose to add or ignore the person.

When the guest joins you on the live video, he or she will occupy half the screen, sharing his video and audio as well (see Figure 18-5).

FIGURE 18-5:
A guest on a live
broadcast shares
the screen with
you until the
person leaves.

Saving Live Broadcasts and Sharing Them

After you've completed your live broadcast, don't forget to save it! After you've
tapped End Live Video, tap Download Video (refer to Figure 18-2, right). The
broadcast is saved to the camera roll on your device.

You must have enough storage space on your mobile device to save the full video. If you don't have enough storage space, only a portion or even none of the video will save.

When you save your Instagram Live broadcast, it becomes a regular video that you can use any way you'd like. Here are some places to reuse it:

>> On your website

>> In a blog post

>> In your email newsletter as a free replay, or as a teaser for your next Live broadcast

>> On your YouTube channel (share the link to your broadcast on LinkedIn and Twitter)

>> On your Facebook business page

You can also edit the video to create sound bites of 1 minute or less, and upload them directly to Instagram, Facebook, LinkedIn, and Twitter. Or create a graphic about the video for Instagram, and then link to the video (on YouTube or your website) via the link in the bio on your Instagram profile page.

You can reuse live content in so many creative ways — don't let it go to waste!

6

Creating Content on IGTV

Chapter **19**

Learning How IGTV Works

GTV was introduced in 2018 as a standalone app that integrated with Instagram. Sound confusing? It is! IGTV was designed to be its own app for viewing and interactions, and yet it's tied directly to your Instagram profile. It's a video-only platform with some unique components.

In this chapter, we show you the various aspects of IGTV, how you can use it, and what makes it different. We also explain why you're seeing what you see in the feed.

Finding IGTV within Instagram

Even though IGTV is a singular component, it's accessible from two places in the Instagram app:

>> **On an account's profile:** If the account is using IGTV and has created videos, you'll see the little IGTV icon just below the highlights on the user's profile page. Figure 19-1 (left) shows you where to find IGTV from an account's profile.

>> **On the Explore page:** On the Explore page (tap the magnifying glass icon in the bottom navigation bar to get there), an IGTV tab is at the top of the screen. Figure 19-1 (right) shows you where that's located.

In addition to these two locations, you can also see IGTV videos recommended for you on the Explore page. The videos will appear in the list of suggested content, as shown in Figure 19-1 (right).

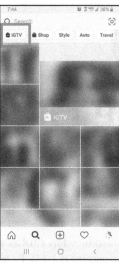

If someone you follow creates an IGTV video and shares a preview of that video to Instagram, you'll also see that preview as a post when you're scrolling through your feed (see Figure 19-2, left). It will appear as a regular post, but you'll see the IGTV icon in the lower-left corner of the video. If you tap that icon, you'll be taken to the full IGTV video; if you watch the entire 1-minute preview, you'll be prompted to watch the remainder of the video on IGTV (see Figure 19-2, center). Tapping that option will open the IGTV video and allow you to continue watching (see Figure 19-2, right).

FIGURE 19-2:
Watching an IGTV
video.

Finding IGTV in the IGTV App

As we already mentioned, IGTV is a standalone app. You can install it from the app store for your device by searching for IGTV. After you've installed the app on your device, you can log in as the same account you use on Instagram. All your profile information and followers will transfer to the IGTV app.

TECHNICAL STUFF

If you unfollow or follow someone on IGTV, that same interaction occurs on your Instagram account, and vice versa. The two are linked and you can't follow different people on IGTV than you do on your Instagram account.

After you have your IGTV account set up and you're in the app, you'll be taken to the home feed (see Figure 19-3). This is where the videos of the people you follow and those recommended for you will all appear. You can scroll vertically through the videos and tap any video to play it.

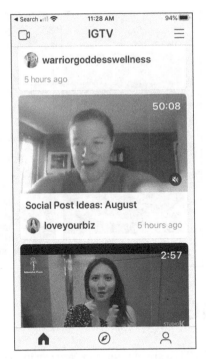

Understanding How IGTV Videos Are Formatted

IGTV was originally designed to be used only with vertical videos. In addition, the video viewer would not rotate when the mobile device was turned to the horizontal position (as most other video players do).

However, in 2019, Instagram announced that it would start allowing horizontal videos to be uploaded and that those videos would rotate with the screen.

TIP

IGTV videos can be from 1 minute to 1 hour in length. They encourage longer-form content that keeps viewers watching longer. In contrast to Instagram stories, IGTV videos are meant to share more in-depth content.

Videos from 1 to 15 minutes in length can be uploaded via your mobile device. Videos over 15 minutes in length can be uploaded only via a desktop computer. We cover the upload procedures in Chapter 20.

Tapping into Whose Videos You're Seeing

Your IGTV home feed is full of the IGTV videos created by everyone you follow on Instagram. Whenever someone you follow adds another IGTV video, it will appear in your list of videos.

To keep you interested, however, much like the Explore page on Instagram, the IGTV home feed will populate videos that it thinks you'll be interested in. These are not accounts you're following but the video content or the account creators are similar in interest to other content you watch or accounts you follow.

TIP

If your IGTV Explore feed has a video that you don't like or want to see, tap and hold down on the video preview in the feed. Then tap the option for notifying IGTV that you're not interested in that post. Or when viewing a video full-screen, tap the three-dot button at the bottom of the screen to access a menu that enables you to notify IGTV that you're not interested in that post, copy the link to the post, share the video, save the video, or report the video. Tapping the Not Interested menu option tells the algorithm to show you less of that type of content.

Chapter **20**

Claiming Your Stake on IGTV

In the preceding chapter, we show you how IGTV works and where you can find those videos. If you're intrigued by the options in IGTV and you want to create your own videos, this is the next step. In this chapter, we explain how to upload videos and format the videos for better results.

Uploading Videos to IGTV

If you have an Instagram account, you can upload IGTV videos. (Before, you had to set up an IGTV profile to upload videos to IGTV.) You can upload videos using your mobile device or a desktop computer.

Using your mobile device to upload

Your phone can upload videos from 1 to 10 minutes long. (Desktop computers can upload longer videos.) To upload a video, follow these simple steps:

1. **Tap the plus sign (+) at the bottom of your Instagram profile page or home page.**

   The Library tab (iOS) or Gallery tab (Android) is selected automatically.

2. **Select an existing video from your library by tapping it (see Figure 20-1).**

3. **Tap Next.**

FIGURE 20-1:
Select an existing video from your library.

4. **Choose Long Video to share the full-length video to IGTV, as shown in Figure 20-2, and then tap Continue.**

   This option also enables you to share a preview to your profile and feed.

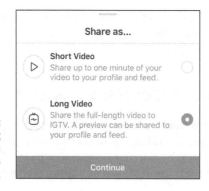

FIGURE 20-2:
Choose Long Video to share a full-length video to IGTV.

5. **Choose a cover photo in one of the following ways, and then tap Next:**

- *Select a frame from your video, as shown in Figure 20-3.*

- *Tap + Add from Camera Roll (iOS) or Add from Gallery (Android), and then add a photo from your camera roll or gallery.*

<   Cover   Next

coreycwalker
Your video title appears here
0 views

To select a cover image, choose a frame from your video or an image from your camera roll.

⊞ Add from Camera Roll

FIGURE 20-3:
Choose a cover
photo.

6. **Type a video title and description, as shown in Figure 20-4.**

7. **If you want to add the video to a new series or an existing series:**

- *To add to an existing series:* Tap Add to Series, select the Series, and tap Done.

- *To start a new series:* Tap Add to Series, tap New Series, type a series name and description, and then tap Create.

- *If you're creating a series for the first time:* After tapping Add to Series, tap Create Your First Series, and then fill in your name and description.

8. **If you want to post a preview of your video on your Instagram feed, toggle the Post a Preview button to blue.**

You can edit the preview or profile cover by tapping the arrow to the right of either of those sections.

9. **If you want to add the video to your connected Facebook page and Facebook Watch, toggle the Make Visible on Facebook button to blue.**

10. **Tap Post.**

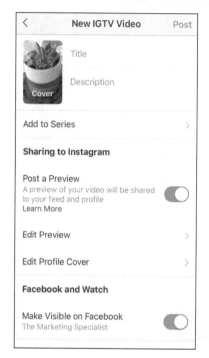

Using your computer to upload

If you prefer to upload IGTV videos using your desktop computer rather than a mobile device, or if you want to upload videos over 10 minutes in duration, follow these steps:

1. **Go to** http://instagram.com **and log in to your account.**

2. **Click the IGTV tab under your bio on your profile page, as shown in Figure 20-5, left.**

3. **Click the Upload button under the IGTV tab on your Instagram profile, as shown in Figure 20-5.**

FIGURE 20-5:
Select the IGTV tab from your desktop Instagram profile and click Upload to get started.

4. **Drag and drop a video file from your computer to the video box on the upload screen, as shown in Figure 20-6.**

   If your video isn't on your desktop or easily accessible to drag and drop, click the + icon to search your computer for the file. Depending on the size of the video, the upload may take several minutes or longer.

FIGURE 20-6:
Drag and drop a file onto the browser page.

5. **Select the cover image by choosing a JPG or PNG file from your computer.**

6. **Give your video a title and description.**

7. **If you want a preview to appear in your Instagram feed, select the Post a Preview check box.**

8. **Select whether you'd like the video to post on IGTV, or both IGTV and Facebook.**

9. **Click the Post button to upload the video, as shown in Figure 20-7.**

FIGURE 20-7:
Your video is
uploaded to
Instagram via the
desktop following
the onscreen
instructions.

Creating Quality Content for IGTV

Now that you're ready to upload videos to IGTV, we want to make sure your videos look amazing and perform well. In this section, we provide some suggestions for making your videos even better for IGTV.

Making your videos shine

If you're looking for some tips to make your IGTV videos look better, sound better, get more views, and longer retention, here are some suggestions for you:

TIP

>> **Get right to the point in your video.** Don't waste time with fluff and ramblings. Hook your audience immediately by getting to the meat of the topic.

>> **Have a good cover photo that describes the video and looks appealing to those viewing it.** If you're showing up as suggested content to people who don't follow you, it helps to have a good cover photo to draw them in.

>> **Film vertical videos.** Even as Instagram allows more video formats for upload, the vertical video is best formatted for and fits in the IGTV space.

>> **Avoid loud introductions or distracting noises in your videos.** If people are playing the video or it automatically plays after the last one, you don't want people to stop watching because the audio caught them off guard.

>> **Keep your content consistent.** Because IGTV is a singular channel, you can't break out types of content. If your videos cover a whole range of topics — from your family vacation, to a recipe, to a business trip, to a party, and more — you probably won't retain viewers. If someone finds you for the recipe you shared, she'll want to see more of the same things, not videos of your dog sleeping. Pick a theme for your channel and keep your content consistent with that.

Using the video description to your advantage

TIP

The description of the IGTV video is a gold mine that most people don't realize is there. Writing a short description about the video may seem simple, but there are hidden tricks to using the description effectively:

>> **Share details about the video and any relevant takeaways, if applicable.** A descriptive caption can appeal to more viewers and increase video views.

>> **Include a URL in the video description.** On Instagram, only business profiles with over 10,000 followers or verified accounts can add swipe-up links to their stories. But on IGTV, any account of any size can add a clickable URL to its video description. Take advantage of this whenever appropriate.

>> **Use hashtags in the description.** Just like Instagram posts, you can include up to 30 hashtags in your IGTV video description. This will help you appear in more searches and have more people find your content. Make sure to follow the same hashtag rules we talk about in Chapter 9.

Responding to Comments on Your Videos

Hopefully, people will love your IGTV videos and want to connect with you via comments to respond to or engage with the videos. When someone responds to your IGTV video, you'll receive a notification in your Instagram notifications. You can reply directly from that notification just as you would any other Instagram post.

Additionally, you can view any comments directly from your IGTV video by tapping the comment icon. The comments screen will open and you can scroll through, view, like, and reply directly to any comments on the video (see Figure 20-8).

FIGURE 20-8:
View, like, and reply to comments on your IGTV video by tapping the comment icon on your IGTV video.

7

Why Isn't This Working?

Chapter **21**

Insta-Diagnosing Instagram

N othing in this world is perfect, and Instagram is no different. Sometimes weird (and frustrating) quirks happen with the app and you may find it difficult to do certain things while using it. Have no fear, though! Help is on the way . . . just keep reading.

In this chapter, we take you through some of the more common issues that users report running into with Instagram and give you steps to correct (or at least get past) them.

REMEMBER

The latest versions of iOS for the iPhone and iPad (version 13.4.1) and Android (version 10.0) were used to create the instructions for this chapter. If you have an older version of iOS or Android, your mileage may vary.

Installation Issues

When Instagram won't install for you, we've got your back. Instead of panicking, read on to discover the common reasons why Instagram won't install and sugges-tions for resolving them. If they don't work, take a few deep breaths because we've thought of that, too, in the "Nothing Is Working . . . Now What?" section, later in the chapter.

Dealing with compatibility issues

If you're receiving compatibility error messages, it may be time for you to upgrade your operating system before you install Instagram because the app requires iOS 8 or later on an iPhone or iPad.

For Android users, the Google Play Store entry for Instagram states that compatibility is dependent on the smartphone or tablet you're using. When you download Instagram, the Google Play Store automatically checks your smartphone or tablet to ensure that it's compatible.

That said, Instagram notes that some Android users receive a "Device not compatible" message. If you receive this message, Instagram recommends that you clear all Google Play Store data stored on your smartphone or tablet and then try to install Instagram again.

Here's how to clear all Google Play Store data from your Android device:

1. **In a home screen, swipe up from the bottom of the screen and then tap Settings.**

2. **Tap Storage.**

   The Storage screen appears, as show in Figure 21-1.

3. **Tap Other Apps.**

4. **Tap Google Play Store in the list. (You may need to swipe up first.)**

5. **Tap Clear Storage.**

6. **Tap OK in the pop-up window that appears.**

Now you can return to the Google Play Store and try to install Instagram again. If that doesn't work, check out Chapter 22 for information on support from Instagram and other online sources.

Checking your space

If you use your smartphone or tablet a lot, you know that storage issues are a bane of your existence. (If it's your only bane, well done.) You can check the memory usage to see how much memory space Instagram is eating up.

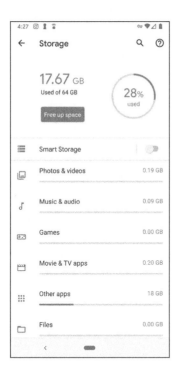

FIGURE 21-1:
Clear your Google
Play Store data
here.

iPhone and iPad

It's easy to find out how much storage space Instagram is using on your iPhone or iPad:

1. **On your home screen, tap Settings.**

2. **Swipe up on the screen if necessary, and then tap General in the settings list.**

   The General screen appears.

3. **Tap iPhone Storage or iPad Storage.**

   The iPhone Storage or iPad Storage screen appears.

4. **Tap Instagram. (You may need to swipe up first.)**

   In the Info screen that appears, the Documents & Data entry shows you how much storage space Instagram is using, as shown in Figure 21-2.

TIP

If you think Instagram is taking up too much space and the app is affecting the performance of your iPhone or iPad, tap Offload App to free up storage space but save your photos and profile data. If that doesn't help, reinstalling Instagram might. Instagram will save your data so that everything will still be there when you reinstall.

FIGURE 21-2:
The storage space that the Instagram app is taking up appears to the right of the Documents & Data entry.

To reinstall Instagram, tap Delete App in the Info screen. Then repeat the steps in this section to see whether reinstalling freed up any storage space.

Android smartphone and tablet

As with the iPhone and iPad, it's easy to find out how much memory the Instagram app is using on your Android smartphone or tablet. Here's how:

1. **On a home screen, swipe up from the bottom of the screen and then tap Settings.**

   The Settings screen appears.

2. **Tap Apps & Notifications.**

3. **Tap Instagram.**

   Recently opened apps appear at the top of the Apps & Notifications screen. If you don't see the Instagram app, tap See All *n* Apps, where *n* is the total number of apps installed on your smartphone or tablet.

4. **Tap Storage & Cache.**

   The total storage appears in the Storage screen, as shown in Figure 21-3.

FIGURE 21-3:
The storage
space on an
Android device.

To clear all the memory that the Instagram app is using without clearing all the app's data, tap Clear Cache.

If you think Instagram is taking up too much space and the app is affecting the performance of your smartphone or tablet, tap Clear Storage in the Storage screen. Then tap Delete in the pop-up window that appears in the center of the screen.

Android clears your Instagram profile data stored on your smartphone or tablet, any photos or videos you've taken in the Instagram app that you haven't posted to your feed, as well as all the memory that the Instagram app is using. If the app is open, it closes automatically.

REMEMBER

If you've already posted photos or videos to your Instagram account, your posts remain in your feed. Photos and videos you've saved on your smartphone or tablet are also safe.

Unfreezing an installation on your iPhone or iPad

If the Instagram app freezes during installation and you've given the App Store a reasonable amount of time to install the app, try a cold restart of your iPhone or iPad by turning the device off and then back on.

After you restart your iPhone or iPad, try installing the Instagram app once more. If this doesn't work, you'll have to contact Apple support, which is easy to access from the Apple website (www.apple.com). Once on the website, click or tap the Support option at the top of the screen. On your iPhone, tap the menu icon in the upper-left corner of the page and then tap Support.

Finding a missing app on your iPhone or iPad

If the App Store says Instagram is installed but you don't see it on your iPhone or iPad, connect your phone to your computer and sync your apps by using the iTunes program on a Windows computer or Finder on a Mac.

If iTunes or Finder won't cooperate, it's time to contact Apple support on its website.

Resolving issues on an Android device

If you have problems installing the Instagram app on an Android device, there may be a connectivity problem between the Google Play Store and your smartphone or tablet.

In this case, you'll need to go through the Google Play troubleshooting wizard, which will take you step-by-step through solving the problem. If the wizard can't help, Google will give you options for contacting its support staff members so they can dig deeper. You can access the wizard at https://support.google.com/googleplay/troubleshooter/6241347?hl=en.

Log-In Difficulties

If you can't log in to the Instagram app, one of several issues may be the culprit. You may have a problem with your username or password, or Instagram may have disabled your account. We'll be your guide in resolving all these problems so you can start Instagramming.

Checking your username

If Instagram won't accept your username, you may have typed the username incorrectly. This may seem silly or even insulting, but ensure that your username is typed correctly. If you have repeated characters, it's easy to miss one of those characters as you type.

Did you add the @ symbol to your username? That symbol is used only to tag people in a comment in Instagram. So ditch the @ when you type your username.

If you still can't add your username, someone else may have changed your username. When you change your username or any other account information, you get an email message from Instagram informing you that your information was changed.

If you didn't get one in your email inbox or in your junk email folder, ask one of your friends or colleagues to log into Instagram, look at your profile, and find out if the username was changed. If your friend or colleague knows how to take a screenshot, have that person take a screenshot to send to you. After you review it, you can send it to Instagram if needed.

TIP

Do you suspect that your account was hacked? Instagram has suggestions for getting more help to secure your account at `https://help.instagram.com/149494825257596`. This page also contains a link to contact Instagram and explain what's happening.

Fixing password issues

If you've forgotten your Instagram account password, here are some suggestions for finding it. Or, as a last resort, resetting it so that you can get back to scratching your Instagram itch.

REMEMBER

If you're using your Facebook username and password to log in to Instagram, you'll have to open Facebook reset your password.

Checking your password

If you use a password manager app, open it to see your username or password in Instagram or Facebook. If you're using your Facebook account to log in to Instagram, you may want to log in to Facebook (or log out and log back in) to find out if your Facebook password is working properly.

Password management apps can become cranky from time to time and not work properly, so if you find that your Facebook or Instagram password doesn't work when you type it, you have several options to fix the problem:

>> Restart the password management app.

>> Restart your computer, smartphone, or tablet, and then try logging back into Instagram to see whether the password management app works properly.

>> Uninstall and reinstall the management app. Before you do this, write down all your accounts, usernames, and passwords . . . in a secure location, of course.

Finding your saved Instagram signup message

When you sign up or change your account information, you receive an email message that contains a link to log into your account as well as the email address you used to log in. Be sure to click the link in the email message so you can log in with the email address Instagram expects you to use. (The link includes your password so you don't have to enter it.)

REMEMBER

If you don't see the Instagram email in your inbox, check your junk email folder. If you find the message, you can tell your email app that messages from Instagram are not junk.

Resetting your password by email

If you don't have the email message you received from Instagram and you can't remember the password (or can't find it the password management app), you can reset your password.

On an iPhone or iPad

Here's how to reset your password by email on an iPhone or iPad:

1. **Open the Instagram app, and then tap the Forgot Password link.**

   The screen shown in Figure 21-4 appears.

2. **Tap Username.**

3. **Type your Instagram username, email address, or phone number.**

4. **Tap Next.**

REMEMBER

   If you mistyped your email address when you signed up for your account, you won't receive an email message in your inbox. In this case, reset your account information using the phone message detailed in the next step.

5. **Tap your confirmation code you received in your email inbox.**

6. **Tap Next.**

   Instagram opens so you can browse your feed. You can also change the password within the app if you want.

On an Android smartphone or tablet

Here's how to reset your password by email on an Android smartphone or tablet:

1. **Open the Instagram app, and then tap the Get Help Logging In link.**

2. **Type your Instagram username, email address, or phone number.**

3. **Tap Next.**

REMEMBER

   If you mistyped your email address when you signed up for your account, you won't receive an email message in your inbox. In this case, reset your account information using the phone message detailed in the next step.

4. **Tap Send an Email.**

   In a few minutes, you'll receive an email from Instagram with a link to reset your password (Android users).

5. **Click or tap the Reset Your Instagram Password link in the email.**

   The Instagram New Password web page appears in your browser.

6. **Type your new password.**

Resetting your password by text message

If you don't have access to your email account, Instagram can send you a text message on your smartphone or tablet (provided your tablet has a data plan).

On an iPhone or iPad

Here's how to reset your password by text message on your iPhone or iPad:

1. **Open the Instagram app, and then tap the Forgot Password link.**

   The Trouble Logging In? screen appears (refer to Figure 21-4).

2. **Tap Phone and then type your phone number.**

3. **Tap Next.**

4. **Tap OK.**

5. **Type the six-digit SMS code and then tap Next.**

   Instagram opens so you can browse your feed. You can also change the password within the app if you want.

WARNING

The link in the password reset email or text message expires, though Instagram doesn't say when. If nothing happens when you tap the link in the message, you'll need to send another password reset email or text message.

On an Android smartphone or tablet

Here's how to reset your password by text message on your Android smartphone or tablet:

1. **Open the Instagram app, and then tap the Get Help Signing In link.**

2. **Type your Instagram username, email address, or phone number.**

3. **Tap Next.**

4. **Tap Send an SMS.**

5. **Type the six-digit SMS code and then tap Next.**

   Instagram opens so you can browse your feed. You can also change the password in the app if you want.

WARNING

The link in the password reset email or text message expires, though Instagram doesn't say when. If nothing happens when you tap the link in the message, you'll need to send another password reset email or text message.

Dealing with a disabled account

Instagram won't tell you that your account has been disabled for violation of its Community Guidelines until you try to log in and you see a message telling you that your account is disabled.

Now what? Enter your username and password, and then follow the onscreen instructions to try to appeal the decision. There are no guarantees that your account will be reinstated.

Finding Relief for Common Problems

If you run into problems uploading photos or videos, sharing with other Instagram users, or receiving notifications, read on to get some suggestions for finding solutions fast (and what to do if you can't).

Instagram won't share

Instagram has noted that problems exist when sharing your photos and videos with Facebook and Tumblr. You may encounter problems sharing your Instagram posts on Twitter, too.

TIP

If you want to learn about other sharing options, including copying a link so you can paste it into another social networking website, see Chapter 7.

You may have problems sharing your Instagram posts on Facebook, Twitter, or Tumblr for the simple reason that your preferred social network is down. In that case, you just have to wait until it fixes the problem.

If you verify on another smartphone, tablet, or computer that Facebook, Twitter, or Tumblr is operating normally, the link between Instagram and Facebook might have become disconnected. You can reset the link from a smartphone or tablet app by following the instructions in this section.

REMEMBER

If you still can't connect after you reset your links, the Instagram or Facebook app may have become corrupted. In that case, it's best to remove both apps and then reinstall them. Facebook and Instagram save your data, so you won't have to log in to both apps after you reinstall them.

Here's how to reset your linked Facebook, Twitter, or Tumblr accounts:

1. **Tap the profile icon in the lower-right corner of the screen.**

   The screen shown in Figure 21-5 appears for iOS (left) or Android (right).

2. **Tap the menu icon (three lines) in the upper-right corner of the screen.**

3. **Tap Settings, tap Account, and then tap Linked Accounts.**

   The Share Settings screen appears.

4. **Tap Facebook, Twitter, or Tumblr.**

5. **Tap Unlink Account.**

6. **In the pop-up window that appears, tap Yes, I'm Sure.**

   Instagram and the other app (Facebook, Twitter, or Tumblr) are now unlinked.

7. **Tap Facebook, Twitter, or Tumblr.**

   This step reconnects the accounts. Try sharing your Instagram post again.

Getting Instagram to notify you

If you turned on notifications in the Instagram app but don't see notifications on your smartphone or tablet, check whether the Instagram app is sending you notifications.

Checking notifications on your iPhone or iPad

Here's how to check and set your Instagram notifications on your iPhone or iPad:

1. **On the home screen, tap Settings, and then tap Notifications.**

The Notifications screen appears.

2. **In the apps list, swipe up and tap Instagram.**

3. **If the Allow Notifications entry is off, slide the switch from left to right.**

If the slider is green and the switch is to the right side, notifications are on.

By default, Instagram notifications appear in Notification Center and on the lock screen. You'll also see a Badge App icon and hear a sound when you receive an Instagram notification.

Checking notifications on your Android smartphone or tablet

Here's how to check and set Instagram notifications on your Android smartphone or tablet:

1. **On the home screen, swipe up from the bottom of the screen and then tap Settings.**

The Settings screen appears.

2. **Tap Apps & Notifications.**

3. **Tap Instagram.**

Recently opened apps appear at the top of the Apps & Notifications screen. If you don't see the Instagram app, tap See All Apps. You might see the total number of apps on your device between the words *All* and *Apps.*

4. **Swipe up on the Application Info screen until you see the Notifications option in the list.**

If notifications are on, you'll see the number of notifications per day below the Notifications option. If they're off, the word *Off* appears.

5. **If notifications are off, tap the Notifications option and then turn on notifications.**

   You can also instruct Instagram to show different types of notifications including likes, new followers, live videos, and more.

Nothing Is Working . . . Now What?

When all else fails, you need to contact Instagram to report the problem. Instagram will need the following information to help you:

» The type of smartphone or tablet you're using

» The operating system and version you're using on your smartphone or tablet

» When the problem occurs and how often it occurs

You can report a problem in the Instagram app on your iPhone, iPad, Android smartphone, or Android tablet:

1. **Tap the profile icon.**

2. **Tap the menu icon (three lines) in the upper-right corner of the screen.**

3. **Tap Settings, tap Help, and then tap Report a Problem.**

   The Report a Problem window appears.

4. **Tap Something Isn't Working (iOS) or Report a Problem (Android).**

   The Feedback screen (iOS) or Report a Problem screen (Android) appears.

5. **Write your report.**

   In Android, you can tap the box with a plus sign (+) to add a screenshot that helps illustrate your problem.

6. **Tap Send (iOS) or Submit (Android) in the upper-right corner of the screen.**

TIP

It's more likely than not that you won't get a response to your problem from Instagram. If you feel that you've waited long enough to get a response, you can follow up with the Facebook Help website at www.facebook.com/help. You can not only ask Facebook about your problem, but you can also leave a message in the Help Community forum to (hopefully) get some answers.

Getting Rid of Error Messages

As with any app, you'll occasionally get error messages in the Instagram app on your iPhone, iPad, or Android device. And like any app, you may not understand why you're getting those error messages. In this section, we list four common error messages and how you can get around them.

Can't add a comment

If you receive an error message that states that you can't add a comment, one of these reasons may apply:

>> You can't include more than five tags in a comment. (You tag other Instagram users by typing the @ symbol before the username.)

>> You can add no more than 30 hashtags in a comment.

>> You can't post the same comment multiple times in one post.

>> Instagram filters out certain words and phrases, such as profanity, to meet its Community Guidelines.

>> You haven't updated Instagram recently to ensure that you have the most recent version.

If none of these reasons applies to you, close and restart the Instagram app. The next step is to turn your smartphone or tablet off and on, and then launch the Instagram app. Still not working? You need to contact Instagram for support, as described in the preceding section.

Can't delete comments

As of this writing, Instagram has a problem telling its users that a comment has been deleted. This problem arises if you try to delete a comment and get an error message that says the comment can't be deleted.

One potential solution is to close the Instagram app, restart it, and then view your post on the screen to see whether the comment is still there. If it is, you can close the Instagram app and clear all Instagram data, as described earlier in the "Checking your space" section. That should clear out the deleted comment from your post.

If the comment is still there and you still get the error message when you try to delete the comment, your best option is to ignore it. By the time you read this, we hope that the problem will have been fixed or at least hidden effectively.

REMEMBER

You can delete only comments you've posted and comments from others about your posts.

Can't refresh feed

When you refresh your feed screen by swiping down, sometimes you won't see new posts. That could simply mean none of your followers have posted anything recently. However, if you can't refresh your feed over a period of time, it could be due to one of the following:

» Your Wi-Fi signal is weak, or you're in an area with heavy Wi-Fi network usage, thus weakening the connection.

» You've reached the limits of your carrier's data plan. You'll need to find a Wi-Fi network or shell out money for more data in your plan.

» Instagram is having some issues. You'll just have to be patient.

If all else fails, report the problem in the Instagram app as described in the preceding section, and see whether Instagram can figure out what's wrong with the app.

Can't follow anyone else

If you receive a message that says you can't follow anyone else, check your profile to see how many other Instagram users you're following. If it's 7,500, you won't be able to add any other followers.

Most people will never reach the 7,500 limit. If you receive this error message and you are below (even well below) the limit, report the problem in the Instagram app so you can work with Instagram support to solve the mystery.

REMEMBER

There is no limit to the number of Instagram users who can follow you.

WARNING

Instagram has an unadvertised limit to the number of people you can follow per hour and per day. The maximum amount of Instagram users you can follow is 20 per hour and 480 followers per day. If you reach this limit, you'll have to wait until the top of the next hour or the beginning of the next day to follow someone.

Chapter **22**

Insta-Help Is on the Way

I f you ever need help using Instagram, plenty of online resources are available to supplement this book. In addition, the app itself contains online help that you can refer to quickly.

What's more, if you can't run the Instagram app, you can find help on the Instagram website, on Instagram social media profiles, and on other social-networking and community websites.

In this chapter, you start by learning about Instagram's online help in the app as well as on the Instagram website. Then you find out how to contact Instagram through its social media profiles as well as the Instagram blog. Finally, see how to join an online community so you can get help from other Instagram users.

Taking Advantage of Instagram's Help

Help Center, shown in Figure 22-1, should be the first place you look for a solution to your problem. To access Help Center on the Instagram website, go to `https://help.instagram.com/`.

FIGURE 22-1:
Instagram Help
Center on a
desktop browser.

Accessing Help Center

If the Instagram app is installed on a iPhone, iPad, or an Android smartphone or tablet, and the app isn't working, you can access Help Center not only on the website but also on the Windows Instagram app if that app is installed. If your smartphone or tablet app is working, you can also access Help Center from the app at any time.

On the iPhone or iPad

Here's how to view the Help Center screen if you are using an iPhone or an iPad:

1. **Tap the profile icon, in the lower-right corner of the screen.**

2. **Tap the menu icon (three lines) in the upper-right corner of the screen.**

3. **Tap Settings.**

   The Settings screen appears.

4. **Tap Help and then tap Help Center.**

   The Help Center screen shown in Figure 22-2 appears.

FIGURE 22-2:
Swipe to view all
options in Help
Center.

Swipe to view all the topics. Tap a topic title to view more information about that topic.

When you're finished viewing information in Help Center, return to the Help screen by tapping the X icon, in the upper-left corner. On the Help screen, tap the < icon to return to the Settings screen.

On an Android smartphone or tablet

You view Help Center in your web browser on your Android smartphone or tablet. Here's how:

1. **Tap the profile icon, in the lower-right corner of the screen.**

2. **Tap the menu icon (three lines) in the upper-right corner of the screen.**

3. **Tap Settings.**

   The Settings screen appears.

4. **Tap Help and then tap Help Center.**

   The Help Center screen appears in your browser app, as shown in Figure 22-3.

If you already selected your default browser app in Instagram or another app, the Help Center web page will appear in your default browser automatically.

REMEMBER

FIGURE 22-3:
Help Center on an Android device.

Swipe in the screen to view all the topics. Tap a topic title to view more information about that topic.

When you've finished viewing information in Help Center, return to the Options screen in the Instagram app by opening the Recent Apps screen and then either closing your browser window or tapping the Instagram tile if you plan to return to the Help Center later. (The steps for opening the Recent Apps screen depend on the device, so we can't list them here.)

Visiting Privacy and Safety Center

Review Instagram's Privacy and Safety Center so you know how to use Instagram wisely and what to do if you think someone is using Instagram in the wrong way (which may or may not be affecting you directly).

In the Help Center screen, open Privacy and Safety Center by selecting Privacy and Security Help. A list of topics appears, as shown in Figure 22-4.

FIGURE 22-4:
Privacy and safety
topics on an
iPhone.

Viewing Instagram Business web pages

The Instagram website has a dedicated business website that you can access at `https://business.instagram.com`. The website, shown in Figure 22-5, contains information on setting up a new business account, promoting your posts, learning how to get the most from your business account, and more.

If you can't access the Instagram Business website or you prefer to work with the mother ship (Facebook), visit the Facebook Business website at `www.facebook.com/business/help/976240832426180`.

The Facebook Business website contains much of the same information as the Instagram Business website, including details on advertising on Instagram, targeting ads for the best results, and Instagram Business Tools. You may want to look at both the Instagram Business and Facebook Business websites to ensure that you get the most complete information about promoting your business in Instagram effectively.

FIGURE 22-5:
The Instagram website for business.

Tapping Social Media

Instagram doesn't keep its communications limited to Instagram. It maintains close connections with Facebook and its Facebook Business website (two billion profiles and counting as of this writing).

Instagram also posts regularly on its Twitter profile, which is no surprise because you can share your posts directly on Twitter from the Instagram app.

What's more, Instagram's blogs for both personal and business users can help you learn more about using Instagram and become inspired to create a post or two.

Sending a message on Facebook

Instagram for Business has a Facebook profile at `www.facebook.com/instagramforbusiness`, shown in Figure 22-6.

You can view posts from Instagram by scrolling down or swiping up. You can access the Instagram Business website by clicking or tapping the Learn More button. As of this writing, you can even call the number on the Instagram for Business Facebook page.

Tweeting and being tweeted

The Instagram Twitter feed, at `https://twitter.com/instagram`, gives you the latest information. You can also find photos, videos, and links to Instagram posts that Instagram thinks are interesting, as shown in Figure 22-7.

Scroll in your web browser or swipe in the Twitter app screen to view recent posts. Click or tap links to view the Instagram post or linked article. You can also send a tweet to Instagram. There's no telling if Instagram will respond, but you never know until you try . . . er, tweet.

FIGURE 22-7:
Follow the Instagram feed by clicking or tapping the Follow button in the upper right.

Reading the Instagram and Instagram for Business blogs

Speaking of the Instagram blog, you can view the general Instagram blog at `https://about.instagram.com/blog/` on your web browser, as shown in Figure 22-8. Scroll down to view blog post summaries. Click a topic title to view more information about that topic.

TIP

If you have the Tumblr app, you can open the blog in Tumblr by tapping Open in App, at the top of the screen. (If you don't have Tumblr installed, you can get the app from the Google Play Store by tapping Get the Tumblr App, at the bottom of the screen.)

Visiting the Instagram Business blog

Instagram Business also has a separate blog, but you can't get to it from your Instagram app. Instead, you need to go to your web browser and type `https://business.instagram.com/blog/`. Or go to the Instagram Business website at `https://business.instagram.com` and tap the News link, in the upper-right corner.

The blog appears, as shown in Figure 22-9. Swipe or scroll to view recent post summaries. To read a post, tap the summary title, photo, or description.

FIGURE 22-8:
Blog post titles appear below the image.

FIGURE 22-9:
The Instagram Business blog.

Joining a Community

Instagram makes it easy for you to join communities — and not just the ones on its Facebook and Twitter feeds. You can also scan Reddit and Quora, two popular discussion websites, to find an interesting discussion — or start one of your own.

Visiting Reddit and Quora

You can also join online communities to talk about Instagram. Two of the most popular (and busy) websites are Reddit and Quora.

WARNING

Some of the messages you'll find on these online communities are inappropriate or even NSFW (Not Suitable For Work). If you're going to search for messages in these online communities, you may want to ensure that no one else can see your screen before you start reading.

Reddit

Visit the Reddit Instagram page (called a subreddit) at `www.reddit.com/r/Instagram/` (see Figure 22-10). As the About Community section says, this subreddit is unaffiliated with the Instagram company. Swipe or scroll to view the list of messages. If comments are included with the message, you'll see the number of comments below the message title.

You can also search for messages with one or more specific search terms. Here's how:

1. **In the Search box in the upper-right corner of the web page, type your term(s).**

2. **Tap or click the magnifying glass icon on the left side of the Search box or press Enter.**

   A list of posts with titles that contain your search term(s) appears on the page. Scroll or swipe up and down to view all the posts.

When you find a post you want to read more about, tap or click the post title to open it. You can leave a comment as well as share the message on your Facebook, Twitter, or Tumblr account.

Quora

Although Quora doesn't have a general Instagram *space*, which is Quora's name for a *group*, check out the Instagram for Marketers group at www.quora.com/q/instagramformarketers. Swipe or scroll to view the list of recent messages, as shown in Figure 22-11.

The number of upvotes, reposts, and comments appears below the message in the list.

You can search Quora for one or more Instagram terms by tapping or clicking in the Search box at the top of the page, typing your search term(s), and then pressing Enter or tapping Return on your smartphone or tablet keyboard. A new web page with a list of all message topics that contain your search term(s) appears.

Tap or click the message title to read in a new browser tab the original question and any answers. To reply to a message or comment, tap or click in the Add a Comment below the message or comment, type your message, and then click or tap Add Comment. Return to the list of messages by closing the browser tab.

TIP

If you have a Quora account and are logged in, you can write your own message for other users to read and comment on by tapping the red Add Question button in the upper-right corner of the screen.

FIGURE 22-11:
The Quora
Instagram for
Marketers group
page.

8

The Part of Tens

Chapter **23**

Ten Brands Killing It on Instagram

I t's so easy to tell you what to do; it's a lot harder to do those things. That's why it helps to see what other great Instagram brands are doing and use them for inspiration.

Throughout the book, we talk about Instagram tactics and best practices. Now we want to show you ten accounts that are great examples of these recommendations.

GoPro

For a big brand, @GoPro understands the effect of using Instagram well. GoPro's content is a mix of people, places, and pets. Although its photos and videos span every corner of the globe, they are cohesive, well branded, and share the same story of adventure and excitement. Figure 23-1 gives an example of the posts shared on the GoPro account.

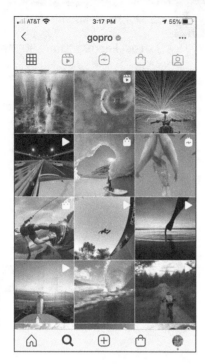

The most unique aspect of the GoPro account is that almost all its content is user-generated content (UGC). Its posts are photos and videos created by its customers, which it *regrams* (repost) to its account. GoPro chooses only the best content and posts that stay true to its brand's styling and personality.

Beyond the branding, GoPro also does a good job of interacting with its audience, posting fun captions and responding to comments and questions on its posts. GoPro builds engagement and loyalty through this method of communication.

Yellowillow

The @yellowillow Instagram account, run by photographer Anne McIsaac, has beautiful styling in which most of her images incorporate the color yellow, as shown in Figure 23-2. She shares images from her work and life, in a range of topics and locations, but are all tied together with her photographic style and the pops of yellow color.

FIGURE 23-2:
The @yellowillow account incorporates yellow into post content.

Anne incorporates effective hashtag strategies as well as a brief description or story about the post, giving it context and personality. She is also dedicated to her audience, responding to comments and questions to build a relationship with her followers.

Thanks to the size of her audience and the value she has as a brand, Anne collaborates with other companies to create sponsored posts. Even though these posts are promoting another product or company, she ensures that the content stays true to her own branding and personality.

LeesFeedBoutique

Lees' Boutique is a modern boutique located in Lees' Feed and Western Store, which is a feed, tack, western wear, and pet supply megastore. Once inside the trendy boutique, you'd never guess that you could buy hay or guinea pig food next door! Lees' Boutique has its own Instagram account at @leesfeedboutique that features its fashion and accessory items.

Owners Tegan Lee and Cori Avila, and their dedicated staff, do an amazing job of modeling new items that come into the store daily, as shown in Figure 23-3. Since they buy small quantities of brands that most other local stores don't carry, fans of her account know they have to act fast if they see something they like! Followers will often ask how much an item costs, if it's available in their size, or what the material feels like. The staff is always quick to answer questions and offer to hold or ship the item directly to the customer.

FIGURE 23-3:
The @leesfeedboutique account staff models all of its new inventory for purchase.

Since starting the Instagram account, Tegan and Cori have noticed an increase in their monthly sales, both from customers requesting items directly online and those stating that they came into their shop looking for an outfit from the @leesfeedboutique account. Tegan says Instagram has been an amazing way to reach customers outside her small Northern California town.

RPMItalian

RPMItalian is a restaurant in Chicago, Illinois, and Washington, D.C., that showcases its cuisine, restaurant, and news via its @rpmitalian Instagram account. Every photo has great staging and lighting. RPMItalian effectively incorporates behind-the-scenes content, such as making pasta from scratch or showcasing chefs in the kitchen, while editing and staging the photos to align with its brand styling of plated dishes.

Black and white is the dominant undertone of the images, yet pops of color add visual appeal. Figure 23-4 shows you how RPMItalian achieves this brand styling on Instagram.

FIGURE 23-4: The @rpmitalian account shares a variety of images from its restaurant.

This account also shares posts on a minimal schedule, at most two to three times a week. In this way, it ensures that its content is of the highest quality and has the greatest effect on its audience.

GymShark

Love to pump iron? Then you've probably heard of GymShark, a fitness apparel and accessories brand based in the United Kingdom and supported by millions of highly engaged social media followers and customers in more than 100 countries.

The @gymshark Instagram account, shown in Figure 23-5, partners with a variety of sports influencers (from jump rope pros to UFC fighters) to showcase athletes working out wearing GymShark gear. By using different types of athletes, GymShark shows how its clothes are comfortable and appropriate for training in any sport. Influencers will often include mini-workouts while wearing the GymShark brand, offering added value to fans of the account. They also tag the influencers, who then typically share the post on their own profiles. Many of these profiles have hundreds of thousands or even millions of followers, who then get exposed to the GymShark brand.

FIGURE 23-5: The @gymshark account uses athletic influencers to promote its workout apparel brand.

© @gymshark

TheLoveBombCo

The Love Bomb Company sells coffee mugs and glassware imprinted with witty motivational sayings. Its @thelovebombco Instagram account is a direct representation of its brand, voice, and style. When you view this account — from the bio to posts and products — you immediately get a sense of what this company is about (whether you love it or hate it), as shown in Figure 23-6.

FIGURE 23-6:
The @thelove-
bombco account
displays its
personality and
branding clearly.

This company understands that always posting its products can get overwhelming and appear pushy. So instead of only showcasing its products, it includes quotes in branded fonts.

It also connects more authentically with its audience by including user-generated content provided by its customers. This highlights its products in various settings and shows the variety of lifestyles, yet commonalities, of its customers.

The.Book.Report

The @the.book.report account on Instagram makes great use of videos and multi-image posts (also called albums or slide shows), two effective but underutilized Instagram features. Michelle, who runs the Instagram account, provides reviews of children's books and uses her Instagram account to share her opinions as well as a look at each book.

She uses the slide show post to share an image of the book cover, as shown in Figure 23-7, and then a series of images or a video to showcase the inside of the book. Her captions contain her insights into the book and its value to other parents.

FIGURE 23-7:
The @the.book.
report account
uses a variety of
features to
provide book
reviews.

To create trust and rapport with her audience, Michelle also incorporates posts about her family and kids, demonstrating their personal life and interests.

LaJollaMom

The @lajollamom account is run by Katie Dillon, a luxury travel blogger. Her account is full of beautiful photos from around the world, but she also does a fantastic job of sharing educational content. Her captions often include insider tips, fun facts, or other information that her audience finds valuable. Figure 23-8 is an example of one of her post captions detailing where to get the best sweets in Japan.

Katie often shares personal experiences of her travels with her family as well. It provides transparency to her audience and builds trust with those who follow her.

The photos on her account are personalized but high-quality images that are edited and selected for best performance on Instagram. As with most of the other examples in this chapter, Katie ensures that she interacts with her followers by personally responding to comments and questions on her posts.

FIGURE 23-8:
The @lajollamom account uses captions to educate and inform Katie's audience.

TSA

The TSA — the agency that ensures traveler safety at airports and other transportation facilities — isn't an account you would expect to follow on Instagram. However, the @TSA account understands how to do Instagram well, as shown in Figure 23-9.

It showcases its working dogs and handlers on Instagram, which helps because people love to see dogs on Instagram! It also shares photos of all the wild and crazy items that have been confiscated by TSA agents. In these posts, the captions are used to remind you of prohibited items, so there's an educational component in addition to the humor behind the odd objects.

To keep its account more lighthearted, the @TSA account will often get involved in trending topics or relevant events, such as handwashing songs during coronavirus or National Apple Pie Day.

FIGURE 23-9:
The @TSA
Instagram
account is full of
items people
have attempted
to pass through
security.

GeneralElectric

For a large engineering company, focused on business-to-business customers, the @generalelectric Instagram account does a surprisingly good job. This account doesn't attempt to focus on large-scale clients. Instead, it builds brand awareness and connects with people on an individual level.

This Instagram account incorporates employee profiles, inside looks at product development, tours of the company's facilities, and information about how things are built. Its posts are informational and educational, yet entertaining to view or read. Figure 23-10 is an example of a fun and informational post about curing manufactured pieces after they are 3-D printed.

This account also effectively incorporates photos, videos, and slide show posts to best generate engagement with a wide range of its audience.

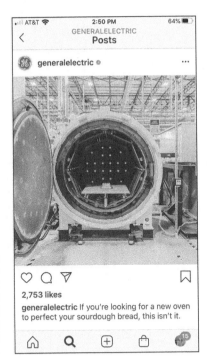

FIGURE 23-10:
The @generalelectric account shares fun and educational content to build brand awareness.

Chapter **24**

Ten Places to Find Inspiration

The tactics and methods for using Instagram for your business are often methodical. But what really connects with people and your audience is good content. Posts that evoke emotions or educate your viewers will always perform well for you.

If you're unsure of where to start or what types of content you want to create, look for inspiration from others on Instagram. Seeing what they are doing can give you the ideas and motivation to create unique and valuable content of your own.

In this chapter, we show you ten great sources of inspiration on Instagram.

Investigate the Explore Page

One of the first places to look for inspiration on Instagram is the Explore page, shown in Figure 24-1.

FIGURE 24-1:
The Explore page displays a variety of content targeted toward your interests.

To get to the Explore page:

>> On your mobile device: Tap the magnifying glass icon in the Instagram toolbar.

>> On the Windows app and the desktop version of the Instagram website: Click the compass icon at the top of the screen (to the left of the heart icon).

The Explore page curates posts from a variety of Instagram users. The content is found and sorted specifically for you, based on the types of accounts you follow and interact with. What you see on the Explore page will always be different than what others will see, because each user receives customized results.

TIP

You can easily refresh the Explore page to see new content by swiping down on the screen on your mobile device.

This page includes a combination of Reels, videos, and photos that might interest you. You can tap any post to view it in its entirety, including the caption and comments.

The content on the Explore page is valuable as a source of inspiration because most of the posts are from people you don't currently follow, so you're introduced to new accounts and fresh content. And that content is usually high performing (reels, photos, and videos that generate a lot of engagement compared to their account follower size), so you'll see the type of content that generates positive reactions.

Review Hashtag Searches Related to Your Brand

Hashtags are a popular way to find content centered on a specific theme or phrase. There's no reason you shouldn't be using this same resource to find inspiration!

You can perform a hashtag search on Instagram in two ways. The first is to tap any hashtag you see in an Instagram post. The corresponding hashtag gallery in Instagram appears, as shown in Figure 24-2, and you see all recent content created using the hashtag you tapped.

FIGURE 24-2:
A hashtag gallery displays the Instagram posts that include the hashtag you tapped.

The second method for accessing hashtag searches follows:

1. **From any Instagram page, tap the magnifying glass at the bottom.**

    The Explore page appears.

2. **In the Search field at the top, type the hashtag you want to search for.**

    To follow along with the example, type **#photography**. The screen shows results from the hashtag you entered, the number of posts using it, plus any related hashtags. Figure 24-3 shows the results of our search for #photography. As you can see, related hashtags that start with *photography* also appear in the list.

TIP

Using this search function with a keyword for your industry is a great way to find other related hashtags that you might want to use on your own content or search for more ideas.

3. **Tap a hashtag in the list to open up the corresponding hashtag gallery.**

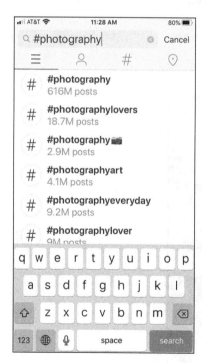

FIGURE 24-3:
The hashtag search screen populates other hashtags with your related keyword.

Searching these hashtags, especially when searching topics and keywords related to your business or industry, is a resourceful way to find fresh content. And best of all, because the content is in line with what you're looking to create, you should be able to get some good ideas of what others in a similar industry are doing and pull inspiration from those posts.

Spy on Your Competitors

Nothing's wrong with a little healthy competition! In fact, it can make for great inspiration. You most likely already know who your competitors are in your business. Look them up on Instagram to see what they're doing and get ideas of what you may (or may not) want to emulate in some way for your content.

If you aren't following your competitors on Instagram, you may need to search for them. Just as you did with the hashtag searches, tap the magnifying glass icon on the home page to display the Explore page. Next, tap the Search field and start typing either the business name, if you know it, or a type of business or a physical location or both, as shown in Figure 24-4. Tapping any name in the list will take you to that Instagram profile.

FIGURE 24-4:
Use the Search field to look up your competitors.

Of course, you don't want to copy what your competitors are doing. But seeing how their content is created, how often they post, and what hashtags they use can give you some direction in your own strategy.

Even if your competitor posts content that you don't find appealing or that doesn't generate much engagement, that information is helpful to know. You can use it as inspiration for the types of content to avoid in your own strategy.

Get Inspiration from Local Businesses

Beyond looking at your direct competitors, it can be helpful to look at businesses in your local area. These accounts may be creating quality content that showcases your city or region. You may be able to draw inspiration from the local flare they utilize in their content. You may also be able to find some good local hashtags to use in your own posts based on what other local companies are using.

If your business is local or has one or more physical locations, consider incorporating content in your Instagram strategy that highlights local or regional attractions. For example, if you own a shoe store, including content related to your local parks, city walks, or even live events can be a great way to connect with your target audience. It reinforces that you are part of the community and reminds active people that they need good shoes.

You can also search using the Places tab in the Search field to see top posts that are tagging your current location or other target locations. You never know who might be a good local partner!

Check Out Your Favorite Products

Many of the brands you already know and love are likely using Instagram as well. And if you already enjoy those products, chances are you'll like the content they're sharing on Instagram too. Check out those favorite products and companies on Instagram to get some fun inspiration for your own content.

Look for brands that are creating content regularly and that you find visually appealing. You might find creative ways to stage your products to make them more flattering or appealing.

Finding content that also showcases humor, education, or other entertainment value is also helpful. Figure 24-5 shows you three examples of products in which the companies got creative with their content to best appeal to their target audience.

FIGURE 24-5:
Products with appealing Instagram posts.

From small and local companies to global brands, there are many brands using Instagram well and which can provide inspiration for your Instagram content.

Look to Photographers

Great photography performs the best on Instagram. Regardless of the value of your message, people will scroll right past your post if you use a poor-quality image. Improve your photography skills and find inspiration by following actual photographers on Instagram.

Good photographers have a sense of composition, alignment, and lighting that helps them create beautiful photographs. Finding photographers who appeal to your style can help you see the types of photo staging that will improve your own photography skills.

Depending on the types of objects you plan to showcase on Instagram, look for photographers with a similar subject. For example, Figure 24-6 shows you a photographer who focuses on business branding and headshots.

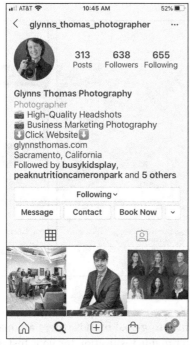

FIGURE 24-6: Photographers often focus on a specific type of photography.

Get Inspired by Bloggers

Many bloggers make good use of Instagram to build their audience and to motivate their audience to take action on the posts they're sharing. Whether encouraging viewers to, say, read something, follow a recipe, or fix up a DIY project, Instagram often helps these bloggers reach their goals.

Bloggers who create beautiful content and drive engagement and interactions are great sources of inspiration. Most of them have vibrant photos with beautiful finished projects. Seeing how these accounts create attractive content can help you determine how to stage and set up your own content to best appeal to your target audience.

Most bloggers also have cohesive galleries on Instagram. Even though all of their posts showcase a different item or project, they have a consistent style and theme.

These posts should help inspire you to create your own style and theme to keep your content branded and cohesive. Figure 24-7 demonstrates a blogger who does this well.

FIGURE 24-7: Bloggers often create cohesive galleries that appeal visually to their audience.

Find Big Brands That Are Being Creative

A lot of big brands get creative with their Instagram content and campaigns. Although they often have the advantage of large budgets and teams of creative input, you can take all their hard work as inspiration for your own content.

Take a look at big brands to see how they incorporate storytelling, employee profiles, company updates, or product launches. When you see how massive organizations are able to connect on a personal level with their audience, you can find similar ways to reach out to your audience.

Figure 24-8 provides three examples of large companies that connect in humorous and effective ways with their audiences.

FIGURE 24-8:
Big brands get
creative on
Instagram.

You can find inspiration in how big brands not only connect with their audience but also take time to create a strong and timely message that resonates well.

Learn from Instagram and Marketing Experts

To stay on top of what is and is no longer working well on Instagram, we recommend that you follow industry leaders in Instagram and social media marketing. These accounts often post breaking news or Instagram tactics to help you better create an effective Instagram strategy. Because Instagram does release updates regularly, having a good resource for current news and tactics is beneficial.

Industry leaders often begin implementing new tactics and features quickly, so you can see them in use and can determine how to incorporate them in your own content strategy.

Some of the best resources for Instagram news and updates follow:

» @jenns_trends

» @coreycwalker

» @smexaminer

» @tylerjmccall

» @suebzimmerman

» @mollymarshallmarketing

Follow the Instagram for Business Account

As we just mentioned, Instagram is always updating the app and adding features. It also does a lot to highlight companies that use Instagram for marketing. Instagram has created @instagramforbusiness, shown in Figure 24-9, to help you better understand Instagram as a marketing tool.

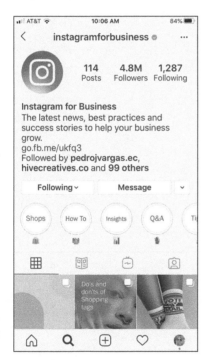

FIGURE 24-9:
The Instagram for Business account on Instagram.

To stay abreast of the latest features and updates, and grab inspiration from other businesses using Instagram marketing, follow the Instagram for Business account.

Index

About the Authors

Jenn Herman is a social media consultant, speaker, and globally recognized Instagram expert. She is the forefront blogger on Instagram marketing and her blog, Jenn's Trends, has won the title of a Top 10 Social Media Blog multiple years. She is a sought-after and international speaker providing tips, resources, and training for organizations of all sizes that need to structure their social media strategies. Her business background includes administration, sales, human resources, and marketing and she enjoys bringing all these skills together to help you grow your business. Jenn has been featured in *Inc.*, Fox News, BBC News, Yahoo Finance, *Entrepreneur*, *HuffPost*, The Verge, CBS Radio LA, and numerous other podcasts and publications. She has authored or co-authored *Instagram For Dummies, Ultimate Guide to Social Media Marketing* (Entrepreneur Press), and *Stop Guessing: Your Step-by-Step Guide to Creating a Social Media Strategy.* Jenn's Instagram username is jenns_trends.

Eric Butow is the owner of Butow Communications Group (BCG) in Jackson, California. BCG offers online marketing analysis and improvement services for businesses of all sizes. Eric has written 36 computing and user experience books. His most recent books include *Instagram For Dummies, Programming Interviews For Dummies,* and *Ultimate Guide to Social Media Marketing* (Entrepreneur Press). When he's not working or writing books, you can find Eric enjoying time with his friends, walking around the historic Gold Rush town of Jackson, and helping his mother manage her infant and toddler daycare business. Eric's Instagram username is ericbutow.

Corey Walker is the owner of the Marketing Specialist in El Dorado Hills, California, which offers social media strategy, content, ad management, and analytics with a concentrated passion for Instagram and Facebook. She has managed the social media accounts of hospitals, medical groups, restaurants, online businesses, and publications. She has also co-authored *Instagram For Dummies.* When she's not online, you can find her at the gym, baking with her kids, or engrossed in a good book. Corey's Instagram username is coreycwalker.

Dedications

To my daughter, who motivates me to do so much more.

— Jenn Herman

To my family and friends.

— Eric Butow

To my dear and much-loved family.

— Corey Walker

Authors' Acknowledgments

I'd like to thank the team of people who made this book happen. My co-authors, Eric Butow and Corey Walker, made it a pleasure and I'm honored to have worked alongside them. My family and friends, who continue to cheer me on with each of these writing adventures. My agent for this book, Carole Jelen. And the team at Wiley, including executive editor Steve Hayes and project editor Susan Pink, made us look good! Finally, thanks to you and every other business owner or marketer who wants to learn how to use Instagram effectively and is willing to invest in that commitment.

— Jenn Herman

I'd like to thank my co-authors, Jenn Herman and Corey Walker, for being such wonderful people to work with. My thanks as always to Carole Jelen, who served as the agent on this book. I also want to thank all the pros at Wiley who made this book possible, especially Steve Hayes and Susan Pink. And I also thank you for buying this book.

— Eric Butow

It was wonderful to once again collaborate with my co-authors, Jenn Herman and Eric Butow. My family was very excited to have another edition of this book out and cheered me on as I edited. Our literary agent, Carole Jelen, was a great help in getting this new book underway, and Steve Hayes and Susan Pink smoothed out all our writing kinks! I also want to thank my friends, extended family, and all future Instagram pros who purchase this book to market their business.

— Corey Walker

Publisher's Acknowledgments

Executive Editor: Steve Hayes

Project Editor: Susan Pink

Copy Editor: Susan Pink

Technical Editor: Hannah Partridge

Proofreader: Debbye Butler

Production Editor: Tamilmani Varadharaj

Cover Image: © PeopleImages/Getty Images